Mistress

Lucina White

Stairwell Books //

Published by Stairwell Books
9 Carleton St
Greenwich
CT 06830 USA

161 Lowther Street
York, YO31 7LZ

www.stairwellbooks.co.uk
@stairwellbooks

Mistress © 2021, 2024 Lucina White and Stairwell Books

All rights reserved. No part of this publication may be reproduced, stored in or introduced into a retrieval system, or transmitted, in any form, or by any means (electronic, mechanical, photocopying, recording, e-book or otherwise) without the prior written permission of the author.

The moral rights of the author have been asserted.

Previously published as ISBN: 978-1-913432-09-6
eBook ISBN: 978-1-913432-18-8
Paperback ISBN: 978-1-917334-15-0

FOREWORD

When Lucina White asked me to edit her autobiography, I was intrigued. When I read the draft text, I felt honoured and privileged. I'd been granted an opportunity to help prepare a wonderful life story for publication.

On the one hand, this book provides a rare insight into the real world of a true Dominatrix. On the other, it's an inspiring tale of female empowerment, not just (indeed, not particularly) in the sense of 'domination', but as an illustration of how a woman with limited formal education and no partner to support her can triumph over adversity through her own unaided efforts and carve out a successful career. Lucina has faced an astonishing sequence of misfortunes and catastrophes without letting them deter her. She compares them with the Seven Plagues of Egypt. They'd have made ninety-nine percent of people give up in despair. However, her story isn't a mere catalogue of disasters; it also reveals a caring, compassionate, impulsive and witty person who loves animals, enjoys an irrepressible urge for adventure, and is steadfast and indomitable.

I promised Lucina I'd do as she asked: edit her autobiography to the best of my ability. She and I talked on the telephone, exchanged e-mails, and met face to face. She proved to be not only a warm, likeable person but also level-headed, charming, intelligent, and blessed with a quiet sense of humour. However, it's evident that she doesn't tolerate folly or dishonesty.

She doesn't match the stereotypical image of the Professional Dominatrix. She isn't six feet tall with flaming red hair and she doesn't carry a whip wherever she goes. She's five feet four with dark hair and spectacles and her hands are more likely to be occupied in cuddling her pet Yorkshire terrier than in brandishing offensive weapons. But what she tells us in this book about the world of 'Bondage and Discipline, Domination and Submission, Sadism and Masochism (BDSM)' demonstrates that *all* the stereotypes around it are misleading, and many of them are the antithesis of truth. Reading her story opened my eyes to a lifestyle that I'd previously no more than half understood, and I was by turns startled, amused, touched, incredulous and delighted – but never revolted – by the details she describes. She seeks neither to shock nor to titillate. Her accounts are direct and explicit when they need to be but they're never prurient. Rather, they're kind, humane and understanding, and you know from the outset that Lucina truly cares about her clients and is protective of them. However, depictions of dungeon activities occupy less than a quarter of the book. The other three quarters portray the many contrasting facets of a remarkable, varied and admirable life outside the Chamber. When I read the text, and again when I edited it, I experienced the range of emotions I expect from a good novel, fluctuating between laughter and tears.

The profession she's chosen wouldn't suit everyone. However, the way in which she's built and sustained her business in defiance of every challenge the world could throw at her provides a glorious exemplar for women (and men) everywhere, no matter what career they choose to follow.

Mark P. Henderson
2020

Chapter 1

The aromas of moist stone and leather were overlain with perspiration and excitement. The warm dim light of the Chamber gleamed on dildos, handcuffs, leather restraints, a whipping bench, racks of canes and paddles, and his naked skin. My lash cracked again and the straps binding him to the St Andrew's cross creaked in harmony with my black leather corset and long black leather boots. The session was nearing its end. Then his gasps and cries subsided and all the tension seemed to evaporate from his muscles. He began to look more like a holidaymaker dozing in a deckchair on a Mediterranean beach than a slave undergoing punishment and humiliation in a converted cellar under a disused mill. And then, to my surprise and consternation, he started not just to cry but to sob uncontrollably. I was so startled I dropped my whip, untied him and hugged him.

"David, are you all right?"

He nodded, wiping his forearm across his eyes.

"Oh yes, yes, I'm more than all right, Mistress. That was wonderful! Thank you so much!"

Obviously, what I'd done to him had released a lot of pent-up emotion. That wasn't unusual. Slaves (it's standard to call our clients 'slaves' in the dungeon, though not outside it!) quite often shed tears. Many of them tell me how well my ministrations have relaxed and de-stressed them. It always gratifies me. However, David's response was of a different order. My feeling of power over the client had made me 'high', as it invariably does. Inflicting pain isn't pleasurable in itself, at least not for me, but the empowerment has an almost drug-like effect. However, David's heartfelt sobbing perturbed me.

"Come on, David, get dressed and let's go and have a cup of coffee in the lounge."

Seated on my sofa he grew calm. Indeed, he looked as though he'd taken a mild sedative.

"Can you tell me about it?" I prompted. I put my feet up. Black leather boots with high stiletto heels are obligatory in my profession, but they're not designed for comfort.

David sipped his coffee, trying to collect his thoughts.

"It seldom happens," he said. "That was an amazingly good session, Mistress. It took me to where I wanted to go, where I needed to go: that glorious stage where you could have done anything you wanted to me, anything at all – cut off my penis, mutilate me, start to kill me – and whatever you did I'd have said, 'Thank you'. Nothing mattered any longer. I was completely at peace."

It was perhaps the clearest and most articulate explanation of the 'sub' experience I'd ever heard. I put down my coffee mug and closed my eyes. I was buzzing.

"Oh. You got into 'sub space', did you?"

"Yes, Mistress. That's exactly what happened. You took me there. Will you allow me to have more sessions with you?"

At last! I'd finally helped a client to reach the ultimate stage of submission, the total, unreserved and entirely *voluntary* subjugation of body, mind and will to the Mistress. I'd learned about 'sub space' when at the age of thirty I'd been introduced to the world of bondage, domination and sado-masochism (BDSM), but as David had said, it's seldom reached. Indeed, it's very rare. That session was a first for me. It gave me a sense of achievement akin to what I suppose winners of major sporting events and Oscars enjoy: the unprecedented achievement, a rare victory.

No one who'd known me when I was a girl in Cumbria would have foreseen such an achievement. None of them could have anticipated my choice of career, still less that I'd succeed in it.

It wouldn't have happened if it hadn't been for Peter.

*

I was thirteen when I first met Peter. My mother had become ill, and Peter was introduced to us via a lady who'd come to our home to read Tarot cards. My father had heard of her and I had inherited his interest for such things, though he himself was a little cynical about them. The Tarot cards fascinated me. For as long as I can remember I've been drawn to spiritual matters from fortune-telling to ghost stories and mediumship. To an extent I grew up with it; my mother often saw apparitions, the earliest being a white figure at the top of the stairs when she was a young girl at home. Their house was very old. Nobody believed her, so I think she doubted her abilities even then. She never liked or even accepted her sightings, which continued throughout her life. They scared her massively and she wished most of those encounters had never happened. I'd grown up with more ghostly experiences than I can recall. Something happened at least once a day in the house to which we moved when I was seven and left when I was thirteen. You wouldn't expect a little two-up-two-down terraced house in the middle of a boring, average street to become so active, but it made 30, East Drive, Pontefract look like a hidden Halloween attraction. I regularly woke with my hair being pulled, unable to move, as though someone was sitting on my legs; and I saw several apparitions. My father thought we were making it all up, but eventually even he started to feel touches on the shoulder when nobody was there and to hear the sounds of someone walking around upstairs, and it scared him.

Peter was holding meditation meetings, helping people relax and find a more peaceful path. I was welcomed into the group and also into the family and became friendly with his daughter, Joanne, who was a little younger than me. After a few of his meetings he offered to teach my father and me to do Tarot readings. My father wasn't interested, but I was. Over the following six months I learned to read the Tarot cards. It proved to be a slow process, not just learning the meaning of each card but enhancing your perceptions of people and their feelings. Peter became a family friend and something of a father-figure for me.

My own father was what's often called a *man's man*. He enjoyed a pint and male company. He made some bad choices during his life but I don't blame him for them, and he was always a good father and looked after us with more than fair intention. We never had a lot of money but both parents had enough time for us, which is priceless. He recently suffered a stroke. I visit him as often as I can to make sure he's as comfortable.

My sister is four years older than me. When Peter started teaching me the Tarot, she was adopting a lifestyle I didn't want to copy. She'd become pregnant at seventeen, but after she'd had the baby she'd fallen back into bad habits and left our parents to care for little Samantha. By then, both parents were in their sixties and in bad health but still working full-time to pay off my sister's debts, for which they'd stood guarantor. They feared that unless they took care of baby Sam, she'd end up in care. I sometimes missed school to look after Samantha because my mother was struggling to manage. I didn't mind helping; my parents were under great stress, and I grew to love Sam. I've remained very close to her, but have little to do with my sister. Sam grew up to be a strong and independent woman and I'm very proud of her. She is like a sister/daughter to me and one of the few people who I can tell my deepest secrets.

As I was learning the Tarot I was introduced to Paganism and became more involved with the Pagan group and their activities. I'd been brought up a Christian and was sincerely religious throughout my childhood, but much of Christianity failed to make sense to me. It left many questions unanswered. Bit by bit, Paganism came to provide the understanding of life I'd been seeking. As a Pagan you believe in Nature and the natural ways of the world: the balance between day and night, the changing of the seasons, how Nature can be kind and cruel but always for a reason. We learn to respect all life, from elephant to fly, and to learn that we share this Earth with the rest of creation; we don't own it and we never will. There are eight Sabbaths annually, and as a group we celebrated all of them, welcoming the changes of the year. The Goddess is just as prominent as the God, but as far as I can see She is absent from other religions. We learn to find peace within death as natural and inevitable, to see it not as the end but in some ways as a new beginning. Paganism is also known as the 'craft of the wise'; there are spells, all of which are natural and enable you to enhance certain energies. The basic laws of the craft are: live your life to the full, enjoy every day, but try not to cross anyone else's path along the way.

Depending on the person for whom I was reading and how open they were, the Tarot cards could prove an accurate guide to their past, present and future. Most people were drawn to the readings by curiosity, but they wanted hope of a better life, or assurance that a forthcoming venture such as marriage was going to work out well. Occasionally someone who was in a dark place or had lost someone dear to them would need real help. Some of those readings became very intense and sometimes I could relay a message from the loved one, whom I was able to describe. That couldn't be planned; either it happened or it didn't. When such people left after the reading, I felt privileged and powerful because I knew I'd helped them. Feelings like that can be addictive.

*

I was born in Barrow-in-Furness, a small town on the Cumbrian coast, and brought up in a household that enjoyed the usual mix of harmony and disagreement. We were far from wealthy but we didn't struggle: my father was a crane driver in the shipyard and my mother worked in a local wool factory. They were in their forties when I was born; they'd endured four miscarriages before my sister and I arrived. My mother had been unable to carry boys. They worked hard to provide, and despite our relative poverty we had happy times. No holidays abroad and no fancy house, but I spent weekends swimming and playing football, evenings out on bike rides, and by the time I was ten I was a mean pool player. In general, my childhood was unremarkable. I went to school, worried my way through puberty with anxieties about spots, body shape and clothes, and was delivered to adulthood equipped with a handful of hopes and plenty of dreams. I faced the prospect of working my way through life as best I could.

As a child I was shy, a nervous loner with little confidence, and I had only one real friend. Susan and I had been close to each other from the beginning of infant school. However, after we left school at sixteen, we drifted apart. I felt ill at ease in large groups and was only willing to interact with those with whom I'd become well acquainted. Preferring my own company, I loved nothing more than to ride my bike out to the lakes. Coniston Water was only twenty minutes away from Barrow and the ride took me along beautiful coastal roads and country lanes. On a school day I'd sometimes wait until my father had gone to work and then set off alone. Relishing the beauty of Nature in solitude was far preferable to the drudgery of schoolwork. I suppose I took it all for granted, the unequalled countryside and the fresh sea air, but whenever I return as an adult I love it.

I said I had only one real friend, Susan. I should have said one real *human* friend. The two Yorkshire terriers we had as pets, Scamp and Penny, were an extension to our family and I quickly grew attached to them. We enjoyed playing together, sharing moments of sadness and of joy, and I mourned them when they died. A personal connection can be forged between human and animal souls as easily as between two human ones. With a pet, we develop a relationship of shared dependency: as much as the animal needs our care and attention, we need its love and companionship. While I was waiting at a street corner, out shopping with my mother or playing in the park with friends, anyone walking a dog would snare my attention. I must have annoyed them.

A dog doesn't pretend to love you. It can't lie. If a dog offers its trust, its companionship, it forms a bond with you for life. On the other hand, a dog that takes a dislike to you isn't likely to change its attitude or behaviour. Dogs are simple and honest. The love you receive from a dog comes from the warmth of the heart; there's no hidden agenda. There have been times in my life when being with dogs has made the difference between insanity and survival, their mere presence my comfort and salvation. I'm not exaggerating.

*

When I was fifteen, Peter opened a little shop called Pagans' Choice in Ulverston, a small market town about twenty minutes' drive from Barrow. Surrounded by farmland, Ulverston still has an old-world feel with its little cobbled side streets and quaint buildings. Specialising in books of magic and spells, crystals and candles and so forth, the shop was aimed mainly at tourists and other visitors who were curious about such matters. There was trouble with the locals during its early days and we were pilloried in the local paper. Should I have recognised that as a sign of things to come in my later life? I was too young to become involved in the unrest, though I remember people outside the shop carrying banners saying the 'Devil Worshippers' needed to go. Peter responded by meeting the local vicar over a cup of tea. Comparing their beliefs, they agreed that each religion just wanted peace and a life of harmony. After that the trouble died down, but some churchgoers continued to maintain that Tarot cards were evil.

I helped out in the shop on Saturdays during my two final school years and read the Tarot cards there. After I left school the work became full time. By then I'd moved out of the family home into my own little flat. I continued to read the cards but soon I was running Pagans' Choice single-handedly. I did so for the following five years, until I was twenty-one. The income wasn't great but I was earning a wage, and I loved working there. I loved the small town. To help me along I studied and obtained a diploma in retailing. The experience made me disciplined in turning up on time and making sure my money lasted. These were things I hadn't been taught in school.

*

Shops of that kind have limited life-spans, and when my mother's emphysema and care needs forced me to leave, Peter decided it was time to sell up. I moved back home so I could help as much as possible. My father was still working full-time and my niece was still under their care. Samantha was seven by then, and we'd become more like sisters than niece and aunt.

My mother's health meant she needed a lot of support from me but she remained independent in spirit, doing as much for herself as she could. As her emphysema worsened she had to make more and more use of a nebuliser, but although the doctors had predicted she'd only live for two more years, she survived for five. During that time, the social isolation of my childhood returned with renewed force. As her full-time carer I didn't work and I stopped responding to invitations to go out with the friends I'd made since school. Eventually they stopped asking. It became my regular evening routine to go out into the country and watch the sun set over the mountains or the lake, or just to watch waves crashing on the shore. This was isolation, but it was beautiful. Even today I miss it.

Every two months my mother went into hospital for treatment, but during her final stay she suffered a stroke and she didn't come home again. Anyone who's lost a parent knows how this feels; but along with the shock and grief of the loss I felt relief, mostly for my mother. It had been horrible to see her suffering and losing all her quality of life. It was almost a blessing for her. But by then I'd removed myself so far from life and society that I had no idea how to get back into it. I didn't even want to. I'd put on weight. I didn't like what I saw in the mirror. I was in a dark place.

*

Peter had been working as a merchant seaman and I'd heard much less from him during the previous four years. By the fifth year we'd lost contact altogether. There was no internet in those days, and no mobile phones. Then one day, out of the blue, he knocked on my door with a big hello and smile on his face.

We went for a drive around the coastal road. As we drove, Peter looked at me and said, "Either you carry on like you are, Lucina, or you do something with your life. If you don't change now you might never change."

"I don't know if I can."

"Well, you can't go on like this. Get out into the world again. At least take a holiday!"

I'd always wanted to travel, and in particular I was fascinated by what I'd heard about Thailand. I told Peter so.

"But," I added, "I've no money."

He nodded. He was about to go back to sea for four months, he said, and then he'd take a four month holiday.

"If you've lost that excess weight and started going out a bit more by the time I get back, then I'll take you on holiday to Thailand. But *only* if you do."

That was the motivation I'd needed. I started to get out more, and lost weight. When Peter returned he kept his promise. There were no strings attached to his offer. I'll never cease to be grateful for his generosity or for his lasting friendship.

To Thailand we went.

Chapter 2

Thailand opened my eyes. The culture, the people and the wildlife could not have been more different from those in Britain. This was a world of wonder, especially to a young and relatively naïve woman. Everyone I met seemed eager to smile, the sun always seemed bright and the streets were filled with bars that beckoned with *foreign* delights. The conservative greenery of suburban Cumbria hadn't prepared me for Bangkok. Most of all, I discovered how open and non-judgmental the people were about sexuality.

Exploring Bangkok's nightlife taught me how our philosophies and principles are governed by the geopolitical landscape of our upbringing. Peter had told me a lot about the bars and in particular the amazing *Pat Pong*. My childhood in small-town Cumbria had pushed me into conforming to strict heterosexual norms. Despite Britain's recent trend towards understanding different sexualities and genders, we're still encouraged to believe that couples comprise two people of opposite sexes and procreation should only occur in wedlock. In Barrow, lesbian Tracy and lesbian Sue had been known to everyone and covert fingers were pointed at them. Most men had been afraid of fighting with Sue and Tracy! I'd been curious about my own sexuality but had never had the opportunity to explore it in full. The social indoctrination of my childhood had made me hide my attraction to women. Also, in those days, you were either straight or gay. I felt myself to be neither.

In Bangkok I became aware of a way of life alien to my upbringing. While I was enjoying the nightlife in the bars I discovered that Thai girls were attracted to me. At first I was embarrassed: everywhere I went, girls would come to sit with me and ask me to buy them a drink.

Of course some were only interested in business, but many just wanted to talk. Some of them liked to touch my skin, fascinated by its pale colour. There was no sexual labelling in Thailand, only the physical attraction that can occur between people. I often sat over dinner watching male waiters going about their business wearing makeup, their nails varnished red. Teenage children wandered from school, girls mixing freely with boys. Just as in the UK it wasn't unusual to see girls linking arms, but in Thailand boys did the same. Physical contact wasn't frowned upon, nor was any outward display of sexuality. In Bangkok I wasn't forced to conform to any specific social expectation but was free to be all I wished, without inhibitions. I paid for a few bar and massage girls and had my first sexual experiences with women, and it was a lot of fun. Thailand started to feel like home because I didn't have to hide who I was.

*

Quite aside from sexual discovery, one of my greatest passions was born in a perfect and purely accidental moment in Bangkok. The memory of it still warms my heart.

It had been a wonderful evening, mostly spent wandering among bars and trying the local cuisine. It was late and I was more than ready for bed. Fortunately, Peter was my chaperone, guiding me through a maze of streets back to my hotel. My feet felt heavy from the day's walking and my head was light with drink. But what happened next drained every ounce of fatigue from me and I was instantly sobered.

There, standing in the middle of the street, was the huge bulk of an elephant.

For a moment, my feet couldn't move. In Britain we're sometimes confronted by a stray dog, or we might catch sight of a deer. But this wasn't merely different, it was incomparable. I had no idea how to react. If it hadn't been for Peter I'd have remained rooted to the pavement for the rest of the night, but he took my hand and led me right up to the elephant.

I'd never been so close to such a mighty animal, but I wasn't intimidated. Slowly, I stretched out my arm, allowing one hand to rest on her trunk. As my eyes met hers, we were alone in the world. Nothing else mattered. The clamour of the streets, the tuktuk taxis with their whining engines, the speeding cars and the shouts from passers-by all faded away. In that moment, this strange and wonderful animal had come to know me, and I knew her, and our hearts beat as one.

Then I was wrenched back to the tumult of the everyday world. A man I discovered was a *mahout* (somebody who cares for and rides elephants) was complaining.

"You must buy bananas," he shouted (so Peter told me), "or move away from my beast!"

That such a perfect moment could be so unceremoniously broken made me seethe. Rage burned my tongue and vented itself in expletives that are known universally. Peter came to the rescue again, handing the equivalent of about two pounds to the mahout. I later learned that fifty pence would have bought an entire sack of bananas in the market. However, right then I was to receive only three bananas, for four times the cost.

The elephant waved her trunk upward, trying to snatch the small ripe fruit with their curved yellow skins. Before she could grab them I hid them behind my back; but the trunk curled around my waist, pulling the treat from my hand. This was my first hug from one of these most beautiful of animals. It was a moment I'll never forget. There are times when a single event has an impact on the rest of your life. That night, on a dusty street in Bangkok, my heart was shaped in ways that changed me forever.

"I have to come back to Thailand," I told Peter on our way home. "Will you bring me again?"

"I will," he said, "but I won't pay for you next time. You'll pay for yourself. So when you get home you'll need to find yourself a job and earn some money."

*

Peter was right, as usual. I was no longer a teenager; I'd passed my mid-twenties. But what career would suit me? What job would I find satisfying? I had a diploma in retail, but Thailand had whetted my already keen appetite for travel, and retailing and travel don't mix easily. I thought about the problem long and hard before I came up with a plan. Suppose, I thought, I trained as a beauty therapist. Cruise liners employ beauty therapists. If I could obtain the qualification and apply successfully for a post on such a liner, I could earn a living and travel the world at the same time. What could be better?

The problem with my plan was that I needed to eat and keep a roof over my head while I was undertaking the beauty therapy course, which meant I had to find temporary work to provide a basic income. There were few options; I was at college three days per week and McDonald's was the only employer that allowed me to choose my hours. So for the next eight months I worked in McDonald's, serving fast food. I hated every moment of it but it was a means to a definite end, and I was paying my own way.

You learn from all life's experiences. The shop in Ulverston and the Tarot cards had taught me that many people need to feel that their lives are overseen and their spiritual wellbeing supported by a higher authority; also, it had given me an incipient taste for power and control. Thailand had revealed the unlimited range of human variety, sexual and otherwise, as well as igniting my passion for elephants. Working in McDonald's taught me something else: to the customers I wasn't a person; I was just part of a machine for taking orders and supplying meals. The uniform made me invisible. They behaved as though I wasn't there, arguing, swearing, shouting at their children, showing no hint of courtesy. Yet when those same women visited the beauty parlour they were refined, friendly, even respectful. I wasn't wearing a McDonald's uniform, so I was allowed to be a person. Lesson number three: people aren't consistent, and even if you think you're close to them there are sides of them you'll never know. Dogs and elephants are straightforward, constant and loyal. Humans aren't.

Recognising those three truths – people often need to feel that someone or something is controlling and caring for them, they keep parts of themselves hidden even from those close to them, and human variety is infinite – was to stand me in good stead in my later career. So was my capacity for caring.

*

My NVQ Level One in beauty therapy entitled me to work in the industry doing most treatments. I applied for a job in Yves Rocher, a posh salon situated in Debenhams, and during Year Two of the course I worked that job around my college days. NVQ Level Two made me a fully qualified beauty therapist. The qualification is recognised as one of the best in the world so it would allow me to work anywhere –

including, of course, on cruise ships, where they loved beauty-trained British girls because the course was so thorough.

I continued to work in a local salon, gaining experience to implement my career plan, and I began to look for jobs on cruise ships. There were many options! However, one of the girls who worked alongside me in Debenhams had previously been employed by Harding Brothers, who were responsible for employing beauty therapists on certain P & O ships.

"They're really good, Lucina! You should go to them."

I followed her advice and wrote to Harding Brothers: "I've just completed my Level 2 NVQ in beauty therapy and I'd like to work with you."

They replied politely: "Thank you for your message. We're interested in your application, but you will require six months' experience in the industry after the award of your Certificate before we can offer you employment on a cruise ship."

I wrote again, telling them I was a hard worker, and reliable, and they offered me an interview at nine in the morning on a certain date on board the cruise liner *Oriana* in Southampton. I loved the fact that the *Oriana* had been built in my home town, Barrow. I drove down to Southampton the evening before the interview, having been booked into the Merchant Seamans' Hotel, which was cheap. After dinner I went to enjoy the beautiful evening on the sea front, relishing the atmosphere of small alleyways and old pubs, which didn't seem to have changed since they were frequented by sailors two centuries or more previously.

In the morning I walked to where the *Oriana* was docked and was taken aback by how huge she was. A person from the beauty therapy department greeted me and led me to the salon aboard the ship. There were about six girls there; the job interview involved doing a manicure for one of the therapists. This was so easy for me that while I was performing the manicure I was able to ask about an employee's life on board. What I'd already been told was confirmed:

"If the ship's sailing, you're working; twelve hour days, sometimes seven days a week. The basic wage is awful so you need tips. The staff food's almost inedible so your money goes on food and drink."

The interview went well, indicating that as I approached the age of thirty I'd become much more confident than I'd been in my schooldays. I was told there and then that I had the job if I wanted it. I was also shown around the ship and the staff quarters, which were Spartan to say the least, and taken to the staff bar, where I was assured I'd be spending a lot of my time and I shouldn't expect to leave with any money. When I asked the therapist for the best advice she could give me, she laughed and said, "Eye drops!"

The *Oriana* was scheduled for a cruise around Miami the following January, leaving from Southampton. I was to fly out to Miami to join the cruise and sail around the coast of America for nine months.

The successful interview boosted my self-esteem. I understood that I wouldn't leave the ship with any of my wages, or if a little was left it would hardly be enough for a short shore leave, but money had never been a major motivator. I wanted the experience, hoping that amid the hard work there would be fun. My main cause of apprehension was that this new life would be hard at first and I'd be homesick, but I was determined not to give up easily and to allow myself time to adjust.

But then something happened that led to a complete change of my plans.

Chapter 3

While I was enjoying a drink and a catch-up with Peter one evening he made a casual remark that altered not just my immediate plans but my whole life. It paralleled my first meeting with the elephant in Bangkok: an accidental but transformative moment. Peter had always taken a 'try anything once' view of life, and I suppose it had rubbed off on me.

"I've tried something you might find entertaining," he said.

"Go on," I said. "What is it?"

"I've been to see a *Dominatrix*."

For weeks, it seemed, he'd been scanning contact magazines for Mistresses and had reduced his shortlist to one based in Manchester. He hadn't really had much of a session with her, but he'd chatted to her afterwards and learned about some of her activities with her clients. Now he was keen to learn my opinion. To say I was startled would be an understatement. But I was also amused and, above all, curious.

I'd heard of BDSM, of course, but knew little about it beyond the popular stereotypes, which I was to learn are misleading. Peter showed me pictures of his new Mistress on his laptop and his choice surprised me. I'd expected a flowing mane of dark silky hair, not a bob of blonde curly locks. I shared most people's misconception that a Dominatrix had to be dark and mysterious. But his first BDSM session had inflamed his interest in the scene; the Mistress had suggested other activities to explore with him at future meetings. Some of the details he recounted were hard to believe. They surprised and even shocked me, but I was oddly excited too, and intrigued.

"She told me about a man who likes to be dressed in women's clothes and then spanked by way of punishment," he said.

I could picture it, but why would a man want to do that? How could he enjoy it?

"She has another submissive who likes to dance to ABBA songs while she throws eggs at him," he added, "or be made to stand on his head while he recites a nursery rhyme."

"Why?" I asked. I knew the range of human tastes was unlimited but I couldn't make sense of this.

"It's about humiliation," he said. "Mistress laughs at your absurdity. It makes you submit totally."

Could anyone really gain pleasure from being forced into abject submission, subjected to humiliation and pain? And what sort of cold, unfeeling person would enjoy inflicting such abuse? No doubt one could make money doing it, of course! Yet I felt drawn to these curious scenarios, and I knew I wasn't cold or unfeeling.

"I'm going for another session," said Peter, "but Mistress told me she wants help in her dungeon. She's looking for a trainee and I've mentioned you to her. I wonder if you'd be interested, Lucina. Do you want to come along to see what it's like?"

"Me?" I laughed. "I'm not sure it would be for me!"

"Why not go and see her?" he urged. "You've nothing to lose, and I think you'd find it fun."

Perhaps he'd seen something in me that I hadn't seen myself. I started to feel tempted. Maybe, I thought, if I was taken on to help in this Mistress's dungeon, I could earn enough money to save. I could put my cruise ship post on hold for a couple of years...

Accepting Peter's suggestion, or challenge, was the most pivotal decision I ever made. Why did I accept it? Partly because Peter had always been an important influence on me and I was willing to follow his lead; partly because I tend to make spontaneous decisions; partly because I was curious; and partly because my sense of adventure made me hunger for new experiences. Maybe there were other reasons, too, that I can't identify. But they don't really matter. What matters is that I went to the Mistress's Chamber, and it changed my life.

*

That first visit to Manchester was unforgettable. The Chamber was beyond anything I'd imagined. I explored a suite of rooms furnished with all manner of devices and torture equipment. I was mesmerised. The dungeon walls oozed dark sensuality. What surprised me most was how comfortable I felt. I seemed to be at one with my surroundings.

The Mistress greeted me, though it wasn't a warm greeting; she seemed awkward with me. Oddly, this put me more at ease; she appeared to be more nervous than I was! We sat down in a tiny lounge made cosy with sofas and well-placed mirrors and chatted over a coffee. Then she told me that one of her slaves, who worked for the M.E.N. Arena, had managed to get hold of Robbie Williams tickets for that night. She was excited.

"Perk of the job," laughed Peter.

She was expecting a client so she started to prepare herself, still chatting. By then she'd begun to thaw and even managed a few smiles. She seemed to have warmed to me completely by the time the client was due, and she asked if I wanted to watch the session.

I accepted, though I was nervous. What was going to happen? We walked into the dungeon and there, at the far end of the room, was a huge gilded throne padded with red velvet. Its grandeur and aura of power were enhanced by the three steps on which it was raised. A grovelling slave would be forced to look upwards. Mistress sat upon the throne and I stood next to her.

"Come on in, slave," she shouted.

The door opened and in crept a little old man, stooped, almost cowering, and totally nude.

"It's a naked man!" was my first thought.

I'd seen undressed men before, and I ought to have expected to see one here, but this one was a stranger and he was old, probably in his eighties. I was half surprised, half shocked. He stumbled awkwardly towards the throne, still half-bowed.

"Kneel here, slave, and worship my boots," commanded Mistress.

I was transfixed. The man crumpled and crawled on all fours to her feet. As the experience unfolded, it seemed to me that both Mistress and slave were gaining from it, each giving, each taking. Dominatrix and submissive seemed to be acting and reacting with an almost psychic connection. It was as if each had an understanding for what the other required without having to utter a word. There was something pure and beautiful about their interaction. As he grovelled at her feet she bellowed at him: "Lick my boots, I said! Lick them harder!"

He obeyed, more and more quickly, almost squirming at her heels. I believe his pleasure was heightened by having an audience, and a new one at that. It was a chance for him to show off.

The session continued with his frail body strapped to a rack while needles were poked and pushed at his unprotected flesh and an electric charge was sparked through his genitals. Occasionally he screamed, yet he longed for more. I laughed, not with contempt or even amusement, but with the joy of witnessing true pleasure and satisfaction achieved in a way I could never have anticipated. Each time Mistress hurt him I laughed. Each time he screamed I chuckled. At each chuckle he glanced at me and then took more punishment. He was enjoying my delight at his pain and humiliation. But Mistress, I noticed, wasn't laughing. She was quite a stone-faced Dominatrix.

"That's just her way," I thought, "so I suppose I ought to be like that, too. I'd better stop chuckling!"

But I couldn't, and the slave loved my merriment! It became natural for me during that very first session and so it remains, seventeen or more years later. I've never held back on a good smile or laugh during session. In fact, I've had sessions where tears of laughter have rolled down my cheeks.

When the session ended I asked the old man what he'd gained from it.

"A place in *sub space*," he said, "far from all my troubles. I can be myself here, exploring things I can only dream about otherwise. There's nothing so relaxing and de-stressing as total submission to my Mistress, completely relinquishing control. The fact that it has to be kept secret adds spice, too."

The phrase 'sub space' puzzled me, but this was a moment of epiphany. A voice in my head said, "You can do this, and you can enjoy it". I felt alive. My senses were buzzing. For the rest of the day I was as high as a kite and I knew I had to explore the BDSM scene further. It had taken until I was nearly thirty years old for me to recognise my dominant nature, and I said so. The Mistress agreed to take me on as her helper and train me in the arts of domination.

"You need a Mistress name," she told me.

I thought about it and decided I would henceforth be Mistress Tanith. It seemed a professional career had been born for me, or at least conceived. But could I *really* do it? Did I truly have what it took to become a Dominatrix? Did I have the confidence?

*

It was a steep learning curve. There was much to discover. My early days as a Mistress buzzed with unbounded excitement as I explored the potential of my role. I was able to spend my days being paid for something I found I enjoyed. In my heart I knew this was right for me, though at the start of my journey I was full of trepidation. I would wake each morning motivated by the promise of new, exciting and ultimately addictive prospects, but I remained apprehensive. The discovery of my latent needs and abilities was gradual.

Do you suppose that a woman capable of domination must be oozing with confidence? Wrong! While I was training to become a Mistress I was shrouded in doubt, afraid I wouldn't be good enough to hold a submissive's interest. Would my skills meet the clients' expectations? And how did I look in this or that outfit?

All the Mistresses I've met have had similar misgivings at the start of their careers. Self-confidence is essential but it can take a long time to build up, and a single comment can flatten it again. However, if there's a good Dominatrix inside her, she'll recover!

"You'll be fine," said my mentor. "No two Mistresses are alike. We're not all cut from the same cloth. Over time you'll discover what you're comfortable with doing and what you need to leave to others."

What, I wondered, is the plural of 'Dominatrix'? Most of us say 'Dominarixes', though I wonder whether it ought to be 'Dominatrices', as in helix-helices, matrix-matrices, and so on. No matter: Mistress had reassured me, at least partially. The cliché of a statuesque woman clad in leather and wielding a whip is most people's image of a Dominatrix, but Mistress was telling me that there's no single or specific template; the BDSM culture encompasses a wide and varied range of activities from corporal punishment through to role-play and from total power exchange to fetishes (in the Freudian sense of 'fetish'; the accepted technical term is 'paraphilia'). A Dominatrix adopts attire and appearance best suited to the areas of the scene in which she specialises.

"I can't say I'm entirely comfortable dealing with naked people and doing things to their bits," I admitted.

"You get used to it, pretty quickly." Mistress grinned. "And they don't get to see *your* bits, let alone do things to them. You stay covered up, even if you choose to wear something provocative."

Indeed, I discovered that only a small minority of Dominatrixes (Dominatrices?) allow sexual contact with their clients. Most of us state explicitly on our websites that we don't offer sex and will block contact from men who ask for it. Many *escorts* offer a certain amount of domination among their services, which obviously do include sex, but they're not specialist Mistresses.

"I don't get why some clients like being made to stand on their heads and recite nursery rhymes, or have eggs thrown at them, or be dressed as women or babies," I said.

BDSM, explained Mistress, is an umbrella term describing a wide array of activities. To try to encapsulate all BDSM sessions in a single image is like trying to say all colours are blue. What happens in the session is just the *means*, and the means are as numerous and varied as the clients. But the *end* is always the same: total submission, abdication of responsibility, relinquishing control: ultimately, albeit rarely, the 'sub space'. Different clients need different ways to reach that *end*, and each of them is best advised choose a Dominatrix whose skills and preferences provide the *means* that suit him.

"Yes, some of us dress in leather," she said, "and whipping is fairly widespread in the scene, but that isn't what all clients want so it isn't what all Mistresses do. It's like any business: the customer's always right. The Dominatrix accommodates the client's wishes as far as she's willing and able to compromise."

*

She told me that domination in its purest form is expressed through a lifestyle. It's part of your inner being and manifest in everyday life.

"I offer a professional service, but I dominate because it is a part of me and it brings me great pleasure. You don't 'become' a Mistress, you just allow yourself to explore that part of your nature. You either have the urge to dominate or you don't. If you don't, you can't be a Dominatrix."

I'd learned a simple distinction: a professional Dominatrix takes a fee (usually called 'tribute') and a lifestyle Dominatrix doesn't; though as Mistress had pointed out, if you don't have something of the lifestyle Dominatrix in your makeup you'll never make it as a professional. A subservient might prefer to connect with a lifestyle Dominatrix because it enables the pair to form a close bond and a durable relationship, even a marriage. This kind of subservient might feel he loses something if he has to pay for the service. But another subservient might prefer a professional who will match his needs to the services she offers without the tie of obligation; he can enter and leave her dungeon at will.

"I believe I'm going to prefer clients with whom I can form a lasting bond," I decided, "so I suppose that makes me a lifestyle Dominatrix who happens to work as a professional."

Many of my assumptions and prejudices were being put to bed. I no longer imagined BDSM to be a culture of dark rituals and nefarious practices, shady actors in seedy back-street dens plying their trade by the pale light of red lamps, haunting grubby corners of the sex industry. The trappings of torture were all around me, but this was nevertheless a place of harmony, of balance and mutual trust, pairing those who sought to exercise their natural subservience with those who hungered for domination and control. However, I was afraid of injuring or harming clients who asked for hard physical punishment.

"The submissive can halt proceedings at any time," said Mistress. "You give the slave a *safe word*, which he can say if he needs you to stop what you're doing. Mind you," she grinned, "the session works better for both parties if you push the slave to the limit!"

Pushing the boundaries, I discovered later, is an important aspect of BDSM.

"I suppose it will take time and experience before I'm confident about judging the level," I said. "But I'm afraid of breaking the law."

"Everything we do here is legal," she said. "Stop worrying about it. A BDSM session is a consensual matching of deep-seated needs and very specific interests – on both sides. That's all. And don't forget, the means to the common end of control and submission are infinitely varied."

*

An experienced slave called Mike booked a session with me and I led him into the dungeon with Mistress keeping a watchful eye on my performance.

"So, slave, what sort of domination do you want?" I asked.

"If you impose rules, Mistress Tanith, I might disobey them and have to be punished." He gestured towards the rack of canes and paddles.

"Then we must talk about limits," I said. "Do you want to be marked or not? If you do, do you want the marks to last a day, a week, or what?"

Mike wanted marks that would last a day or two, so I gave him a safe word: 'Red'. Then I ordered him to strip, kneel and lick my boots. I decided he hadn't licked them properly, so the thinnest cane made half a dozen stripes on his buttocks. He knew the etiquette, counting the strokes and expressing gratitude:

"*One*; thank you, Mistress… *Two*; thank you, Mistress…"

He gasped with pain at each stroke but obviously wanted more. Then he proved incapable of reciting the seven times table correctly, so the cane-welts were overlaid with stripes from the paddle. His arithmetic slowly improved under my guidance. Perhaps I should have been a school-teacher. Out of the corner of my eye I saw Mistress nod in approval. I was giving slave Mike what he needed.

After the session I asked him how long he'd known he was a submissive.

"I used to break school rules on purpose so I'd be punished," he said, "and I'd engineer situations that would make me humiliated."

Mike had known his place in the BDSM scene from childhood. Later, I found that it's not uncommon for submissive and Dominatrix alike to recount stories indicating their incipient nature even as early as primary school. As he'd grown older, Mike had been forced to conceal his irrepressible need for submission to avoid being scorned by society. It was gratifying for me to help him satisfy that need.

"It doesn't seem fair," he sighed. "If you're born gay, everyone congratulates you on your courage when you 'come out'. Everyone at least *pretends* to respect the LGBT commutity these days. But if you're born submissive you're a deviant, to be ridiculed and ostracised. You have to wonder whether people who ridicule BDSM devotees are just ignorant, or afraid of recognising something in themselves they don't want to acknowledge."

I couldn't disagree with him. Would 'Mummy Porn' have seen half the success it's enjoyed if it had been delivered to those with no interest? I don't have statistical evidence, but everyone associated with the sex industry at any level will tell you that submissive tendencies are at least as widespread in the population as homosexual or bisexual orientations. The sustained marginalising of submissives (and, by extension, Mistresses) seems bizarre.

Sessions like the one with Mike became more frequent and before long Mistress didn't need to watch me so closely. Each slave took me on a fresh journey, sometimes long, sometimes short, but always unique and exciting. Of course, in the early days of anything – the warm glow of new love, the challenge of a new job or the excitement of an adventure – the first few sips are the sweetest. I found I was pushing my own limits while venturing on to unbroken ground and tasting the outrageous. I was becoming the thrill junky of the BDSM world, looking for the next big thing that would make me tick a bit more loudly. Perhaps familiarity always breeds the need for more. You don't reach the imagined place where the grass is greener, but you can keep grazing your fill.

There are times when any job, even domination, can become routine and tedious, and there are mornings when you don't want to go to the work and rejoice when you find you have no bookings that day. But those occasions were rare for me. For the most part I was truly enjoying myself.

*

One day a client came to the Chamber for a thirty minute appointment, the shortest session time we offered. He was middle-aged, more than six feet tall and well-built. He wore a good suit.

"Well, slave, what do you want to be done to you?" asked Mistress.

"I'd like to be bent over and fucked, please."

I'd heard of sessions of this kind but I'd never witnessed one. Mistress ordered him to strip and then bent him over the whipping bench, his hands almost touching the floor and his arse held high. She secured a strap-on dildo to herself, lubricated it, and then started to penetrate the hole between his buttocks. Her thrusts became faster and deeper. He grunted and thrust himself back at her.

"Whose little bitch are you?" she shouted.

"I'm your little bitch, Mistress," he squealed.

I found this so funny – a big man in a suit, stripped naked, bent over, begging to be fucked and calling himself 'Mistress's little bitch'!

I loved watching it. The power exchange was amazing. Then Mistress took off her strap-on and handed it to me.

"Would you like to have a go at this slut, too?" she asked.

My initial reaction was shock. "No!" I thought. "I liked watching, but this is a man's arse!" Then another thought came into my head and pushed out the first one. "If you don't do it now you never will. Are you really a scaredy-cat? Come on, Lucina! When in Rome! *You* never bottle out of anything!"

All of that went through my mind in about three seconds, and then I took the strap-on, put it on and fucked the slave's arse as hard as I could. It was wonderful! I knew the feeling of power would become addictive. It was a defining moment for me. I've lost count of how many arses I've fucked since that day.

After the session, Mistress laughed.

"Sorry I put you on the spot like that, Lucina, but I presumed that since you like women you'd have used a strap-on many times before."

As a matter of fact I hadn't. Nevertheless, I'd now broken my strap-on virginity and it felt great!

Since then I've seen the same scenario with many new Mistresses who say they don't want to do strap-on, mainly because they think it will be messy. However, once they've seen other Mistresses do lots of anal, they decide to give it a go; and none of them ever look back. It's not uncommon for me to be sitting on the sofa when a Mistress comes out of one room to go into another with a huge dildo hanging from her strap-on harness. They can rarely resist the fun of doing a little dance and wiggling their cocks around as they walk by. It's ironic that slaves' cocks are often targets for our mockery and humiliation, and they're certainly the most vulnerable areas for punishment; but when a Mistress wears a cock it becomes one of the most powerful of symbols. Maybe Freud had a point!

The downside to anal play is that the client might not be clean. Surely it's obvious that if you're going to see a Dominatrix for this, you should make a special effort to be sure there won't be any mess. Most slaves respect this and are clean. Sometimes there are small accidents, which can be tolerated especially if the penetration is deep and hard. Sometimes, however, Mistresses have to stop a session because there's far too much poo, and this is unacceptable. Most of us make it clear on our websites that clients must be clean if they want anal.

*

The idea that we can obtain joy from making a routine living isn't consistent with the accepted norm. Yet although I still depended on Mistress's support and continued to lack confidence, I was truly enjoying being a Dominatrix. As I left Mistress's dungeon each afternoon, having just flogged the naked rear of a deserving young slave, it amused me that while I pondered the advantages of using a crop over a paddle I would seem a picture of innocence to everyone out there who bothered to notice me.

I meandered the worn paving where human automatons scurried, their minds enslaved by burdens of work, their time given to duty, bustling like ants, each occupied with their role in the collective. I was an island in a sea of nine-to-five existences, people who made being busy their reason for living, their eyes closed to the world. They didn't notice me, and even if they had they'd never have guessed how I was spending my days.

I chuckled to myself. I'd been liberated from the shadow, my eyes wide open as I stretched my wings and soared.

Chapter 4

My mother used to tell me I should build my own life and not marry and have children.

"I love you and I wouldn't want not to have you," she said, "but if I could have my time over again I'd stay single and childless and make my own way in the world."

She said it so many times, especially while she was ill, that her advice stayed with me. It made me decide I wouldn't marry or have children unless I found someone who was one hundred percent right for me. I wasn't going to marry just for the sake of it.

"If a soulmate appears in my life," I thought, "then great; otherwise I'll be happy with my own company."

The truth is that I was as much of a loner as an adult as I'd been during childhood. In any case, none of the married people I knew seemed especially happy.

"If you could go back to the beginning, would you still get married?" I used to ask them.

Some said, "No". Most said, "I would, but not as young as I did. I'd do more for myself first and leave the marriage and kids until later."

For a woman to lack maternal feelings, not to want children, is considered almost taboo. For years I half-expected the maternal urge to kick in, to find myself suddenly wanting or even needing a child, but it never did. I don't seem to have quite the same fondness for children that many women have. Perhaps caring for my niece Sam when I was a teenager – the nights spent awake, the nappy changes and all the rest – had been enough to drive the urge out of my system, much as I'd loved her (and still love her) and much as I'd felt joy at witnessing her developmental landmarks: first steps, first words, first day at school. All I'd missed out on was childbirth itself, and I didn't crave that! In 2018 I had a hysterectomy because of a benign uterine tumour and it was one of the best things I've ever done. Being single and childless suits me. I've no regrets.

During the most challenging times in my life I've recognised that it's more difficult to manage alone, without the support of a partner, but I've had practical help from slaves who've acted more out of friendship than submissiveness. Emotionally, however, I've never needed much support. Peter is there for me, but when he isn't around I've never felt the need to turn to anyone else. I've had a few intimate personal relationships that have been great in their way, but only two have lasted more than a few months. When I come home from work I need my own space and I want to be alone in it. I have a few close friends, but I prefer to limit my social life. I relax best in my own company.

Anyway, here I was, following my mother's guidance: living alone and starting to make my own way, building my own business. I prefer to put my misfortunes down to experience, but I do have one regret. When my mother was alive, the little money she had was spent on bills. I remember her crying at Christmas because she couldn't afford to buy presents, and I was in no position to help her. When I started to earn money as a Dominatrix I thought how lovely it would have been if I'd been able to go to my mother with a hundred pounds and say, "Here you are, Mum", or, "Don't worry about that gas bill, I'll pay it". I'd have done that and more if she'd lived. But I never got the chance.

*

After I'd worked a few months as her trainee, the Mistress rang me one day and told me not to go back. No explanation. She wouldn't even allow me to call to pick up the bits and pieces I'd left in the Chamber. Needless to say I was shocked and upset; I'd always been honest with her, as I am with everyone. I hadn't minded giving her fifty percent of the tribute from my submissives; it was a high levy but she had a Chamber to run, and even then I appreciated the expenses involved. Whenever a slave gave me a tip I told her; she always took it off me, except once. Nevertheless I regularly walked away from my day's work with more money in my pocket than I'd ever had, and I'd never spoken ill of her. So what had happened?

There were two people who might have caused trouble. One was a new slave who when he sessioned with me alone kept asking me to meet him outside the Chamber.

"I'll pay you to have dinner with me, but don't tell the other Mistress."

Of course I'd said "No". He was a creep. I think Mistress only accepted him as a regular because he had money. I heard that her next trainee accepted his offer and sessioned behind her back. Later, when I was established in my own Chamber, he contacted me and begged for a session.

"No!" I said. "You're a mischief-maker and I don't want to see you."

The other possibility was a transvestite maid who helped out in the Chamber. He too asked for secret sessions. Again I refused.

"I'll only session in private with you if you ask Mistress and she agrees," I told him.

Whichever of those two pests lied to Mistress, they did me a favour. I'd been happy in her Chamber 'learning the ropes', if you'll forgive the phrase, but her summary dismissal gave me a push. My immediate reaction was to return to Cumbria and sit feeling sorry for myself. However, that didn't last long.

"You know, Lucina," said Peter, "she isn't the only Mistress in Manchester who's asked for help."

"You're right," I agreed.

That little conversation turned the upset into something positive. I started to consider how I could face a brave new world of domination alone. Of course I was grateful for Mistress's teaching and support; but in any profession, it's natural for apprentices and students approaching graduation to feel they're outgrowing their mentors. Her experienced guidance in matters of safety as well as in the arts of domination had been invaluable and I'll always appreciate it. You can't learn such things from a book. However, I'd become increasingly aware of the difference in the way we treated clients after their sessions. She was quite cold and often rude, whereas I wanted a little chat.

"That's not the way it's done," she told me. "After the session they should be gone within five minutes."

I couldn't come around to her way of thinking. She saw the clients as pathetic men with money and she called them 'pieces of shit'. I'm sure some slaves want to feel like that, but I was learning many of them didn't. Most were intelligent, professional men; they didn't want to be treated like shit after the session; they appreciated a simple conversation while they were readying themselves to leave. This difference between Mistress and me had started to create bad feeling, so an eventual rift was inevitable.

*

Those reflections were only half-formed as I set out to launch my solo flight as a Mistress. Excited though I was, and much as I felt I'd found the right career for me (would it seem pretentious to call it a 'vocation'?), I was still new to the industry and still far from confident. Partly because of insecurity and partly to stimulate business, I began my new career by messaging other Mistresses around Manchester:

"I'm a Dominatrix new to the area and I'm keen to work in partnership with another Mistress. Would you be interested in teaming up with me?"

After weeks of frustration, unreturned e-mails and a series of 'thanks but no thanks' messages, a Mistress wishing to set up a new dungeon in Manchester replied. She gave her name as Anita. This was what I'd been waiting for. However, nothing is ever as it seems. A golden goose seldom flies into your nest by invitation. Far from discovering riches, I found myself burdened with the responsibility of training a woman with even less experience than I had.

Anita had decided to set up a domination business with the help of a man called Roger, whose goal seemed to be to get into her pants. I soon recognised his intention and it made me uncomfortable. As far as I could tell, she was playing him to get what she could from him. Their plan was to rent a tiny penthouse flat in the centre of Manchester. This was among the first of the posh new flats being built in the city at the time when the Hilton Hotel was under construction. I soon discovered that Roger was the mastermind behind their scheme. Anita wasn't only inexperienced, she didn't even seem very interested. She often failed to turn up for bookings and then she disappeared for days and we couldn't contact her.

"This isn't going to work," I realised. "Her heart isn't in it."

I put my name on the flat rental because Anita's credit wasn't good enough, and Roger was married and didn't want awkward questions. In the end, this proved to be a good thing for me. The apartment had one bedroom, which we converted into the 'play area'. I had to sleep on a pull-out sofa. However, the balcony doors opened on to Deansgate, so the city was right on my doorstep. It was all very exciting, though I loved returning to Cumbria every weekend to breathe the beautiful sea air.

As my mentor had said, you're either attracted the BDSM scene or you aren't. You can't teach a woman to become dominant, or for that matter submissive; all you can hope to do is unlock abilities and needs already there. For some people there are hints of a penchant for domination from a very early age; for others (such as me) it's brought to the surface later. But if it isn't there at all, it can't be created.

"Are you sure this is for you?" I asked Anita, certain that the answer was *No*.

She looked uncomfortable.

"Roger's a submissive and he's seen a lot of Mistresses, and he wants me to... Well, you know. He's really intelligent and thinks we can make a go of this business."

I asked her to explain. She said he was going to run the Dominatrix business for her while at the same time taking advantage of her newly-acquired skills, and presumably her body, for his own satisfaction.

"He says we'll make a lot of money," she added.

"I see. But you need to be trained first, and that's to be my job, is it?"

"Yes."

Nice idea, perhaps, but if you want to try car-racing you must first ensure your car has an engine. Roger had assumed that Anita would take to domination like the proverbial duck to water, but he was wrong, so his plan was doomed. It didn't take long for my first-ever trainee to decide she wasn't cut out for the industry. No one was surprised when she quit. However, it wasn't a complete loss for Roger; he did get into her pants. More than once, I returned to the flat on a Monday to find them playing in the play room. Using the apartment as a kinky love nest was unprofessional and it was awkward for me.

"Pity she's not cut out for a Mistress role," said Roger. He studied me. "I'm still keen to run a domination business, though. Are you in? I'll be happy to work with you. We'll make a very good income."

Drawn by the promise of the security I craved, I took Anita's place in his scheme.

"You'll need a new working name," he said, "not the one you used while you were training. A new name will bring new clients." He pondered. "Do you know Rowley's play, *The Birth of Merlin*? No? Well, according to that play, when the most famous of all magicians was being born in a cave in the forest, Lucina brought the Fates to attend his mother and bestow gifts on him. I think you should be Princess Lucina."

"I'm not sure I'd want that much limelight," I said.

"That's the point," said Roger. "Lucina hid in the shadows. As Mistress of the Fates she never wished to be seen."

Seventeen years later, I'm still Princess Lucina when I dominate my clients.

*

My arrangement with Roger functioned for about six months. I found my feet working as a lone Mistress and I enjoyed the support of a partner keen to generate business. We explored other areas of the sex industry, sharing the costs of setting up an escort agency while I continued to develop my skills as a Dominatrix. Unfortunately, after Anita left, Roger turned his amorous attentions towards me. I refused to accept his recurrent offers of allegedly mind-blowing sex and his requests for long domination sessions in the play room. On two occasions his advances became so assertive that I had to leave the apartment for a while. It seemed he wanted to fuck anyone or anything except his wife. To his credit, however, he did take "No!" for an answer, which is why our partnership lasted as long as it did.

Roger also went down to the main door to greet clients, or if they found their own way upstairs he opened the door for them. At the time I presumed this was the way things were done. Also, the presence of a man was good for safety. However, when I started to receive e-mails thanking me for sessions, many clients said they were uncomfortable about the little bald guy who opened the door. Since then I've made sure there are no men around when slaves come to my Chamber and I ensure that my clients never meet each other. It's important for a slave to feel comfortable when he enters the dungeon.

I say 'he' because the large majority of a Mistress's clients are men, though we have female slaves too. Whence the gender imbalance? Here's a possible answer: women have traditionally held subordinate places in the household and at work, and in most varieties of heterosexual intimacy they're the 'passive' partners, *done to* rather than *doing*. Also, our culture makes it harder for men than women to express and release emotion without being 'persuaded'. Perhaps, therefore, while everyday life frustrates submissive men, it meets the needs of most submissive women. I wonder whether we'll see more women seeking domination at the hands of professionals when more of us attain top posts involving major responsibility and sustained stress, increasing women's need to relinquish control in order to unwind. If so, the ones who session with a Dominatrix will presumably have lesbian leanings. The straight ones will have to seek 'Dominators' (Masters) to address their needs. I know such Masters exist, but more of them will be needed if my prediction comes true. I hope plenty of men with the right nature will be willing to brave social censure and take up that challenge. After all, why shouldn't men have the chance to succeed in a woman's world?

The escort agency finally ended my connection with Roger. His interest was diverted more and more to this new business, diminishing the support he gave me as a Mistress. Even though he was taking half my tributes, his presence during sessions was becoming less and less frequent, so if anything had gone wrong I'd have been on my own. While I had a *financial* interest in the agency, my only *professional* interest was in my business as a Dominatrix. When it became clear that we were on different paths we parted company, amicably but irrevocably. He was also mixing business with pleasure, so the girls were doing whatever they wished and walking all over him. This was not a recipe for success. Indeed, I believe his business folded soon after we went our separate ways, mainly because his wife was unhappy about never seeing him. Anyway, I was left to work from the penthouse apartment, completely alone for the first time.

Being alone and inexperienced as a *lifestyle* Dominatrix means not knowing how to find a submissive to share your passion. As a *professional* Dominatrix, being inexperienced and alone means having to learn very quickly how to advertise, market your services and balance the books. Graduating from a protected environment to a world where I had to stand on my own two feet was unnerving. In any business, those first few steps into independence are fraught. I hadn't made new friends since moving to Manchester so I felt very alone. I still had doubts; I was still uncertain I had what it would take to succeed in the industry. I was scared that I wouldn't be able to meet the demands of running a business. Had I taken a wise decision? Was I deceiving myself about my ability?

*

After a while I devised a business system that seemed to work and e-mails requesting appointments began to appear. One morning I received such an e-mail from a new client:

"Dear Princess Lucina, my name is David. I've studied your website and I'd like to meet You. At present I am on business in the south so it will be some time before I can visit You, but I would like to send You a gift."

Perhaps 'David' is the most common male name in England because a remarkably high percentage of my clients introduce themselves as David or Dave! I'll label this client 'David1' (and the one I described at the start of this book, the first to reach 'sub space' in my Chamber, will be 'David2'). One thing was obvious: David1 was an experienced submissive because he knew how to address a Dominatrix. All pronouns relating to a Mistress should be given upper-case initial letters: I, Me, My; You, Your, Yours; She, Her, Hers. That's part of the etiquette required of a slave.

"Of course, slave David," I replied. "What gift do you propose to send Me?"

"May I be permitted to send You perfume wrapped up in twenty pound notes?"

I'd be surprised if any woman reading this wouldn't find the offer attractive. I'd received such requests before, but the promised gifts had never materialised. So when I wrote back, "Yes, that would be acceptable", and named the appropriate perfume, I didn't expect any result. I was to be surprised. A few days later a parcel arrived containing my favourite perfume wrapped in twenty pound notes. Actually, I wasn't so much surprised as stunned; I hadn't done anything to earn this gift. It simply showed that a submissive had met his need by sending a gift to a Mistress.

For some submissives, the need for domination is met by being bound tightly and/or beaten. For others it can be an act such as presenting a gift or providing financial support. In our culture, and others, there's been a long tradition of men supporting women financially, usually in exchange for sex, and some women exploit this by helping men to lighten their bank accounts while entertaining them in bed. The financial domination facet of the BDSM world (usually shortened to Fin Dom) has more devotees than you might suppose. The appeal to slaves seems ambivalent. They enjoy being controlled and financially exploited by the Mistress, but at the same time their relative wealth gives *them* control. Anyway, David1's present boosted my self-belief no end and went a long way towards persuading me that I could indeed succeed in business. It was an important stepping stone in my career as a professional Dominatrix so I'll never forget it. My confidence has grown throughout my subsequent career, fed by the compliments of repeat clients and those special moments where I know I've made a difference to someone. But it was David1's gift that made me realise I'd *arrived*.

"I'm now truly *inside* this amazing world of BDSM," I thought. "I can really do this!"

David1 and I exchanged a series of e-mails over the following weeks. The bond required for a proper Mistress-slave relationship was forming and a friendship was starting to germinate. Once when I'd failed to reply to one of his messages, for reasons I can't recall, he e-mailed again.

"Please, Princess Lucina, message me back, even if it's to say, 'Piss off, you pathetic slug!'"

That made me chuckle! So it was that his slave name was born. From that day forth, David1 was affectionately known as 'Sluggie'.

We did eventually meet. He found a way to come to Manchester, using business as a thinly-veiled disguise for his journey. However, circumstances sometimes conspire to leave the best-laid plans in shreds, and our first attempt at meeting was an example. The appointment was set for eight o'clock on a particular evening. Everything was in place. The anticipation was building nicely. But that very day I developed an abscess on my wisdom tooth. I don't know if you've ever suffered the pain of a gum abscess, but if you have you'll realise that my mind was far from achieving the focus needed by a Mistress about to meet a client.

I hadn't yet registered with a dentist in Manchester so I was forced to travel back to my home town in Cumbria to be relieved of my pain. To make matters worse, Sluggie had no mobile phone, so the only way I could cancel our meeting was by e-mail; and he didn't receive the message in time. As a result, there he was at eight o'clock, standing outside the building, chocolates and champagne in hand, only for an empty apartment to greet him. Naturally he was disappointed and upset, as was I, but he was kind enough to understand that it couldn't have been helped.

It was thanks to that failed meeting with Sluggie that I moved into a bigger and more domination-friendly flat. He'd rung several buzzers outside the building until a blonde woman answered, whereupon he asked if he could leave the champagne and chocolate with her, giving my apartment number. When I called at the woman's door later to collect the gift, she invited me in.

"This apartment's huge compared to my tiny penthouse!" I thought.

I promptly rang my landlord to ask if he had any two-bedroom flats available for rent. He had. I moved to the second floor of the same building and at last I had my own bed instead of the pull out sofa. The second bedroom was large for a city centre flat and I converted it into a perfect little Chamber, making the most of every inch. It served me well for seven years; I didn't need much play space because I used it economically.

"*You* could dominate in an empty room!" one client told me.

It was a huge compliment, but I thought, "That's what I've been doing for the past year!"

*

"You will buy a cheap mobile phone," I ordered Sluggie, "so there will be no risk of further wasted journeys."

Sluggie wasn't attracted to pain and had no interest in a dungeon setting; instead, he was driven by a fetish for feet and a love of shoes. Rather than using our time in session, we'd visit the Trafford Centre where I'd order him to buy me new shoes or perfume. I'd tie a rope around his balls and cut a small hole in his trouser pocket so I could pull the rope through. While we sat drinking cocktails I could tug the rope, pulling his balls and thus controlling him in front of crowds of people without any of them knowing. I found this very funny and it also made me feel powerful.

I was happy with our arrangement; it required no effort on my part and it was easy to maintain. Whenever I wanted new perfume or a new pair of shoes I would simply order Sluggie to buy me the gift; and sure enough, within a few days a parcel would arrive containing whatever I'd demanded.

Sluggie's love of Fin Dom didn't mean his BDSM interests lacked kink. He liked being ordered to masturbate into his wife's shoes and then to clean up the mess. He enjoyed nothing more than to be made to wear lacy knickers beneath his trousers while he was at work or to play with himself in the toilets. This kind of fetish play, quite common within the BDSM scene, seldom crosses over into the cliché scenario of bondage and discipline.

Sadly, my wonderful arrangement with Sluggie couldn't last forever. When it came to subservience he was far from faithful. That in itself didn't trouble me. Submissive men often show their loyalty on various levels, some sticking to a single Mistress, others sessioning with more than one Dominatrix. However, Sluggie had sworn his loyalty to me, often begging to become my 'contract' slave, yet he still sought services with others. It created an unstable situation. A number of years passed before it finally came to a head when another of his *owners* ordered that he no longer be permitted to contact me. I was hurt.

Throughout our adventure my interest had been invested in the journey we were taking together. We'd become friends and we'd bonded as Mistress and slave. His particular fetish had been a new experience for me and part of my growth as a Dominatrix. It was pleasing to receive gifts to order, but that hadn't been my motive for becoming David1's Mistress, for continuing as his Mistress, and becoming a friend and confidante. I recalled many conversations in which he'd shared his private worries with me.

'My sons are going to college soon,' he once told me. 'My wife and I will be alone together for the first time in seventeen years and I'm terrified. What will we have to say to each other? I'm due for retirement and I don't want to take it.'

Helping him to come to terms with such worries was every bit as important, for both or us, as providing the kind of domination he'd wanted. Little wonder I was hurt by his departure.

Later, he realised the error of his ways and begged me to take him back, but the damage had been done. We'd both learned a valuable lesson. From that day forward, David1 understood that taking a journey with somebody who wished to share in his needs was more valuable than buying a quick fix to ease those needs temporarily. For me, the lesson was that while it's good to make an investment in the needs and wishes of your slave, such things are seldom meant to last. I refused David1's request to return to duty as my slave. Was I allowing pride to get in the way of a good thing? I don't think so.

Chapter 5

No matter how much we enjoy our work we all need time off. Although my business was starting to prosper, I needed a holiday; and true to his word as always, Peter took me together with my niece Samantha on another visit to Thailand. This time I paid for myself, as agreed. I'd felt compelled to seek another encounter with elephants. There was no shortage of opportunities; many trips on the backs of these magnificent creatures were, and are, available. The hotels offer countless pamphlets about parks where you can watch elephants perform or paint, but it was the elephant excursions that appealed to me because they appeared much more natural than tricks and performing. There seemed no better way to explore the wonders of Thailand than from the back of an elephant, so I took every opportunity to do so. At the time, I thought nothing could be more glorious than to ride on one of these splendid animals. I was completely safe, sitting on a chair on the elephant's back; even snakes are scared away by the vibrations of an elephant's footsteps.

It wasn't until I took a day trip into the mountains in the north of the country that I discovered such excursions to be nothing more than packaged thrills for tourists. Peter, Sam and I arranged to visit a sanctuary dedicated to elephants that had been hurt, abandoned or abused. We went to an office in the centre of Chiang Mai, the old capital of Siam (Thailand), less hectic than Bangkok and surrounded by jungle and open land. There we were met by a truck driver who took us along a winding, potholed road to the base of the jungle, also the base of the elephant sanctuary.

There were three parts to the sanctuary, but on a single day trip I could only visit the first part, low-lying and down the river. Across the river, through the dense jungle and far up the mountain, was Elephant Haven, where once a week the volunteers would trek with the elephants who could manage the journey. There, the volunteers slept in a hut while the elephants roamed free in safety. To make the trek you sat on an elephant's neck, with no chair, hanging on for dear life while you crossed the fast-flowing flooded river. There was no other way to cross, but you could depend on the astonishing resilience of the animals. During the rest of the week the volunteers stayed with the elephants in the third part of the sanctuary a few miles upriver, where the jungle was less dense. Here, the elephants had to be chained at night in case they wandered into the fields in search of food, because farmers had the right to shoot them. Chaining wasn't necessary in Elephant Haven because there were no farmers for miles around. There, the volunteers and mahouts stayed in one hut with no electricity, just torches and candlelight. In the dead of night they could hear the subtle calls exchanged by the elephants as they slept.

In the morning I had to go out with my mahout to find the elephant on which I'd ridden to the sanctuary. He panicked because he couldn't find his girl. Trying to keep up with a skinny, fully-fit Thai man who runs through the jungle like Usain Bolt isn't easy. But we discovered his elephant, safe and sound, happily munching on fresh branches.

In the sanctuary on that day trip I met Max, the second largest bull elephant in Thailand. When he was standing, his bulk arched so high that at five feet four inches tall that I could walk beneath his belly without having to bend. Max had been a working elephant trudging the busy streets of Bangkok, but he'd suffered a serious accident. There was an open lesion in his face and he had a massive infection.

"The bonnet of a truck hit him," I was told. "As well as the infection he has severe pain in his hips."

He'd been at the sanctuary for only a few months. Because of his injuries he couldn't yet make it up to Elephant Haven, so his mahout stayed in the lower camp with him. I spent that unforgettable day with Max, helping to feed him and washing his aching limbs. As the mahout bathed the wound, this gentle behemoth drew his trunk to his mouth as if trying to ease his pain. It was a pure moment, unpolluted by fake tourist packaging. I sat at the huge feet of this glorious animal, looking up in awe. Not for one moment did I feel in danger. Every now and again the elephant glanced down at us.

"He's telling us he understands. He knows we're trying to help him."

When another elephant was brought down from the Haven, a bull like Max, I saw one of his tusks was missing.

"He was used for illegal logging," said his human companion. "While he was tied to a tree, a poacher cut his tusk off with a motorised hacksaw, as close to his face as possible. Poachers want to ensure the maximum profit."

This elephant's mahout had originally brought the unfortunate animal to the camp to have his wound treated, but he'd been persuaded to sell him to the camp's founder. I was honoured to be given the opportunity to ride on him, not as a tourist sitting upon a throne but perched upon his head, as is right. It was an unforgettable experience. I couldn't believe how high I was seated or how little I could hold on to. There was nothing like the safety and comfort of the cushion of a saddle, but this was so much better. The elephant's head was covered in stiff, spiky hairs that stuck upward and prickled my behind. As he trundled forward and wandered beneath trees with large branches, forcing me to bend, I fought for balance. But at no time did I feel in danger.

"He's caring for my wellbeing," I said. "Every time he feels I might fall he clamps my legs with those huge ears. It's amazing!"

Watching this elephant bathe was incredible, the mahout clambering on board and scrubbing the skin while the animal wallowed in the depths of the river. I stood close by, throwing water over his massive bulk, loving every moment. All of a sudden the elephant rose to his feet and the water rushed forward to fill the vacuum left by his body. Taken unawares, I stumbled under the power of the current. I had just enough time to thrust out my hands, pushing against the elephant to prevent myself from being pulled beneath the murky depths.

It was easy for me to decide to become more involved with the elephant sanctuary. No sooner had I landed back in England than I'd begun to plan my return, this time for four weeks in the mountains as a volunteer.

*

Such a trip takes more than a little preparation, but before very long I was on a plane heading back to my new-found passion. This time I didn't have my suitcase full of clothes and makeup for nights out but a new rucksack full of the essentials for living in the jungle for a month, including a torch and batteries and just enough money to survive. I don't think I'd ever felt so nervous as when I reached the sanctuary's tiny office. I was a long way from my Chamber; I'd retreated from my Dominatrix persona and felt like just a small town girl on a jungle safari, completely immersed in the unknown. But this was where I wanted to be, and I was excited as well as apprehensive.

I was joined on my adventure by a band of intrepid explorers all of whom shared my passion. We'd travelled there from all over the globe, divided by language but united in our common cause – our love for the magnificent elephants. One by one we slipped into the back of a small truck and wound our way into the mountains. We passed the camp where I'd befriended Max, reviving wonderful memories. I asked about him.

"Max eventually made it up to the Haven," said the guide, "and he's living there, though his hips still aren't good."

Our journey ended some distance from the site of my previous adventure. It was a constricted piece of land with huts nestling in the branches of trees, forming a village in the sky. Although each of those tree-bound lodges was compact, they'd been built to be practical. A mattress filled one snug room almost entirely; mosquito netting hung from the ceiling, protecting the bed from the winged vampires. A second room, equally small, housed a toilet and a large bucket. The bucket filled with water that dripped continuously from the roof, a basic but effective fresh water supply. There was no electricity; no light switches to flick, no bulbs to glow. Navigation during twilight was conducted by the light of a battery-powered torch or undertaken with stubbed toes and curses.

This odd hamlet of roosting shanties was huddled around a single larger hut, the communal area. Here we met to share meals and enjoy various forms of recreation. It also housed the village's only source of electricity, a tiny generator chugging petrol fumes into the jungle air so we could cook meals and make toast.

"No phones, no laptops, no newspapers – this is life in isolation!" I laughed. "I love it!"

Each day began like a scene from a Disney animation. I rose to the warmth of Thailand's sweltering furnace and carefully climbed from my Ewok-style shelter. As I traversed the steps of the neat wooden ladder, the friendliest elephant greeted me. We quickly became pals. This wonderful beast had taken a liking to the fruit that surrounded my home. His trunk rose into the air and he munched the sumptuous flesh of an exotic pear while he waved a warm welcome to me. Could there be a more perfect start to a day?

As well as elephants there were many stray dogs, all now cared for with kindness. Their homes had been the streets and their lives had been hard, but now they lived under the luxurious green canopy of the jungle. One of these dogs volunteered its services as my protector, standing sentry at the door of my hut, keeping me safe while I slept.

"Hello again," I said, responding to his morning greeting with a stroke and a cuddle. "Are you coming to the breakfast hut with me?"

He always followed me there. But there was no time to linger. After a thirst-quenching guzzle of water we were off to work. The first job of the day was to clean the area where the elephants slept. Basically, this involved a shovel, an aching back and a distinctive smell. It wasn't the most glamorous of occupations but it was honest, useful work and I enjoyed it. The texture of elephant faeces is different from that of any other animal because of the diet; it's so full of fibres it can be used as paper.

"Can you imagine a world where what passes from the body can thereafter be used to clean up the mess?" I said. "It adds a whole new dimension to the concept of recycling."

After a quick cup of coffee it was a time for a bath, not just for us but for the elephants too. This involved a walk to the river and a shared dip with our four-legged friends. No thought was given to safety. There was just unlimited trust and lots of fun. I'd sit on an elephant's back as he waded into the river, and slowly the water would come up to my bottom. All I could see was the elephant's head and trunk. I'd scrub until its head was clean. Elephants have the gentlest of souls and I never felt at risk. I swam beneath their bellies and moved with ease around their legs with never a hint of danger. We just had to make sure we weren't down-river if they did a poo; parts of the river were fast-moving so it wasn't easy to get out of the way!

There were a couple of babies who'd been orphaned, their mothers having been shot by poachers just after giving birth. These beautiful creatures loved to play, often hiding beneath the water with only the tips of their trunks peeping out. If you walked within range of that waving grey periscope, it wrapped itself gently around your leg and pulled you beneath the waves. They were enchanting.

Living here amongst those delightful creatures, escaping the hustle of modernity, was a process of detoxification for me, all things material being gradually shed from my life. I slept in my hut in the jungle canopy. I had only ten pounds in my wallet. I've never been happier, and perhaps I never will be.

After the bathing was finished a truck arrived laden with bananas. The elephants always appreciated this lunchtime snack and set out to devour every last one. After lunch they were attached to long chains, rather like putting a dog on a leash but with much bigger collars. The long chains were needed to protect the animals. When the mahouts weren't about, the elephants would wander away, and because the sanctuary had no fences they could easily get into farmers' fields; where, elephants being elephants, they'd eat all the crops. Farmers therefore poisoned some crops or just shot the intruders.

Then it was time for us to relax, which for me meant an opportunity to renew acquaintance with my old friend Max. After the other elephants had had their baths in the river it was Max's turn. He liked to bathe alone because he was quite unsteady on his huge legs. When I'd first visited the jungle camp Max hadn't been given a mahout, but he had one now: Karl, an Australian guy who like me had come to the jungle as a volunteer but had decided he was going to live there. Max was full-time work; he needed constant medication and attention and there are no days off. But Karl was dedicated and we shared the same love for Max.

The short walk to the river took time for Max's slow legs. It was usually midday when we arrived and the sun was overpowering, so I always walked in his shadow to keep cool. Max would cover himself in mud as a sun block and return to his hut dirtier than when he'd left. Nevertheless, being in the water to wash Max was an experience I truly appreciated, one that the other volunteers didn't share. I believe Karl saw my love for the big fellow, and I certainly saw Max's love for him.

"Is there any civilisation around here?" asked one of the volunteers.

"Tiny village, not far away." A mahout pointed out the direction. "You can buy a few things."

I decided to take a look. The village was indeed tiny but I could purchase beer and cigarettes. Those weren't items I wanted for myself, but they enabled me to put the ten pounds in my wallet to good use. As I walked up to the village I saw children playing around their little huts-on-stilts. They were almost in rags, but I noted how happy they seemed.

"For you," I said, handing my purchases over for the mahouts to share. "I just want to show how much I appreciate your remarkable work with the elephants."

When an elephant is assigned to a mahout they're usually partnered for life. If the mahout dies the elephant will pine, and this often ends in its own untimely death. I've known the same thing happen with loving human couples; one partner dies and the other soon follows. Mahouts are decent men who carve out an honest living, taking what they can from the land. They care for their families and live the simplest of lives with crops and a handful of chickens. They deserved my gifts. It felt good to show they were valued for their care of the elephants.

Each evening the cook arrived with batches of colourful powders and odd-looking produce that was magically transformed into a feast. Bonds soon formed among everyone present. We were always glad of each other's company. After dinner the mahouts joined us and we shared a few beers.

"We want to learn more English," they told me.

"Well, I want to learn to speak Thai," I replied, "so let's spend a few hours exchanging language lessons."

*

One morning, after I'd decided to sleep in the communal area with all the dogs, I was awoken at sunrise by the shouts of a mahout who spoke very little English: "MAX, MAX, MAX!"

The panic in his voice told me something was very wrong. I followed him to where Max was lying. Elephants like to sleep lying down as long as they feel safe, but Max could only sleep standing up because of his hips. This time he'd lain down to sleep and now he couldn't get up again. He was trying but he was clearly in distress. As I stood next to his prone form, his head reached almost the same height as mine and our eyes were on the same level. I stayed and stroked his trunk, trying to reassure and comfort him, until Karl arrived; then Max's trunk rose and wrapped around him. Such was the bond between them that the elephant knew all would be well now Karl was there.

Meanwhile, other mahouts had gathered and were talking rapidly in Thai, debating what to do. They fetched Lilly, the largest elephant in the sanctuary apart from Max. We put a chain around her and managed to get the other end around Max. With lots of shouting, and lots of determination from Lilly, who surely knew what was happening, Max slowly struggled to his feet. There were a few false starts because he was in pain, but more people had gathered now, and as Lilly pulled him we all got behind and pushed, shouting encouragement to both elephants in Thai and English. I'm sure they understood. Eventually, Max was on his feet with a look that said, "I'm never doing that again".

I hadn't had time to put on my mosquito cream and I'd been standing in deep undergrowth for over an hour. My legs were covered in sores and bites that took months to heal. While I remained in the jungle I used Max's face cream to ease the pain.

*

I was honoured to meet the founder of the sanctuary, an amazing lady called Lek. She'd dedicated her life to elephants, often risking her own life to do so. The Thai government didn't want the plight of elephants in their country to be highlighted; elephants bring tourist dollars so any bad press is viewed dimly. Lek was a diminutive woman but surprisingly strong, and not just in will. Together, we travelled what she called the Jumbo Express.

"It means a trip down to the city," she said, "so you can see at first hand just how badly tourism harms elephants."

This is where the truth was laid bare: I saw overworked animals poorly fed and kept in appalling conditions. The seats on their backs had rubbed their skin and caused painful sores. Lek had opened my eyes to what my own tourist dollars had once fostered. The Jumbo Express was her way of administering free medication and providing the care the elephants needed and deserved. I stood and watched the tourists coming in on the backs of those lovely animals, all smiling and taking pictures, oblivious to the pain and suffering they were causing. But of course I'd been oblivious, too.

As tourists we live in a beautiful dream, unaware of the truth hidden in shadow. My time at the sanctuary was a valuable lesson in not taking everything at face value. Thailand is a paradise that holds much appeal, but we need to take care in our choice of activities. Elephants have been used in Thailand for many years now, for war among other purposes, but more recently they've been exploited for logging as well as to entertain tourists. Some have been looked after and well fed, but others have been terribly abused and overworked. In 1989, logging was banned by the Thai government owing to a shortage of trees. You'd have expected this to lead to tighter guidelines, reservations and sustainable farming. However, it had the opposite effect. Instead of curtailing the rape of natural resources, it increased it. Rather than working set hours, the loggers now operated in short bursts around the clock so they couldn't be caught, resulting in the wholesale destruction of areas of forest. The effect on the elephants was devastating: they were pressed into hard labour, drugged to ensure they were willing to work longer and abused when they couldn't, forced to go on even when they were exhausted. Some were worked to death. Some gave birth while they were pulling logs and weren't allowed to go to their babies. It was elephants such as those that ended up at the sanctuary.

An elephant named Lilly May had been used for illegal logging although she was pregnant. She gave birth at the top of a hill and her baby fell down the slope. Chained to the logs, Lilly May couldn't help her newborn. The baby died. Instead of compassion for her loss she was met with violence. Losing her calf had made her aggressive, so in order to control her she was stabbed in both eyes. When Lek discovered her she was blind and in a terrible condition. Remarkably, while she was being cared for at the sanctuary, another elephant took her under its wing. We speak of humanity, empathy and kindness, yet the burden of guilt lay entirely on our species; it took an elephant to show benevolence, and an elephant to save Lilly May's life. Gently, using her trunk, this surrogate nurse led her patient to the river. Together they ate bananas, slept and played, their lives joined by a loving bond.

One baby elephant came to Lek via a local village. His mother had fallen victim to poachers so soon after his birth that he hadn't even had an opportunity to suckle. Filled with terror, the baby had fled to the jungle where he was later found starving and close to death. Again the sanctuary came to the rescue and nursed him back to health. This beautiful animal was to be called 'Hope'. No name could have been more fitting.

*

By the time I took my leave of the jungle, my heart had been bruised by the cruelty the elephants often suffered. So deeply had my soul been touched that I considered buying land and starting my own sanctuary. Unfortunately it isn't easy for a foreigner to acquire property in Thailand so the plan fell by the wayside. Over time, life and priorities change. I can't say *my* priorities changed; I'd still like to make a difference out there; but sometimes things are just not meant to be.

Despite my preference for a solitary life it's in my nature to become attached, especially to animals, so I tried adopting a rescue dog from a sanctuary I'd discovered. He was a Jack Russell called Milo and it had seemed impossible to rehome him because he was randomly aggressive; indeed, I seemed to be the only volunteer who could approach him without being attacked. If I hadn't taken him on there'd have been no alternative but to have him put down. Sadly, and despite my best intentions, Milo only lasted for two months in my apartment. During that time he launched an unprovoked attack on my niece's face. She was unharmed, fortunately, but frightened. Finally he had a go at me when I went to put his lead on to walk him. I'd no choice then: I called the sanctuary and they collected him (he seemed overjoyed at the prospect of going somewhere exciting), took him away and put him to sleep.

The episode traumatised me. I wanted a dog of my own, but because of Milo I couldn't then face the prospect of another rescue dog. What should I do? My love for our pets Penny and Scamp when I was a child in Barrow had left me with a lifelong affection for Yorkshire terriers, and this helped to make my decision. I learned of a litter of Yorkshire terrier puppies that hadn't all been given homes and I adopted one of them, an effervescent little fellow I called Charlie.

Thereafter I found myself rooted in one location. I hadn't intended to become more home-bound, but the deepening bond between Charlie and me altered everything. Before long, he and I had become inseparable. Wherever I went, he followed. It was hard to leave him behind because he pined. On one occasion I left him with a sitter to attend a wedding.

"He wouldn't eat," the sitter said when I went to collect him again. "He spent the day lying beside the door and crying."

Of course a dog is for life, not just for fashion. I'd made my bed and now I needed to lie in it. But even if I'd anticipated the impact Charlie would have on the way I lived my life, I wouldn't have changed a thing. Nevertheless, he's the main reason I haven't yet been back to Thailand.

*

Sadly, Max has passed on since I returned from my sojourn in the Thai mountains, but the cruelty inflicted on those majestic animals continues in the name of tourism – and of logging. Nevertheless, as long as people give selflessly to such a good cause, there will be 'Hope' for the future. The bond between human and elephant, like that between human and dog, is never broken. Although my planned future visit to Thailand is on hold, I know I'll return one day. Spending time with elephants deepens the soul and creates lifelong memories.

If you visit Thailand and wish to know and understand these most regal of animals, please do so with your eyes open and your heart filled with care.

Chapter 6

In 2009, while I was still living and working in my two-bedroom apartment at the end of Deansgate in Manchester, my life was relatively simple. I'd been there for nearly seven years. The room I'd converted into a small dungeon contained everything I needed and I'd built up a great regular clientele. Things were going well and I loved living in the city. I didn't frequent many of the restaurants or nightclubs but I still enjoyed being able walk straight out into the urban bustle at any time for a nice lunch or coffee.

Working from home had massive advantages. Apart from not having to commute in city traffic, I was available at short notice for sessions, which suited a lot of clients. It also suited me. From arising in the morning I could be ready in forty-five minutes: tea, shower, makeup, and then a fifteen second walk to work. It was great. Outside sessions, I spent most of my time alone. I didn't mix much with other Mistresses or indeed anyone else, though I'd made good friends with a couple of my clients and I'd go out for dinner or a drink with them.

Although I'm something of a hermit, there were times when my life felt restricted. I could go days without leaving the apartment and weeks without chatting to anyone except clients. However, little Charlie had just entered my life and we were starting to discover the lush parks around the city and its environs.

One morning a regular client arrived for the session he'd booked: Mike, or as I called him, 'Mr Noodles'. The nickname arose from his love of needle play. He'd sign off his text messages 'Mr Needles', but predictive text can play tricks, so throughout the many years we knew each other he was 'Mr Noodles'. He was an old hand at BDSM and visited both male and female escorts. He knew how to have fun and was happy to try anything at least once. On the day in question, Noodles told me about a Mistress he'd visited not far from my apartment.

"She's stunning," he said, "really beautiful. But more than that, she's got what it takes to be a Mistress." I knew Mike was experienced enough to spot quality a mile off, so I listened. "She's just started to Domme," he told me, "and she's working from home. She only has a little table with a flogger and crop on it but her potential is definitely there. Should I put her in touch with you, see if she wants to session from here instead?"

"Yes," I said.

Since Anita, I'd never thought about having another Mistress use my little room, but if Mike's lady was the right kind of person, why wouldn't it work? And extra money is always useful.

She and I began to communicate through text and I knew we were going to hit it off, though we were different in many ways. Lady Zara, as she'd named herself, was a stunning olive-skinned beauty from Colombia with long flowing locks of black hair. Brought up in London with private school education she had one of the poshest English accents I've ever heard. She was also fluent in French. After college she'd made a very good living from modelling, but when life brought her to Manchester this career had dried up so a friend had suggested domination.

Zara loved the finer things in life. She adored her designer clothes, shoes and handbags. I remember going shopping with her one day while she tried to educate me about the best designer shoes. I'm afraid she might as well have been talking in her fluent French. You can take the girl out of Cumbria but not Cumbria out of the girl.

Any experienced slave will tell you that a good-looking woman doesn't always make a good Dominatrix. Looks can give you short-term success as a Mistress (or as an escort), but to continue for long in this profession you need charisma and depth of personality, plus 'that certain something', which a person either has or hasn't; it can't be learned. Zara had 'that certain something' and she was very keen to learn. I didn't have to do much training with her; she picked things up very quickly, did her research and put a lot of effort into advertising. She soon became very popular, and it was nice for me to have someone around whom I could chat with and laugh with about things most people wouldn't understand.

*

One evening as I sat by my computer checking e-mails a message came through from Zara, forwarding an e-mail from a client. She asked what I thought about it and what she should do. When I read it, a cold shiver went down my spine. The e-mail was an angry rant threatening to destroy Zara and everything she was. His only desire was to make her miserable and hurt her in any way he could.

"What the hell is this?" I thought.

I'd had clients who'd mistaken warmth for something more and asked me out on a date; indeed, it still happens. It's not uncommon. Sometimes the rejection, however kindly worded and subtle, can lead to a touch of anger, but that seldom lasts. However, this e-mail rant seemed very different. I called Zara to get a fuller picture.

The back-story was that Mr X had visited Zara at the apartment about three weeks earlier. He was in his 40s and very well presented, over six feet tall with dark hair, quite handsome. He owned a kick-boxing club in Manchester and was high up in the sport himself so he had a huge physique. He also owned a construction company, and he had a large house and two children with another on the way. On the surface, therefore, he lived an ideal life. I can't remember what his fetish was, but Zara recalled that at the end of their session he'd started to cry.

"I'm so unhappy... My wife doesn't understand me..."

Zara gave him a hug, which she subsequently regretted. In fact, after this incident, she never again showed affection to a client.

"Will you go out with me on a date?" asked Mr X.

"No," said Zara. "I don't date clients and also I have a boyfriend."

Since then he'd bombarded her daily with e-mails. Most were threatening, but every now and again there'd be one saying how sorry he was and he didn't know why he was being like that. The next day there'd be an aggressive one again. Now his e-mails had become menacing, saying he'd hurt her. Short-term anger at rejection is normal, as I said, but two weeks of sustained harassment wasn't normal at all.

"How have you replied to him? I asked.

"I haven't replied at all since his first nasty e-mail," said Zara.

An alarm bell rang in my head. The answer was simple.

"You go to the police!"

On Monday morning, Zara went to the police station and reported the threats. I waited all morning to hear from her. We were both nervous. Professional Domination isn't illegal but you don't want to become involved with anyone official if you can help it. (Little did I know what was to befall me in later years: inquests, Health and Safety violations, planning permission and all the rest!) We weren't even sure if the police would take us seriously, given our profession. But that was just what Mr X was counting on, and we couldn't let him get away with it.

Zara eventually phoned, her voice a little shaky but full of information. The police had looked into Mr X. He'd been in trouble before for violence, and one charge was for assaulting a policewoman. Zara was passed straight through to C.I.D., who took the situation seriously and confirmed that they saw this guy as potentially dangerous. Zara told them honestly how she'd met Mr X and they read all the e-mails.

By this point I too had started to receive e-mails from Mr X; not nasty, like the ones Zara was receiving, but apologizing that I'd been caught in the crossfire though none of it was my fault; unfortunately, because I knew Zara, I'd suffer the same as her. I also went to the police and gave the C.I.D. an interview. I could tell they were concerned. They wasted no time in visiting Mr X and formally ordering him to stop the harassment, pointing out that his actions were abusive and threatening and if they continued he'd be arrested and charged. They told us his manner towards them was calm and conciliatory. He said he'd stop all contact and get himself together, and he was very sorry and regretful. The C.I.D. seemed hopeful that this would end the problem.

Now they were involved I was sure he'd back off. He was happy to try to intimidate women but he couldn't ignore the police. Could he? In my mind I tried to put the affair to bed, but the feeling in the pit of my stomach wouldn't go away.

*

The renewed harassment started with simple things. The buzzer would ring on my street-door monitor, but when I looked at the screen there was no one there. That wasn't too concerning at first; it wasn't unusual for people to ring several apartments to try to get access to the building. However, when it started happening two or three times a day, I began to feel alarmed. The buzzer might go at eleven at night and then at eight the following morning. Then the hammering on my door started; loud knocks, thudding and banging, followed by feet running down the hallway. This was unnerving, especially late at night when I was alone. We told the C.I.D., but as I hadn't actually seen Mr X and he hadn't made explicit threats they weren't prepared to do anything.

At eight one morning I got up and walked into the lounge, rubbing my eyes. I did what I always did first thing: let Charlie out on to the balcony for a pee. Standing there in my dressing gown by the wide patio doors I looked over to my left. The apartment block was a large L shape, and through one of the big windows I saw Mr X standing and glaring at my balcony. When he saw me looking he jumped out of the way, but my hair stood on end.

This guy was obsessed. He knew Zara didn't live with me. I wondered why it hadn't crossed his mind to follow her home, but for some reason his attention was solely on my flat. At one point I thought, "Maybe I should just tell him where she lives, then he'll leave me alone. She has a boyfriend to protect her; I have no one." I didn't, of course. I'm not that kind of person.

Again the C.I.D. said they couldn't do anything; although he was watching the apartment he hadn't made threats. The banging on the door continued, but now there were no running-away sounds. It's scary when your dog alerts you to someone sitting outside your door. Charlie told me exactly when Mr X was there by sniffing frantically under the door and barking. The man was unpredictable. His behaviour was frantic and persistent. I wouldn't have put it past him to flip and really hurt me if not kill me. You didn't need to be a psychologist to see that the problem wasn't going to go away on its own.

One Friday evening I was watching television when Charlie once again started growling and sniffing under the door. I could hear Mr X shuffling around outside as though he was trying to get comfortable. Then the letters started. They were pushed under the door, ramblings in red scribble. Most of it I couldn't understand, but it was clear he wanted to harm Zara, and to harm me too because I was there and he couldn't get to her. I wasn't sure what he was planned to do that night; he seemed hell-bent on destruction. But after a few hours he went away.

He wasn't going to give up, though. At least now I had written proof of his threats. However, it seems the C.I.D. don't work on Saturdays and Sundays. My report would have to wait until Monday morning. Meanwhile, Mr X had other plans.

*

Saturday was a beautiful day. I'd arranged a drive out to the country with a client who was also a very good friend. We'd take Charlie for a walk. Zara had a booking in the afternoon. I didn't think it wise for her to be in the flat, but she wanted to earn money and to be fair she hadn't experienced Mr X's menaces except by e-mail.

My client and I enjoyed a long walk with Charlie and were sitting in a dog-friendly pub when the call came from Zara. She was in a total panic. A poster had been pushed through the flat door. It showed a photo of her in her full Domme gear with a slave at her feet, which Mr X had taken from her website. Beneath the picture were more crazy ramblings: "Lady Zara of 42 City Gate is escorting from this flat. The guy in the photo is her boyfriend, John, who encourages her to be pimped out." Her boyfriend wasn't called John and the slave in the photo wasn't him; it was a chap from Birmingham we affectionately called 'Wormie'. But Zara discovered that Mr X had posted this drivel not only through my door but through every door in the building, and on all the cars outside and every lamppost in the vicinity.

I couldn't believe it. I'd tried so hard to be discreet and mind my own business, but now this rubbish was everywhere. The only good side was the leaflet read like the drunken ramblings of a bitter ex-boyfriend. I rushed back from my day out to find the flat empty: Zara had summoned her boyfriend, who'd grabbed as many leaflets from outside as he could and then got her safely out of the building. Mr X must have been hiding somewhere nearby where he could see her boyfriend through the windows because later that night sent her a photo he'd taken saying, "I can't believe how ugly he is". This was going from bad to worse!

On the Monday, the first thing Zara did was to call our previous contact at the C.I.D. The police went to Mr X's house that afternoon and arrested him. They'd normally have sent two officers but in this case they sent four because Mr X was huge and known for aggression.

"We arrested him yesterday evening," the C.I.D. man told me. "He didn't resist. He admitted what he'd done. He got bail from court this morning but he's forbidden to go near your apartment or Zara's."

That night, bizarrely, Zara received an e-mail from his wife! She said she now knew what had been happening and was sorry for his behaviour. She realised he had major issues that needed to be dealt with, but she was going to stick by him and help him as much as she could and make sure he wouldn't bother Zara any more. Could this get any stranger?

Our C.I.D. friend told me how the situation stood.

"I hope the court order will be enough to stop Mr X's aggressive behaviour," he said, "but to make sure, I've put the case on the system as an emergency. If he shows up again, ring 999, ask for the police and give the case log number, and it will flag up for instant response."

That made me feel much better. I had a bit of back-up now. A week passed quietly with no incidents and I began to relax.

"Maybe his wife's taken control of the situation, as she promised, so everything's now in hand."

*

I was wrong. Around one o'clock the following Saturday afternoon I was relaxing with Charlie when I heard shouting from the car park. I couldn't decipher many of the words but they were abusive and threatening.

"Someone's having an argument," I thought.

I went to the window to look out, as most people would. There was Mr X, two floors below, glaring up at my window, shouting threats with the most angry and bitter face I'd ever seen. I backed away from his line of sight, my heart racing. He was back, and he was pissed off. I stood there for a second or two to compose myself and then it started: huge stones being thrown up at the window like missiles. His strength and anger propelled them at such speed they were cracking the double-glazed glass.

"OK, this is it," I thought, "he's snapped."

I grabbed my phone, dialled 999 and asked for the police. I gave their switchboard attendant the case log number and explained the emergency. Mr X was still shouting and hurling chunks of stone at my window.

"I'm sorry, there's no record of that log number," she said.

"There is," I insisted. "The C.I.D. gave it to me in case the stalker came back, and he has, he's out on bail and not allowed near me!"

Very calm and without any urgency in her voice, she said: "I'm sorry, Ms White, but I cannot count this as an emergency. I'll put you through to Greater Manchester Police and they can send someone out."

I couldn't believe it! The phone rang for the Manchester police. The stones kept coming up, interspersed with brief intervals of calm when I presumed he was collecting more to throw.

A woman answered eventually and I explained my situation. Again she confirmed there was no log number.

"This guy is dangerous!" I repeated. "The C.I.D. gave me the log number in case he came back!"

She was having none of it. She sounded bored and more or less called me a liar.

"The best I can do is to send an officer around when one's free."

What? Did Mr X shit gold?

The stone-throwing suddenly stopped and I peeped out. He was gone. My heart still pounding, I called Zara, obviously in a panic, and told her what had happened. She sounded angry, as if I was spoiling her Saturday afternoon.

"What do you expect *me* to do?"

I was furious.

"Come and sort it out!" I shouted. "He's your stalker, not mine!"

"Well, I don't see what I can do. I'll call the C.I.D. on Monday and tell them what's happened."

I was gutted. I'd protected Zara for weeks and now she was happy to leave me to this maniac's attentions unsupported. I could have thrown a piece of paper down to Mr X with her address on it so he'd harass her instead of me, but of course I didn't. Yet she never rang back that weekend to see how I was. It would be an understatement to say I was angry with her. I never got a thank-you from her and to this day I've never quite forgiven her.

About an hour later a policeman turned up. He was a quiet, thin guy who walked towards my door as though he was kicking pebbles on a beach. He came in and was instantly scared of Charlie, my Yorkshire terrier. What was the point of him being there? However, I told him the whole story.

"Well, there's nothing I can do," he said. "If this is true then you need to contact the C.I.D. when they're in the office."

"So in the meantime he's allowed to come round and do what he wants?"

"Nothing we can do, Ms White."

He left. I was raging! Soon after he'd gone, the stone-throwing started again. It was as though Mr X had been waiting for the officer to go. This time a stone penetrated the lounge window and landed only inches from Charlie. I called the police again, knowing it would do no good. They said there was no record of Mr X, so all they could do him for at that moment was criminal damage.

"Am I going mad?" I thought.

I waited until the stone-throwing stopped again, packed a small bag for me and Charlie and left the apartment to stay with a friend for the weekend. I feared for my safety. This maniac was capable of committing serious injury if not murder and he was bitter and twisted enough to do it. I felt like a sitting duck in my own home. My main concern was for Charlie. He was just as vulnerable as I was.

*

First thing on Monday, Zara called the C.I.D. and told the man in charge what had occurred over the weekend. I very quickly received a call from him, apologising profusely.

"I'm so sorry, Lucina. This is all my fault."

What he'd done was put the case into the system as an emergency, with the log number, but he'd missed off the date so it didn't register.

"I can't apologise enough," he said. "We're going to arrest Mr X this morning and we'll keep you updated."

Later that afternoon I received another call saying Mr X *had* been arrested and would be in custody until he appeared in court the following morning, charged with breaking his bail conditions and with criminal damage. I could breathe again, knowing he wasn't going to come round and set fire to the apartment or something equally awful. I returned home to sleep safely in my bed once more.

Tuesday morning came. I knew he'd be in court. Surely the judge wouldn't let him out on bail this time? But I couldn't count on the justice system any longer! I got the call later that day telling me what had happened. The judge had wanted Mr X to spend a minimum of six weeks in custody while he underwent a psychiatric evaluation. However, his wife had pleaded for him to be released under her care so she could take him to her relatives' house in Scotland; he could have his evaluation there. She promised he wouldn't return to England.

"That bloody woman!" I thought. "Like she said she'd keep him out of trouble last time. Well, that didn't exactly work, did it? She clearly has no control over him at all."

However, there was nothing I could do. The C.I.D. promised again to keep us updated.

Four weeks passed without incident, though I was continually looking over my shoulder. One call from the C.I.D. informed us of the midway psychological report. It seems the *female* psychologist was quite impressed with our Mr X. He could display charm and a quiet manner when he chose, and he'd taken her in. "From what I can see so far," the psychologist said, "he doesn't pose a threat to anyone." To say I was angry is an understatement. Not only was this guy not intimidated by the police or the justice system, he also knew how to charm and control those around him.

Another week passed and one more call came from the C.I.D. Mr X had been asked: "Have you ever had fantasies about killing Zara?"

"Yes," he'd replied.

They explained that by law they therefore had to notify Zara. Then that was it. Nothing further!

"OK," I thought, "nice to know. Now what the hell are we meant to do with this information except dwell on it? Good night's sleep all round, eh?"

Only during the sixth week did things turn our way. Mr X finally showed his true colours to everyone around him. Before he could complete his six-week evaluation he'd turned on someone he was staying with, a member of his wife's family. From what I could gather it was a vicious attack, which resulted in the family member pressing charges and his wife washing her hands of him completely. He was now in custody in Scotland and would face charges there before returning to England to face the other charges. The C.I.D. later told us he'd been sentenced to six months for his aggressive assault, and (needless to say) they'd keep us fully updated.

*

My life returned to its usual tranquil routine, walking Charlie and whipping men without fearing I was going to be cut up or have petrol thrown over me. About six months later, around ten o'clock on a Tuesday morning, the sun was shining through the large patio windows of my flat and I'd just brewed my second cup of tea when multiple thuds sounded on the door, aggressive and all too familiar. My heart jumped into my mouth and the memories flooded back. I walked quietly to the door and looked through the peephole; nobody there.

"This can't be," I thought.

But that old familiar feeling was back in the pit of my stomach. It was an alarm that went off whenever he was close. I phoned Zara.

"It *could* be someone or something else, but I know it's him."

She called the C.I.D. It seemed our friend had been released from prison in Scotland and immediately summoned to appear in court in England for his earlier offences. They hadn't notified or warned us. In fact, they'd put him up in the Travelodge just down the road, unescorted. He hadn't been able to resist the temptation. He'd just *had* to come by!

He received an eight month sentence for his aggressive, threatening and stalker behaviour. From my point of view, it had been a long time coming. We were told we'd receive a call when he was to be released so we could be prepared in case he came round again, but we never heard another thing from the C.I.D. Upon his release, the first thing Mr X did was contact Zara to say he was sorry for everything. Fortunately, that was the last either of us heard from him.

Going through that experience affected me in many ways. To be so vulnerable in your own home isn't nice. It's also not nice to feel helpless, knowing it's someone else's responsibility to sort out the problem but they're not doing the best of jobs. Also, when I asked if I could legitimately defend myself, I was told I couldn't. "Just call for help."

It wasn't long after this episode that I decided to move from the apartment. Even though things had settled down, there were too many bad memories. Zara was also affected by the experience and was never warm or kind to her clients again. And our friendship was never the same again, either. Mike, 'Mr Noodles', would have been upset to discover how his recommendation of Lady Zara had worked out. Not that it was in any way his fault.

Women in general are vulnerable to the kind of menacing nuisance we'd experienced from Mr X. Being a Dominatrix doesn't protect you against stalkers.

Chapter 7

My working/living apartment in Deansgate had served me well for seven years. I'd become confident in my ability to satisfy my clients' needs and run a successful business by doing so. My en suite toilet and shower was separate from the slaves' facilities, which suited me. Other Mistresses apart from Zara had approached me about renting the room. This was great, but it meant the apartment never closed down, and having a six foot tall Dominatrix strutting around your living room in the evening when you're trying to watch *Coronation Street* verges on the surreal. My days needed a cut-off point. Even before the troubles with Mr X I'd started to think of moving to a bigger place so I could keep work and home separate. Work was taking over my life. I needed my own personal space. To have a safe haven to go to, as Zara did, had become very appealing.

It isn't easy to find the ideal place for a dungeon. It has to be discreet but easy to reach. It needs enough rooms for privacy, with accessible toilet and shower facilities. There's much to take into account. I discussed the problem with friends.

"I'm using a unit for work," said one, "but the walls are too thin."

"No good for our needs," I said, thinking of the noises that emanate from a busy dungeon.

"Well," she continued, "I know the manager of a large mill, and I'm sure he said there were empty rooms in the basement."

She gave me the manager's number and I called him to arrange a viewing. He sounded friendly.

"Yes, Lucina, the cellar was a storage place, but it's been disused for years, so it's available for rent if it's any good for you. What will you want to use it for?"

"If it looks suitable, I'd like to convert it to a dungeon," I said. "I'm a Dominatrix."

There was a pause before he replied, "Yes, that's fine. Do you want to come and take a look?"

A friendly landlord is a bonus for any business, not least mine! We arranged a date for the viewing. The mill, I discovered, was a big redbrick edifice more than a hundred years old, mostly divided among various businesses, and the location was perfect. The manager greeted me in his office with the grin and the twinkle in the eye that usually welcomes people in my profession. He took me through a huge basement to a door that opened on to three small units. The place was filthy but the layout looked usable.

"I like the independent outside door," I said, "so there's access from the street without going through the rest of the building. And two back doors leading into the basement... How about electricity and plumbing?"

He said there were basic electricity and plumbing supplies, so heating and lighting could be installed and so could toilet and shower.

"That's fine," I said. "It'll take work but it has real prospects. How about the walls? Will it be OK to fix things like restraints and St Andrew's crosses?"

"You can do what you like, Lucina. Just don't burn the place down!"

I wondered whether cleaning and converting the units into a Chamber would be too much work and too expensive. Should I take the rental? I couldn't decide, but sometimes Fate seems to take a hand in our lives. A few days after viewing the mill property I received a letter from the court telling me that the landlord of my Deansgate apartment had had his assets seized, so the property would be repossessed and sold at auction. I'd wondered whether the landlord was dodgy; he'd never come to check the flat. Anyway, my seven year tenancy of the apartment was about to end. The court letter finally made my decision for me.

I agreed the rental price for the basement, which was reasonable given the state of the place, and I was offered three rent-free months to get it into working condition. It turned out that I'd underestimated the time and effort that would be required to turn the cellar into a functioning Chamber. Cleaning the place took a month and generated a skip full of rubbish. I couldn't have done it without the help of a couple of dedicated friends (who were also slaves). Then I invested most of my savings in converting it into reception room, lounge and two dungeons. I equipped one of the dungeons with the wide range of implements and devices suited to my clients' various tastes and needs and installed appropriate flooring and carpets. The units were separated by partition walls and a toilet and two showers were plumbed in. The electricity supply was inadequate for the heating I needed; I moved into the place in the middle of a very cold winter and the temperature was minus seventeen. This would remain a problem for some time. To begin with I only had equipment for the one dungeon; the second dungeon was established slowly over the succeeding year, along with cells and various other additions. Soon, however, I was mentoring other Mistresses, some of whom had the requisite dominant streak in their characters. A few of them continue to work in my Chamber to this day. Zara came with me to Stockport, too. She sessioned there for six months before she left to start a family.

*

"It's about sex, isn't it, even though we don't offer sex?" said one of my trainees.

I tried to explain the psychological aspect of sex as it relates to submissives, but I was still struggling to understand the nature of 'sub space' myself. At that time, no slave had explained it clearly to me, and I doubted whether I'd managed to take any of my clients as far as that desired Shangri La during the early days of my career. Most slaves said they were satisfied and happy after sessioning with me, which was reassuring; but could I take them further?

"Well, most of them become aroused," I said, "but you don't have to let them have orgasms. One effective psychological torture is the 'ruined orgasm'. You get them nearly there, right on the brink of coming, and then you stop. If they're tied up they can't do anything about it."

"Except be angry, I suppose."

"Oh, no, that isn't allowed. They have to say, 'Thank you, Mistress'."

My trainee digested this. I don't think she was convinced. No matter, she'd learn; at least she would if she had domination in her nature.

"But what about you? Us, I mean? Do we get satisfaction?"

I had to think about that.

"I can't speak for all Mistresses," I said, "but for me... Well, put it this way. You know what it's like when you're sexually aroused. You're not in control of your emotions and you easily lose control of your behaviour. In fact, losing control of your emotions and behaviour is what you want to do. *Need* to do. You can't direct your energy anywhere else. For me, being a Mistress is different. To dominate, I need to keep control over my emotions and behaviour and I have to focus my energy. So no, I don't get sexual pleasure during a session."

In fact, I've known Mistresses who *are* turned on by caning slaves, and arousal certainly happens during private play, for instance between partners. We're all different. I always try not to tell trainees 'how things are done'. I can only say, "This is how I do it", but each individual has to find what works for her.

She shook her head.

"So what's the attraction?"

"It's a 'high'. It's exhilarating, particularly the sense of power I achieve. People who use cocaine describe something similar. I don't allow cocaine or anything of the kind in my Chamber, by the way. A conviction for having illegal drugs on the premises would spell the end for the business. And I certainly wouldn't use cocaine myself – I've seen the harm it causes. But that's what a good session of domination with a willing slave does for me: it makes me 'high'. It seems all Dominatrixes get 'high' during sessions, whether they become sexually aroused or not."

One of my clients, a doctor, explained this 'high' to me. He said it was something to do with catecholamines in the brain. Apparently 'catecholamines' are substances like adrenalin that are found in the brain as well as other parts of the body and are involved in feelings of excitement and joyful intoxication. If you're a Dominatrix, punishing a slave sets the catecholamines in your brain dancing and fills you with warm, satisfied smiles.

But would they dance even faster and longer if I managed to carry a slave into 'sub space'?

*

The first time it happened in my Chamber, at least to my knowledge, was with 'David2', the client I described at the start of this book. He was an experienced submissive and he knew in detail what he wanted to do or have done to him. Established and confident though I'd become, I was still at a point on the learning curve where I was most comfortable with slaves who were practised in the art of submission. Novice submissives, people who aren't sure whether they really want to become a Mistress's slave, are advised to visit an experienced Dominatrix, who'll give them the guidance they need.

"Very well," I said, having listened to David2's requests. "You are now my property. Your sole purpose is to serve me. You will obey whatever order I give you. Is that understood?"

"Yes, Princess Lucina."

"Strip. Then lie there, face down."

David2 was obedient. During the next hour he was flogged, ball-busted, mocked, humiliated, tied to a St Andrew's cross and generally abused. Finally, as I described earlier, he reached 'sub space'. After he'd described this state of bliss, while we were drinking coffee, I asked about his earlier experiences of it. He told me a little about his marriage. He was a widower and he missed his wife.

"Some of the games we played in the bedroom were fem-Dom scenarios," he said. "We didn't do it often – sometimes I dominated her instead, tying her to the bed and so on – and most of the time it was fairly conventional sex, though usually brilliant because we loved each other. Anyway, when she was Domme and I was sub, she used to tie me up, cane my buttocks, kick my balls, make me lie face down on the floor so she could stand on my cock and crush it into the carpet, tie my balls to a suitcase and make me crawl the length of the room dragging it behind me, push vibrators up my arse, urinate into my mouth... She could get me into 'sub space' doing all those sorts of things, and my reaction really turned her on. I had to use my tongue to bring her to orgasm after we'd finished playing games of that kind. So what happened with you this afternoon reminded me..."

He broke off as emotion welled up in him again. I was touched by his recollection and by his openness in revealing such intimate and treasured memories. At the same time, I realised that having achieved this success I could do it again. I knew now that I could take other slaves into 'sub space'. Nevertheless it remains very rare; in all the years I've worked as a Dominatrix it's only happened half a dozen times. David2 had also confirmed what I'd told my trainee: during private

BDSM play between couples in love, the 'high' of domination is accompanied by sexual arousal.

Incidentally: urinating on a slave is a game known as 'water sports' in the business. But like any other dungeon activity, it's just one more *means*. As always, it's the *end* that matters, the slave's submission and abrogation of responsibility. The means are just whatever works for each particular slave-Dominatrix pair.

*

David2 was unique in travelling all the way to 'sub space' during his first session with me. Usually a more or less prolonged journey is necessary for the slave to get anywhere *near* 'sub space', and increasingly intense treatments are required to bring him closer to the goal as session follows session. For the submissive, BDSM can be compared to eating hot curries: at first, Madras seems far too hot, but in time it becomes almost bland and you have to move on to a Vindaloo. At the same time, while the slave's submissiveness deepens, the 'high' I experience becomes more and more intense. By remaining open to new ideas and willing to explore the imaginations of those prepared to share their fantasies, I find that horizons are broadened for both of us and the spark between us is fanned into a flame. While I'm indulging the needs of a client I'm also feeding the inferno inside me. The further I travel, the more I need to see; the darker the shade, the more I long to experience black. Being drawn into the fantasies of those I choose to dominate, I venture deeper into myself and meet my own ever-growing needs.

A BDSM relationship, when it works for both parties, is truly a symbiosis. The closer the slave travels towards a state of total submission, the more the Dominatrix's needs are met and the more delirious her 'high'. The relationship that emerges is intense and durable; it might be confined to session times in the Mistress's dungeon, but it might evolve into a genuine friendship. It's done that for me, several times, and David2 is not only slave whose emotional release has been manifested by tears. That aside, it's not unusual to see noticeable changes in subservients as they develop and explore aspects of their characters that they might previously have denied. In some cases the bond can grow further, the Mistress becoming a trusted counsellor and friend.

I expect the first moment of the first session with any new submissive to be the beginning of a journey that will explore the needs, imagination and limits of both parties. When I meet a novice subservient, it's essential for him to surrender to his needs as well as submitting to my bidding. Before subjugation can be complete, the masks imposed by society have to be shed. Those masks are a barrier to success, and only by establishing the appropriate Mistress-slave relationship at the outset can we dispose of them. After that, the necessary connection between Dominatrix and submissive can evolve: complete trust on both sides, complete honesty, and an unlimited willingness to explore.

Of course, some clients spend a single hour with me and never reappear. Either they've found another Mistress who suits them better, or they've discovered after the single experiment that submissiveness isn't for them. That's fine. I respect them for trying it.

*

I'm willing to explore all facets of my own actual or possible needs. The greater your self-knowledge the better you succeed in your career, at least in a profession such as mine. With that in mind, I once decided to try being a slave. This wasn't because of a sudden personality change but through a wish to gain a better understanding of those I dominate. Some Dominatrixes switch naturally. Some even believe that to become dominant you have to learn to be submissive, or vice versa. I never shared that view, though I don't denounce the belief as heresy as some Mistresses do. Anyway, I was interested in experimenting.

The attempt wasn't a total failure because I learned something important from it: namely, that hell would have to freeze over before I'd willingly submit again to the desires, discipline and guidance of another. You can't be something you're not. You can't be submissive unless you have the feelings and needs that submissives have, and I don't. Trying to be submissive made me grumpy. It rubbed me up the wrong way and it didn't *feel* right.

Some Dominatrixes do have a submissive side, as I said. A few years ago I contacted a Mistress called Valerie who wanted to sell the furnishings and equipment from her Chamber. After a number of years in the business, Valerie had decided it was time for a new venture. I bought several of the items she'd offered. She and I spent a little time together in her establishment and we formed a connection. Even then

I had an inkling of what might follow, so I wasn't surprised when she later decided to visit my Chamber. I pointed out the items I'd purchased from her and felt the atmosphere grow ripe with anticipation.

Over the following six months Valerie, former Dominatrix that she was, not only knelt before me but also served time on every piece of apparatus I'd bought from her Chamber. She became my slave, with all the thrill and enthusiasm of other submissives.

All things are possible in BDSM. Well, most things are. There are exceptions. For example, it isn't possible for me to become a submissive, as Valerie did.

*

When I talk about my profession to anyone willing to listen, I find most people are interested and indeed curious to the point of fascination. That shouldn't surprise me; after all, it was the way I'd reacted when Peter first told me about visiting a Dominatrix and encouraged me to visit her dungeon. Nevertheless it seems paradoxical that activities considered socially unacceptable or even immoral by many people tend to make the most interesting conversations. Consider: which of the following two conversational gambits is most likely to capture attention?

"Would you mind passing the peas? And have you noticed how the FTSE one hundred index has fallen?"

or

"May I have the recipe for your wonderful gravy? And have I told you about the guy I whipped in my dungeon last night?"

At a wedding dinner some time ago I was seated beside a very tall, eloquent gentleman. He was well-spoken and while obviously well-heeled he didn't speak down to me from a lofty perch. His wife sat opposite us, smiling reassuringly as he engaged me in conversation. It quickly became obvious that he not only knew about my profession but had actually asked to be seated next to me.

"Of course I understand that you'll change or suppress names to protect the innocent, Ms White, as indeed you should, but I'd love to hear tales of your dungeon games if you're willing to tell them."

I obliged with a selection of true-life anecdotes, mixing the psychologically revealing with the light-hearted and amusing. He was riveted. He insisted on continuing the conversation after the meal, after the speeches were over and the wedding guests had started to dance to the strains of the invited band. His fascination showed no sign of fading; he remained hungry for more and more of my slave-stories. I began to think he might be a potential client, sounding out a chosen Dominatrix despite his wife's presence. However, I was wrong. He was just curious.

"Well, enough about my working life," I said at last. "What do you do for a living, if I may ask?"

"Me?" He shrugged. "Oh, I'm just a royal bodyguard. It's a lot more boring than your career."

It seemed that taking care of the safety and security of the British royal family was as humdrum in his estimation as being an accountant. Familiarity hadn't bred contempt for his duties so much as a kind of blasé apathy. Nevertheless I prompted him to tell stories about his experiences, and he obliged. His revelations amazed me. I hung on every word, wanting to know more. It was like chatting to James Bond without the spy recognising that he was in any way special.

This elegant gentleman and I were similar in one obvious way: each of us had a career or profession that seemed exotic, mysterious and fascinating to others, but to us it was our normal everyday work.

Chapter 8

In 2003, while I was still training as a Mistress, a client called Chris booked a session with me and my mentor. It must have left an impression on him, though I can't recall it. Indeed, I've no memory of Chris before I'd started working alone, which is surprising because he wasn't an easy man to forget. I suppose the reason is simple: a double-Domme session has a different dynamic from a one-to-one encounter. It's less intimate so it's harder to forge a personal connection. However, Chris captured my interest from our first one-to-one meeting. His obvious intelligence complemented his articulate, polite manner, making him a joy to be with. He always liked to look smart. He was about five feet six inches tall, not physically imposing but quite fit. He was knowledgeable about a range of different subjects but was always humble. I found his modest demeanour endearing.

As a man in his mid-forties he'd experienced enough of life to be at ease with his submissive nature, notwithstanding his career success and position of authority. Being deferential was part of his makeup. People with submissive natures are often successful in life, their achievements made possible by inner strength.One of the many popular misconceptions about the BDSM scene is that submissives must be meek. If ever there were a man to prove the opposite it was Chris. He was in no way aggressive, but I found his presence a little intimidating.

Those who enjoy submitting to a Mistress usually seek specific BDSM disciplines, the aspects of domination they particularly enjoy. There's a vast array of equipment you can buy to enhance each individual's BDSM experience. With a little imagination you can augment your collection with everyday items as well as specialist ones.

Chris had compiled just such a collection. This included a steel cock ring from which weights could be hung, and an electric charge could be passed through it.

"And these," he said, presenting a nail brush and a breath freshener. "Breath freshener sprayed on delicate areas of skin creates a tingling sensation."

As you'll gather from this, Chris's preference was for what's commonly known as 'cock and ball torture', CBT for short. (The abbreviation could be confusing, since 'CBT' also stands for 'cognitive behaviour therapy'. However, it seems that clients like Chris find cock and ball torture therapeutic, so perhaps the two definitions don't really conflict.)

Over a period of five years, while I was still working in my Deansgate apartment, Chris came for a session every few months and stayed for around an hour. All his toys were used to the full. His bookings were always last minute and always started with 'Just on the off chance...' After the session he didn't hang around. He always seemed in a rush, as though he'd just taken a cheeky hour out. He'd get ready quickly, chatting a little as he did so. However, when I moved to my new Chamber under the mill in Stockport in 2010, my sessions with Chris began to stretch to around two hours and to occur more or less monthly, and I started to get glimpses into his life.

Perhaps the increased session length was as much down to changes in his professional life as anything to do with my new Chamber. Chris had worked in quite a stressful I.T. job. I don't know exactly how his circumstances had changed but he no longer suffered as much hustle and bustle. He was also taking up photography and exploring small business ventures with friends. He was certainly affluent. After a couple of visits to the Stockport dungeon he said:

"I've decided to put more dedication into my life as a sub and my path into BDSM."

Between visits he'd e-mail ideas for the next session, excited about any new toys he'd purchased. He now stayed for coffee after each visit. He began to keep a blog of his journey into BDSM so he could analyse his path more precisely, though BDSM wasn't his only sort of intimate adventure.

"I spend around a thousand pounds per month on girls offering personal services," he once told me. "It's my 'play money'."

Wanting to explore every facet of his personality he visited escorts and sub girls too. He told me about going to one sub woman so he could express his dominant side, but she was too hard-core for him, scornful when he turned up armed with only a slipper. We had a good laugh about that story, and about others he told. He certainly knew how to have fun.

Over time I learned that Chris had a partner, though he said they lived separate lives. He supposed she had an inkling of his BDSM activities but was convinced she had no idea of the level at which he played. Respecting his privacy I was careful not to pry. I never inquire into slaves' personal lives. I need to know certain things such as whether they're allowed lingering marks from canes or paddles, but I don't ask personal questions. Nevertheless, slaves do often talk to me about themselves and reveal private information, as 'Sluggie' did. I listen, I treat what I hear as confidential, and I don't probe.

*

It's a challenge for any Mistress to keep sessions fresh and novel. The BDSM scene has so many facets that no subservient is likely to be interested in all of them. A submissive with a taste for all options would be like a gourmet who loves all possible kinds of food. However, too much of the same thing can become boring. The more often a client visits you, the more ways you must find to adapt and evolve. The Mistress needs to maintain her clients' interest in her, and her interest in them.

Chris offered an intelligent and creative approach to our session time, participating in the planning process and helping to maintain diversity and interest. In one area of BDSM, known as role-play, the Mistress and her subservient adopt roles different from their real-life characters. Examples can include interrogation, kidnapping or school-style punishments. Such sessions aren't scripted; the participants *ad lib* their parts so there are no predetermined conclusions. Chris was an eager participant in role-play games. Sometimes he wore clothes that could be ripped from his body. On one occasion we played out a kidnapping. We arranged for him to arrive looking like a plumber on a call-out. On the way to my Chamber he called at a superstore to buy the appropriate clothing.

"I'm playing out a kidnap game with one of my customers," I told the manager. "I thought I'd better tell you in case Security think something's amiss."

"It's fine, Lucina." The manager chuckled.

A few minutes later, Chris phoned: "It's the plumber. I'm outside the mill. Where should I go?"

"I'll be out to get you in a moment," I said.

I went out to the main street, nodded to Chris and said, "Hello. Follow me."

To unnerve him, I led him the back way into the Chamber, through the cold dark basement and to the large scaffolding poles that hold up the ceiling behind my units.

"The plumbing problem's here," I told him.

He bent down to take a look and I handcuffed him to one of the poles and ripped off his shirt.

"You're going nowhere," I said, "until I've used you for my sadistic pleasure."

We didn't stay out there for long because it was too cold, but the kidnap role-play game had been fun for both of us.

Chris liked to experiment. His experiments included the use of nitrous oxide, which at that time was available in cartridge form as an agent for whipping cream. Carefully regulated, it can render a person drowsy for anything up to a minute. It was legal to use it, and provided it was treated responsibly it wasn't dangerous. Since then it's been made illegal, but by the time the law changed I no longer allowed it in my Chamber anyway.

"Can we use it in a role-play game?" wondered Chris.

He fantasised about being kidnapped and drugged, and nitrous oxide seemed a safe way of playing out the scenario. I allowed it since there were no legal objections. He provided the small canisters and we used them to render him helpless in kidnap role-plays. Then he began to use nitrous oxide regularly, and not just in my Chamber.

"I take some when I visit escorts," he said. "It enhances orgasm. For me, at least."

He was becoming obsessed with an aspect of BDSM known as 'breath play'. This involves restricting the oxygen supply to the brain in order to increase the sensitivity of the sexual organs and enhance the resulting orgasm. There are different ways of achieving it:

asphyxiation, strangulation, restriction of air via a pipe – or the substitution of other gases such as nitrous oxide.

Some facets of BDSM can become addictive. At first the submissive is satisfied by a mild application of the chosen discipline. Over time, however, fulfilment demands increased intensity. Chris's need for ever-bigger-and-better led to him scouring Ebay and purchasing tanks of nitrous oxide together with a mask fitted with pipes and regulated by valves. I'd hold the mask over his face and remove it when he became dazed. The sessions were carefully regulated. His safety was never at risk.

"Do you ever use nitrous oxide at home?" I asked him. "It would be dangerous on your own."

"No, I'd never do that," he said. "I want to keep it just for here, and for some escorts."

I'd no reason not to believe him. Desire for breath play is one of many reasons people visit a Dominatrix, so they can satisfy their urge in a safe environment with no risk to life. I can push someone to the edge with breath play, far enough to make it exciting but not so far that I can't bring them back. To have control of someone's breathing, to have them trust you with their life, gives you a great sense of power. For it to work properly the submissive has to have total trust in you and must relax. It can be hard to relax when you're short of breath, but this is essential if the true feeling of euphoria is to be captured. The submissive has to rely on you to know when enough is enough, and that enhances the Mistress-slave bonding.

I know a few people who do breath-play at home alone, or even while their wives and kids are in bed. It isn't a good idea. Unsupervised, it's dangerous.

*

The increased use of nitrous oxide in our sessions led to an even closer acquaintance. Chris wanted to be sure that the gas didn't affect his ability to drive safely, so he remained in my Chamber for longer after each session, providing more time for us to talk. We discovered a shared interest in motorbikes and travel. Our friendship, built on a solid foundation of trust, was no longer one-dimensional. Our discussions became wider and more varied, encompassing more of him. He shared stories from work, brought me gifts from his travels and dropped by to show me his bike. We were no longer constrained by the BDSM connection alone, though his interest in the scene hadn't dwindled. On the contrary, he often sent clips of YouTube videos and detailed ideas we could try.

Wanting to expand his circle of friends, he searched the internet and settled on a fetish club that held events throughout the month. Its name, 'The Dark Side of BDSM', appealed to me. The difficulty was that those visiting for the first time had to be part of a couple, so he sent me an e-mail with a link to the event and asked if I fancied going. I have a very strict rule: although I can go for a drive, a drink or even dinner with a client, I'd never 'go out' with them. There's a line between professional and personal life that can't be crossed. Most Mistresses impose the same rule, as do most escorts. Also, I tend to avoid fetish parties as they're too much like work. I'd only ever been to two and hadn't much enjoyed either of them. Nevertheless, I accepted Chris's invitation. Perhaps I no longer viewed him as 'just as a client', though the line between my personal life and my life as a Mistress remained clear. I trusted him. I was also intrigued about this 'Dark Side'.

Perhaps I should explain my dilemma more fully. In general, friends talk informally together; there's no hierarchy. In contrast, a Mistress and her submissive adhere to a definite etiquette. Formal titles are used. Respect is shown. A wife and her husband can switch from loving couple to Mistress and slave in the blink of an eye, but the switch entails a change in attitude and behaviour. Over time, a Dominatrix and her submissive can learn when and how to switch between everyday life and the animal within, and they can develop a friendship. What they can't do, unlike the loving couple, is to become sexually intimate, or allow their friendship to develop in a way that could lead to such intimacy. I didn't feel any romantic attachment to Chris, though I liked him enormously. His company was never dull, and he'd boosted my sense of power by saying, "You're the only person who knows every aspect of me. I hide nothing from you." I expect slaves to be open with me, though I never take it for granted; but this was lovely to hear from a man of whom I'd become so fond.

One of the many things I liked about Chris was his sense of humour. He was one of the funniest people I've ever met and even during sessions he had me clutching my sides laughing. His humour was very dry, delivering quick hilarious one-liners. So I knew we'd have a laugh at the fetish club even if I didn't enjoy the party.

*

The Saturday of the party gave way to one of those magical midsummer nights. The air was fresh and warm with a stillness that seemed to slow the passage of time. Chris had offered to drive me there so I could have a drink, but I needed to be in control, so I arranged to take my own car and meet him outside the venue. That way, I could leave whenever I wished. I suspected he'd want to make an evening of it, perhaps continuing after the party for drinks and a meal, and having come dangerously close to 'crossing the line' I felt caution was indicated. In any case I'd left Charlie with a dog-sitter and I never like to take advantage of people who help me. Also, this was the first time Chris and I had been together outside the world of the dungeon and I couldn't anticipate how things would go. People who know me as Princess Lucina in the Chamber can find it unsettling to meet Lucina. Chris might find it weird. It seemed best to focus on the party and see how it went, with an exit strategy planned.

You probably imagine a fetish party as a niche activity involving trendy underground bars and secluded city streets, not country lanes and quaint rural locations. My journey to that party made me feel like Alice tumbling through the looking glass or down the rabbit hole. Traversing winding lanes among fields, missing turnings, I kept pinching myself to be sure I was awake. The venue proved to be a small mill opposite a butcher's shop in a village straight out of the TV series *Last of the Summer Wine*. So Alice reached her Wonderland, decked in heels and draped in a manner befitting the occasion, to be greeted with a smile and a hug by the Mad Hatter and then stumbling over the uneven cobbles to the party. Nora Batty would have twitched at her curtains more than once as the curious and curiouser arrived.

The interior of the mill was unexpected; cramped, with just a few tables and a scattering of chairs. We were greeted by a lady with generous curves, an antithesis to the desk before which she sat. Entry seemed to depend on answering her many questions while giving the appearance of being a couple:

"How long have you been together?"… "Where do you live?"… "Have you been to fetish parties before?"

We gave bland answers, avoiding the lasers from her lie-detector eyes, and at last we were admitted. Adrenalin coursed through my veins as we explored our surroundings. It was the yellow brick road and the magic of Oz, doused in childish excitement and delivered to our senses in ways seldom encountered. We discovered a playroom furnished with all the trappings of a Chamber: bondage equipment littered the floor and the walls were lined with restraints. Behind us, a skinny man in a leather thong had been packed tightly into a full leather body bag.

"He's annoying," whispered Chris. "Talking at the top of his voice about how much BDSM experience he's had."

"I know," I agreed. "Maybe his thong's too tight. But everyone else here is so quiet!"

In the room's centre was a large lady arrived wearing only a babydoll nightdress. She was joined by a heavy-set man decorated from head to foot with tattoos. He donned a pair of red boxing gloves and the lady begged, "No, please, mercy!" He patted his leather-bound fists on the backs of her arms and gently swung at her bum, careful not to hit her too hard and avoiding her most sensitive areas. We were sitting close to them.

"Is it OK to watch?" I asked.

The man turned and smiled. "Yes, of course."

Even knowing the act was consensual I found watching difficult, but the fact that it was all done in near-silence made it mesmerising. He built up the level of punishment over some thirty minutes and for the last ten he was hitting so hard she was crying. There was no holding back. Finally she fell to her knees, tears flooding from her eyes. Her partner removed his gloves and wrapped his arms around her so tightly and protectively that no one could have got past him. After an act that appeared violent there was love, intense beyond most couples' dreams.

"That was so private I felt I shouldn't have seen it," murmured Chris. I agreed.

At the other end of the room a man entered with two pretty girls, perhaps half his age and a third of his weight. He was smiling with gleeful abandon. Soon the two girls had been stripped of their tops and one had been tied to a chair. Pegs were attached to her nipples and an electric charge was passed through them. When she began to scream with pain the pegs were removed and other girl massaged away the soreness.

"How has a guy as old and fat as him got those two girls to play with him?" I asked.

"I was wondering the same," said Chris. "He seems to have no charisma. I suppose he's rich."

As more people arrived we began to drink from a paradise of voyeuristic delights. There were no more than twenty people in the place, but they were cheerful and friendly and their colourful diversity filled the room. The skinny man in the leather body bag was vibrating wildly, his arousal evident. A humming filled our ears. A boy in a heavy metal T-shirt flicked a switch and the hum ceased. His acne-infested complexion beamed with delight as he re-started the vibrator.

I was engrossed by this vignette of BDSM life, privileged to participate in activities that made those people whole. In that place and at that moment they were the same people as they were in their everyday lives, but more honestly so. Liberated from the pressures of social norms, they were behaving as they wished without risk of judgment. From transvestite drifters to large ladies in baby-doll nightwear, the room brimmed with the sincere and the true. As the evening wore on we were joined at our table by a smorgasbord of remarkable characters. Chris fitted into this scene with consummate ease, his happy face and cheerful disposition a magnet to all who came near. He and I talked to a young couple who played and were looking for another couple to play with. The conversation didn't go much beyond exchanges of names and questions such as "Where do you live?" and "What's your job?" but I think Chris meant to follow up the contact. In the event, he never did.

*

I stayed longer than I'd intended, intoxicated by what I'd seen, but sadly the time came for me to leave. Being the perfect gentleman, Chris walked me to my car. It was a balmy night, the late twilight still lingering.

"Wow, what an evening!" he said.

"Memorable, for sure. It's opened my eyes to lots of possibilities!"

"I think I've got a taste for this. I'll probably come to more of these parties. How about you?"

"Yeah. That would be good, Chris."

"I'd like tonight to go on a bit longer. How about a quiet drink somewhere, just the two of us?"

I admit I was tempted. As always, Chris had been great company, funny as ever. But perfect moments remain perfect because they end when they're supposed to. I shook my head, gave him a hug and made my way to my car.

"I'll be in touch to arrange another session," he called after me, laughing. "I have so many more ideas now!"

As I drove away from that little mill opposite the butcher's in the idyllic village, I realised I was at risk of becoming more than just fond of this wonderful man. At that moment I wanted to turn my car round and go after him, to stretch the moment beyond its acceptable limit.

"You need to take care," I told myself. "In any case, you have a little dog to get back to."

However, I felt surprisingly sad as I drove away that night. I had deep feelings for Chris and a strong connection with him. It wasn't sexual attraction, at least not for me, but I felt more at ease in his company than I've felt with almost anyone else. He'd become a very good friend.

Where might that friendship have taken us if subsequent events hadn't turned my life upside down?

Chapter 9

I thought about Chris a lot after the party. We were kindred spirits and his personality attracted me. There was no sexual chemistry and I never contemplated an intimate relationship, but the shift from what we'd been to what we'd now become might nevertheless cause difficulties.

He e-mailed me about our evening in Wonderland, sharing his highlights, thanking me for my company and – as promised – outlining ideas for our next session. His enthusiasm for BDSM was undiminished.

"I enjoyed the party," I emailed in reply, "and I'd be willing to attend another one."

Then came another e-mail: "Fancy going out together to walk our dogs?"

If I'd accepted that invitation I'd have crossed the line irrevocably. I honestly didn't know what to say in reply so I decided to not to answer at all. Any activity within the BDSM area was fine, and going for a drink or even dinner with him could have been acceptable, but walking the dogs together would have been much more personal. I was aware he had a partner, and although he'd played down the relationship I was now concerned he might grow too close to me. No woman likes another woman to be too familiar with her man, regardless of who they are and what the connection is.

He never e-mailed me again. I awaited a message arranging a date for his next session but it didn't come. Days became weeks, then a month, then two months. Still there was no communication. His 'disappearance' was unprecedented. He'd always been reliable. The long silence was totally out of character for him, and it was especially odd for him to forego a session that he'd anticipated with such excitement in the wake of the party. Perhaps, I thought, he'd begun to share my concerns about the incipient change in our relationship. A submissive can become confused if he gains access to his Mistress's private life. But I worried about Chris and even started dreaming about him. In the end I had to do something.

He'd entrusted me with his private phone number. "You can contact me any time," he'd told me more than once. "It's fine."

Despite his assurance, I'd never have used the number if there'd been another option. However, there wasn't. I made the call; the phone was switched off. That was odd, because he was one of those men who live with a phone to their ear. I tried again the following day and the day after that. No answer.

I had to find an explanation. At first I brushed aside the thought that something bad had happened, guessing that demands at home had consumed his attention or he'd had to go away somewhere. Nevertheless, the thought kept coming back, insisting that something wasn't right. For weeks I scanned obituaries, probed blogs and investigated organisations in which I knew Chris was involved. I'd have looked more the part if I'd donned a deerstalker and smoked a pipe. But I learned nothing. At last, I was contacted by an escort whom Chris had visited regularly. She and I had met previously: she'd used my Chamber for a photoshoot and we'd done some modelling together.

"Have you heard anything from Chris?" she asked. "He broke an appointment and he's never done that before. I was expecting some photos from him."

"I expected him to book another session with me, but he hasn't," I replied. "I've been trying to contact him for weeks."

"So have I. I've used adult social media. My messages to him haven't been opened."

Neither of us had any contact with Chris's family (which was hardly surprising!) but we were both worried. Our shared anxiety testified to his charisma and personal magnetism.

Finally, I found a social media page relating to one of Chris's friends. There, staring back at me from the screen, was a eulogy to my companion, together with a photo of his smiling face. Everyone who'd known him would treasure his memory.

He'd died.

*

I'll never forget the moment I learned the truth. A tide of nausea rose into my throat. Bile burned my tongue and my head spun. I felt myself falling into darkness, deeper and deeper. My mind refused to accept that Chris had gone. The discovery was torment, the knowledge a prison, my grief hell. I wanted to return to my state of ignorance. We humans never consider mortality; we'd rather hide our heads in the sand. But ageing is insidious. Someday there'll be no tomorrow. Yet Chris had been a young man, full of life. How could I deal with my memories of him, my feeling that I'd lost control? Where might the road of friendship have taken us? I'd never know. I only knew there was an empty space in my heart.

I set out to learn more. It seemed he'd died suddenly; a brain haemorrhage. Why? He'd been so fit!

Weeks passed and I couldn't get him out of my mind. Of course there was no closure for me: I'd been a secret in his life so I couldn't share my grief or leave a tribute. My memories would always be private. Usually when we're bereaved we can turn the page and move on, but it would be a long time before I could come to terms with losing Chris.

I kept my business running as normal, dealing with my clients as they needed. I don't believe any of them knew I'd suffered such a loss. Then one day as I was finishing work and ready to leave my Chamber for home I played back my voice-mail messages, as I usually do before tackling the city traffic. One message cut the ground from under my feet: an authoritative-sounding gentleman from the coroner's office needed to talk to me about Chris. I replayed the message, my heart leaping into my throat and dancing pirouettes. *The police were going to question me.*

I'd done nothing wrong but I became very worried. Was I under some kind of suspicion? Had I been responsible for giving Chris too much punishment, or too much nitrous oxide, and causing his haemorrhage? Would I be trading my Chamber for the bare walls of a cold cell and my leather corset for a stripy suit? I tried to return the call immediately but the coroner's office was closed, which gave me no comfort. So I rang Peter. Of course, Peter put my mind at rest.

"Lucina, if you were in trouble they wouldn't have left a voicemail. They'd be at your door."

Nevertheless a sleepless night lay ahead as yin and yang joined in battle over my conscious mind. Yin, echoing Peter: if my situation were really serious they'd have come to my door, not left a phone message. Yang: why would they want to talk to me at all unless they believed I was involved? At dawn, yin and yang declared a temporary ceasefire and promised to stay quiet. Time flowed like treacle until the hour hand reached nine, and then, shaking with dread, I rang the coroner's office number again. This time I got through, but the call was an anticlimax. The polite officer who answered seemed grateful I'd returned his call so quickly and thanked me for doing so. He took my details and made an appointment for a visit the following Tuesday.

"We just need to talk to you about the events leading up to Chris's death."

Three days to wait, and still no clue as to why they needed to talk to me about those events! Yin would never agree to such a long ceasefire, and yang would retaliate. Within the three days, what was possibly a storm in a teacup had become in my mind a tempest raging over an ocean. Sometimes we want the things we most dread to happen immediately, to be over and done with. Uncertain and under duress, our minds change white to black. I wanted Tuesday to come. When it finally did I greeted it with a wrecked mind, but I knew I'd find my answers now and the death of uncertainty would give me peace. By the time two smartly-dressed police officers, probably in their midthirties, had appeared at my door, shown me their warrant cards and camped on my sitting room sofa, I was ready to face the truth irrespective of pain.

*

"Would you like a cup of tea?" I offered.

They accepted, which relaxed me a little. Before the inquest, they said, they needed to establish a better understanding of Chris's secret life with me and the escorts he'd visited. Few had known this side of him, perhaps none better than me. I confirmed the nature of our relationship. Then the tape deck appeared and they started to record our conversation; the *interview*. One of the officers made it clear he didn't want to be doing this.

"Chris's family have been through enough without them being dragged through this side of his life as well. But the boss said we had to come and interview you, so here we are."

I didn't want to be doing it either. However, they had questions to ask and I had to answer them. As they turned on the tape recorder the officers took out their notes and studied them. One of them looked up at me and asked:

"How do you spell 'Dominatrix'?"

"Try and use your spell-check," said his companion.

"Spell-check doesn't recognise it. I'll try Googling it. Lend us your mobile."

"Not bloody likely! What if my wife sees it? She already thinks I'm up to no good!"

The slapstick exchange calmed me a little. Answering each of their questions was grasping a nettle, but the officers were kind and told me more about the tragedy. Chris had been found on his bed wearing a mask filled with nitrous oxide. Despite his assurances, despite knowing the danger, he'd administered the gas while alone, and he'd lost consciousness and haemorrhaged. The revelation squeezed the air out of my lungs.

The officers thought Chris had simply been playing at home, even though he was clothed, but having known Chris for so long I knew better.

"It wouldn't be like him to play on his own," I said. "He'd get nothing from it."

They described the mask he'd been wearing. It was one I hadn't seen.

"He was probably trying out a new idea," I suggested.

"Probably," agreed one of the officers. "The mask had only been delivered that very morning."

I now knew exactly what he'd been doing. He'd been trying out the mask for our next session, probably seeing whether he could fit the pipes on and organise the rest of the arrangements. Underestimating how quickly nitrous oxide can make you pass out, he'd suffocated. It gave me a little comfort to realise he hadn't suffered. It must have been like falling asleep and never waking up.

At least, that was my guess. Had Chris come to need bigger and more frequent hits to feed his growing need? A submissive can reach a point where need outweighs reason and the urge to gratify it becomes irresistible. The danger can add to the thrill. We'll never really know what happened to Chris, only the pain that resulted for his family and friends – and for me and his regular escort.

The officers revealed something else that embarrassed and upset me: Chris had been married. He'd told me he and his partner lived separate lives. He'd never alluded to a wife. I had the impression that the officers genuinely liked his wife – widow – and wanted to spare her any further pain. But the news made me numb. I hadn't known him as well as I'd thought!

Of course, BDSM-related needs often push people into living secret lives. To his family, Chris had been a loving husband with a successful career and a zest for life; they'd known nothing of his other side. Now the dark and the light had collided and shattered the image. The evidence was damning, from the discovery of BDSM equipment he'd hidden in the house to the unearthing of e-mails and photos. In the eyes of his family, Chris hadn't been the man they thought they'd known. Indeed, there was a whole world about which they'd known nothing. One crumb of comfort was that he had no children. He hadn't wanted any.

It seemed to me he'd almost wished he was single, and being in a relationship was in many ways holding him back. That's probably why he'd never said he was married; it was as if he *wasn't* married, provided it wasn't mentioned. He'd played down his relationship so much that one day I asked him: "Why don't you just separate?"

"A lot of things happened when we first got together," he said. (He never explained what those things were.) "It kind of bonded us. Also, we bought a house together, so things are complicated."

I'd been a mere traveller on the road Chris had chosen to take, but I feared that what I might have to divulge would cause his family still greater pain. He'd had a wife, a dutiful and caring partner providing support and love. Her world had been taken from her. All she'd known must now seem like a lie. She'd been shown a window into her husband's other world, so ignorance could no longer protect her. Nevertheless, each of us is the sum of all our parts. Chris's wife hadn't known all his secrets, but I'm certain she'd known *him*. I believe he'd been every bit the man his family had loved. He'd had a dark side but it hadn't defined him; it had been just one facet of his life, one of many.

"We've read all the e-mails you and Chris exchanged," the officers told me.

This meant there'd have been no point in my lying about our connection even if I'd wanted to; not that I had anything to lie about.

"How long had you known Chris?" they asked. "What kinds of BDSM activities did you get up to?" But most of their questions, of course, were about the nitrous oxide. "How often did he take it?" ... "Did you know he was taking it at home?" ... "Did you and he ever take it together?"

I could answer all those questions and answer them truthfully, and at last the interview petered to a close. Their searching questions had been accompanied by schoolboy smirks and embarrassed grins. They were curious about my profession, a typically male interest, but I was grateful for their politeness and sensitivity. I signed my statement, beating another nail into the coffin of memory. I wasn't family, not even officially a friend; what right had I to be affected by this tragic death? But affected I was.

Then came a blow I should have anticipated.

"You might be called to give evidence at the inquest," said Officer One.

"I hope you won't," said Officer Two, his eyes sympathetic. "His wife and family will be there."

Again I felt they wanted to save Chris's family any more hurt. I had the impression they'd worked very closely with them since his death and tried to shelter them as best they could. They both seemed very fond of his widow. I could understand that. Any woman capable of attracting Chris was bound to be a lovely person. I didn't want her to suffer any more hurt either.

*

I found it hard not to be angry with Chris. He'd known the dangers. He'd devastated his family. What could be more brutal than seeing your world dismantled, discovering that you've been living a life of illusion? The inquest would be difficult for them to bear even without my involvement. Of course I was anxious on my own behalf, too. Every time the post rattled through my door, dread swamped me.

But time passed with no further word about the inquest, and life had to go on. My Sundays were my days of rest, my Mondays were spent with rescue dogs, and from Tuesday until Saturday I worked in my Chamber. Several other Mistresses now wanted to session in my dungeon and the less experienced sometimes asked me to join them in punishing their slaves, though I always preferred one-to-one encounters with my clients, which helped to build personal trust. Finding ways of satisfying a slave's need to achieve total submission is as rewarding as bringing love and comfort to an abused animal, but it's best done with just one Dominatrix, not two.

Perhaps this is the connection. When a Dominatrix-submissive relationship achieves true synergy, the submissive becomes as loyal, trusting, honest and dependable as a dog, and the Mistress enjoys that love and trust just as she might with a pet. It truly is a reciprocal dependence. Yet the comparison isn't exact. The dog's devotion and trust and dependence are spontaneous, inbuilt, and need nothing more than the owner's love and care to sustain them. The slave's devotion and trust and dependence have to be gained through an investment of effort by both parties, and the submissive often discovers long-buried or dormant aspects of need and personality. This discovery can be transformative. Submissives such as David2 have cried with emotion when their suppressed or unrecognised needs are finally expressed in my dungeon. Such moments are among the most rewarding and gratifying for a Dominatrix.

But a Mistress-slave bond as strong as the one Chris and I had forged over the years is as rare as blue diamond. It wasn't something I'd be able to replace.

Chapter 10

Before the two police officers left my flat after the interview I asked them how soon I'd learn whether I was to be summoned to the inquest.

"Should know in a couple of weeks," they said. The more senior of the pair stared at me and repeated: "If I had my way I wouldn't have you there. The family's been through enough. It couldn't do them any good to have you present. But it isn't my decision."

His words gave me a little comfort; perhaps I wouldn't be summoned. Many weeks had passed since then and nothing had happened. The shadow of the inquest still hung over me but I was daring to relax a little, and clients continued to visit my Chamber.

"It must have gone ahead without me being needed," I thought. "After all, I'd given a long in-depth interview, so what good could it have done to confront the family with me?"

*

Tony first came to see me around that time. Like many subservient men, his ideal would have been to find a lifestyle Mistress rather than a professional. He chose me as a lifestyle Mistress who provided services as a business because, it seemed, I was as close as he could find to that ideal. He was a professional man, well dressed and slight in build. As a slave he was very submissive although his tastes were precise.

"I wish to be caned or disciplined, Princess Lucina, with your permission."

"Ah. You enjoy being beaten, do you, slave?"

I knew he didn't. One of the commonest misunderstandings about BDSM is that submissives enjoy being beaten. Wrong. It's because they *don't* like being beaten that an act of genuine punishment is therapeutic for them. They need to be punished for an actual offence. The caning won't work for them if it seems contrived or if it's too gentle.

To begin with, Tony wrote confessions to various offences. Some of them might have been fanciful but many were real. He reported these confessions to me so he could be punished for his wrongdoing. Over time, our sessions evolved into lifestyle improvements, forcing him to change what he'd become to the man he wanted to be.

"I've taken a year off to write a book," he explained. "I've sold my house and moved into a much smaller flat in the centre of Manchester. But instead of spending my time putting pen to paper I've been gambling, drinking and staying up late."

Any author will tell you that there are times when such distractions are alluring and strict focus is required. Tony lacked the strict focus. I would impose it.

"We shall proceed by creating a number of rules by which you'll be required to live," I decided. "You'll complete a regular report card to declare misdemeanours."

It might seem surprising that a man in this position would be honest in recording any breach of the rules, but the trust between Mistress and slave ensured it. A submissive man will often be more honest with his Dominatrix than with his wife or partner. The slave *could* choose to lie, but he doesn't because any deviation from the truth would diminish future sessions.

"This isn't a game," I warned Tony. "The punishment for any lapse will be real and severe. You need to be afraid of failure."

"I am, Mistress," he said. "If it were a game there'd be no deterrent, so I'd gain nothing."

Ten years later, Tony is still reporting to me to control his behaviour. When he's good I'm kind and when he's bad I'm horrid, but I'm always completely genuine. We've become good friends and he's come to rely on me in ways that govern his lifestyle. He admits he'd now find it hard to enter into a more conventional relationship. Over the years his report card goals have altered to reflect the changes in his life, but there's been no change in the strictness of his Mistress if he fails to fall into line. By his own admission he needs to be genuinely scared of me, to know that if he doesn't go to bed on time, or has an unauthorised orgasm, his pleasure will be extinguished by the fear of seeing me afterwards. Perhaps, in the early days, I hadn't caned him as hard as I should have done. Perhaps I'd greeted him too warmly when he arrived. He's complained about that.

"I need to be afraid to come here if my report card's bad. The more you hurt me, the more I love you."

*

Clients often ask me to indulge in role-play scenarios, as Chris did. Role-play is a slightly grey area of BDSM because the subservient seems to have more control than in other types of session. Nevertheless it doesn't contradict the desire common to all submissives, i.e. to *be* controlled. The slave specifies the game, often in detail, but when the game is played the Mistress is unequivocally in charge. I discourage clients from planning the session too precisely or in too many facets because that kills spontaneity, but it's useful to know at least in general terms what they have in mind. If some of the planning is done by the client then I seldom need as much preparation time as I do for other types of session. However, the activities still have to touch upon those areas of the scene that I enjoy so I can indulge the client as he (or she) wishes, otherwise they're not as much fun for either party.

Role-play can be as simple as a schoolroom scenario or as complex as a scripted interrogation scene. Many submissives wish to use role-play to enact a favourite fantasy; they can spend hours or even days planning the session. It can lead to regular repeat sessions and potentially the bond of a new friendship. It can provide a safe means of experiencing new and exciting areas of BDSM that they might not otherwise have considered. It can also be something from childhood that has stayed with them over the years. What might begin as a vague fantasy can become something beautiful, brought into existence through the imagination and creativity of two willing minds, and then enacted through their partnership.

Some of the most common role-play scenarios involve corporal punishment, CP for short, as in Tony's case. The fantasy often has its roots in the submissive's childhood experiences, such as school punishments or spankings administered at home. One example is the client Mike whom I met while I was being trained as a Mistress. For a submissive with that sort of background, the need for CP tends to intensify during puberty. Mike, for instance, had deliberately sought special attention from teachers he knew had a penchant for administering punishment. He'd even created situations that led to spankings by his parents' housekeeper.

Another client was caught by his aunt in her bedroom when he was sixteen, trying on her silk panties because he liked the feel of them. He'd done it many times before but now he'd been caught. His aunt was so angry that she sat on the bed, pushed him over her knee and beat his bottom as hard as she could with her hair brush.

"I got a huge erection," he told me, "which made her hit me even harder."

He wanted to relive that moment in session while I told him off for wearing my silk panties.

Such early experiences can persist long in the memory and exert a very strong influence. Many boys have had their lives shaped by female interactions during their teenage years. They might have gone on to do 'normal' things such as marrying and having children, but the recollection remains so powerful that even as elderly men they try to relive it over and over again. Most have never even told their wives about it.

One client had been bullied by girls at school. They'd found it fun to chase him every day, pin him down and push grass up his nose. On one of those occasions he'd experienced his first erection. Now he wanted to be restrained and bullied so he could recover that old feeling.

Some men report having been touched up or seduced by female teachers when they were teenagers. You might think stories of that kind are just fantasy, but having met such men I believe many of their accounts. Of course, they'd never complained about the 'inappropriate contact'!

*

What is technically known as 'paraphilic infantilism' is one of the more curious subcultures within the burgeoning ecosystem of BDSM. Players of this game (mostly men, as far as I know) are more commonly known as 'adult babies'. They want to role-play age regression and can exhibit a range of behavioural needs such as drinking from a baby's bottle, wearing nappies and being nurtured with maternal care. Some adult babies have a need to soil (pee or poo) their nappy or be punished for bad behaviour.

This game seems to fit the general pattern of submissiveness: loss of control and abrogation of responsibility, reduction to a state of helplessness. As small children we're helpless and have to be looked after. Also, infancy is a period in human life when we're free of problems; we have no real say in what happens so we have no worries. In that sense, the adult baby game might be a form of escapism. I think the associated feeling of peace is part of what the paraphilic-infantilist seeks.

For many years I refused to entertain sessions with adult babies and I made that clear on my website. My main objection was the soiling. Deliberate defaecation into a nappy was, and remains, a step too far for me. Eventually, though, I did start to accommodate this area of BDSM. My attitude changed one evening thanks to an e-mail from a man I didn't know.

"I noticed on Your site that You don't offer adult baby," he wrote, "but I promise I don't soil my nappy in any way. I simply like to be put in a nappy and left for a while."

This e-mail gave me a positive feeling and I agreed to see him. When he arrived he proved to be a very pleasant if slightly nervous little fellow who true to his word just wanted to be put in a nappy and left for a while. Sometimes I cuddled him like a little boy. From the moment we met he changed my whole perspective on adult babies and he became a lifelong friend. I remain grateful for his guidance. But I still never allow soiling of nappies.

Adult baby sessions can be amongst the easiest for a Mistress. Some adult babies, like the client who changed my views, simply want to be dressed in a nappy and left to watch television. Of course, others have different wishes; each one is an individual. But in my experience, players in this particular area of BDSM are kind, well-educated professionals who're simply looking for their own personal variety of comfort.

A good-looking, highly intelligent and successful middle-aged man wanted me to put him in a very tight nappy and tell him that if he complained I'd make him wear it to school in front of his friends, and that I'd take a photo and send it to his mother. That was the essence of his session. However, he wanted to explain his request. Indeed, his need to explain it in depth was almost as important to him as the session itself. He told me his mother had given birth to another son when he was eight years old. Feeling left out, he started to play up, and one day he climbed into the baby's high chair. His mother dragged him out.

"If you want to act like a baby then I'll help you!"

Furious, she strapped one of the baby's nappies around him very tightly and made him keep it on until she chose to set him free again. This wasn't a one-off event; it became her way of punishing him, using ever-bigger nappies, until he was fifteen. Sometimes she made him go to school in them. When the practice finally ceased, with no explanation, he felt deprived. At sixteen he went for work experience in a care home and was asked to clear out a store room. There he found a box full of nappies that were used for incontinence. He couldn't resist; he put one on and experienced a massive orgasm.

His mother's actions seem to me to have bordered on abuse. I don't understand what she hoped to achieve. Was she trying to warp him for life? If so, she succeeded. You might ask what role a Dominatrix can play in such a situation. Wouldn't the client be better advised to see a professional counsellor? I asked him that very question.

"I've done so many times, Mistress," he said, "and it hasn't helped in the slightest. The only thing that helps is seeing a lady like you who'll live out a little role-play. I can't explain it, but it's the only thing that relieves my feelings. Without visiting a Dominatrix occasionally I become depressed and confused."

Thanks to my experience as a Mistress I've become non-judgmental about almost all fetishes. Dominatrixes encounter so many strange requests and hear so many deep secrets that it becomes hard to shock us. For me, those deep secrets are fascinating. I don't pretend to understand psychology; I haven't read the books or done the courses. However, I do know when a session with me helps someone, and our sessions helped that client. I'm sure the counsellors he consulted, shocked or not, wouldn't have treated him by putting him in a tight nappy and threatening him, but their 'textbook' approach seems to have been ineffective. He was an extremely intelligent man with a good job in the London stock markets and he was of sound mind. The occasions when I've had to halt a session because I've doubted the client's mental stability have been few and far between. I didn't doubt this man's sanity. He had unorthodox needs, but they were understandable.

*

The submissive might recall, or imagine, formal and procedural punishments such as facing the wall for a certain length of time before being made to bend over and touch his toes. When his fantasy leads him to approach a Dominatrix he'll probably want her to be fully dressed and to re-enact a particular scenario. Being made to face a wall is degrading and humiliating. Humiliation is a common thread among a wide range of BDSM activities. When he faces the wall, the submissive is on display, his bad behaviour a voyeuristic treat for the Mistress and anyone she invites to witness his shame. His helplessness in the face of inevitable punishment excites him. Being ordered to disrobe, fully or from the waist down, and being punished by a fully clothed woman adds to the intensity. It's a symbolic act of submission that heightens the embarrassment and deepens the humiliation. As in all BDSM scenarios, the submissive relinquishes control. Therein lies the satisfaction.

Such sessions aren't about inflicting pain; at least, desire for pain is unlikely to be the main psychological driver. Indeed, the submissive's pain threshold might be low. His need is usually more complex, often a wish to confess to a genuine infraction and be punished for it. So it was, and is, for Tony.

*

Another type of role-play scenario is a kidnap. I'd done it with Chris, as I described earlier, but it isn't something to be undertaken lightly. It can be delicate. I seldom provide kidnapping as a service and never for a client I don't know well. It's a dark, dusty, difficult and potentially dangerous corner of the role-play world.

"Imagine hustling someone into the back of your car," I told a Mistress who was planning such a scenario with a client she hadn't met, "only to discover you've got the wrong man!"

"I'll get a recent photo of him," she said, "so I can't make that mistake."

"It wouldn't be fool-proof," I said. "Suppose this client's trying to play a practical joke. What if he sends you a photo of his intended victim, not himself?"

"Oh, come on, is that likely?"

"It's been known. You know the warped tricks men sometimes play on friends who're getting married. What better way to send the groom from stag party to wedding than via a terrifying kidnap ordeal?"

Such stag-party games are generally harmless in the long run, though as a Dominatrix I'd resent being manipulated into participating. However, some kidnap scenarios have untoward or at least embarrassing consequences.

"We'd overlooked the risk of witnesses," one Mistress told me. She and a colleague had planned and enacted a double-Domme kidnap scenario. "We pushed the client into the back of my car, and an upstanding pillar of the community who recognised him saw what we were doing and called the police."

"Oh, my God! How did you get out of *that*?" I asked.

"Oh, we were fine. The witness didn't get my registration number. The police had to investigate but they didn't knock on our doors. They were soon knocking on *his* door, though, so his powers of quick thinking were challenged. He was censured for wasting police time. I don't suppose it did much for his marital harmony."

You can see why I seldom offer kidnap role-play as a service. However, when I've felt able to do it, the results have provided considerable interest and excitement.

*

My client John is elderly, a tall man with a lanky physique and a number of endearing qualities, not least a warm and gentle heart. He's a submissive who loves to share time with his Mistress. Over time we've established the best kind of Dominatrix-slave bond: he's become a regular client and a good friend, and I've learned the strings he likes to be pulled and those he prefers to be left alone. He can't tolerate pain; his perfect session involves being bound tightly and thus rendered helpless so I can subject him to a range of torments targeting his mind. Once we'd become well acquainted he helped me with new photos for my website and took me for lunch in the pub. Our mutual trust had reached a level where there seemed little risk of 'crossing the line'. That meant I could indulge some of his more challenging fantasies as well as stretching my own limits.

"Here's your shopping list," I told him one afternoon.

I sent him into the shopping centre, list in hand, and followed him. I made myself just conspicuous enough for him to know he was being watched while he sought the women's clothes he'd been ordered to purchase. Once he'd bought them all he was taken back to my Chamber and made to dress in them. Then I tied him to the bed and did what he most enjoyed.

Subsequently, he wanted to take things further.

"Princess Lucina," he suggested, "please will you abduct me from home? It's all right, I live alone. Then perhaps you could tie me up and dump me in a place I don't know and leave me there as long as you wish."

He gave me a copy of his house key so the abduction would be easy. Breaking into someone's house without them knowing isn't easy when they're at home! However, we'd agreed a time so he'd know I was coming. I'm sure he heard me entering because I was so clumsy, but he pretended not to, and it worked.

"Don't you dare to struggle or cry for help," I whispered. "I have a knife and I'll use it!"

John was pushed outside at the point of my imaginary knife. Soon he was in the boot of his car, being driven out to Saddleworth Moor to be tied up and dumped in a secluded spot. I had to use *his* car because at that time I drove a sports car with far too small a boot to accommodate him. His vehicle was a classic Rover; he'd got me insured for the day. The boot was large – but it was enclosed, so I wasn't sure how long he could keep breathing. Still, that was part of the fun. I've always feared that my compulsion to push limits will get me into trouble someday, but clients love my sense of adventure and willingness to try almost anything, even when it isn't the wisest move. Anyway, John survived. After I'd dumped him I drove away, but the weather had turned wintry and I was soon shivering. Realising that my prisoner would be frozen, I left him for only a short time before returning to set him free. It was the right judgment; the cold had turned him slightly away from his 'sub zone'.

"The best bit was being bundled into the boot of my own car," he said.

*

It was a reasonably successful attempt at kidnap, but the weather had cut the game short. We needed to adapt the scenario before a second attempt, partly because of those safety considerations and partly to satisfy John's growing appetite for this kind of BDSM.

Careful planning would be needed. In the end a scheme was agreed: I was going to have to kidnap a man a foot taller than me in a public place. However, I'm always up for a challenge, and I can be inventive.

"Go to that McDonald's," I instructed, pointing out the restaurant, "and order a meal. I shall arrive when I choose."

I entered the McDonald's car park and saw John sitting at a table in the window, taking nervous sips of hot coffee. I was nervous, too. This was going to be difficult. Taking a deep breath I parked my car, clamped one bracelet of a set of handcuffs to my left wrist and hid the rest of the cuffs under the sleeve of my jumper. Then I entered the restaurant. It was crowded: customers were queuing, waiting to be served, while others were munching burgers at Formica tables. John had wanted his abduction to be public, but this was *seriously* public. The plan could easily fail, with embarrassing consequences.

Assuming an air of calm I slid into the seat next to my victim and asked him for the time. He spluttered, coffee dripping from his nose. The shock of my arrival had undone his self-control. He lifted his arm to look at his watch, and I pulled the other bracelet of the cuffs from my sleeve and clamped it on his wrist. Before he had time to blink I pulled our arms downward, hiding them beneath the table.

"If you don't do exactly as I say," I rasped, "I'll scream and tell everyone *you're* kidnapping *me!*"

The words had been carefully rehearsed and I delivered them with menace. If I *had* screamed, which of us would have been blamed for kidnapping the other? A woman my size couldn't abduct a man well over six feet tall by force, but the leverage of blackmail brought him under my control. I ordered him to stand. Together we left the restaurant and returned to my car. I held his hand tightly with my sleeve pulled down over the cuffs. Soon he was lying on the back seat of the car with a blanket over him, his wrist handcuffed to the door, and I drove him away.

The plan had worked: John had no choice but to comply with my orders and I was free to do as I wished with him. The scenario had developed brilliantly and he was well satisfied.

*

"Mistress," he asked on a later occasion, handing me his key again, a back door key this time, "I'd like to know what it feels like to be held hostage and at the mercy of my captor. I'm at home most of the time.

I tend to open my curtains when I go out, but when I'm in I generally have them closed."

We discussed this new fantasy and agreed a scheme.

"At some point during a three-day window I'll 'break into' your house and hold you captive for twelve hours," I told him. "But you won't know exactly when I'll appear. It might be on the first of those three days, or the second, or even the third."

I knew the anticipation would build tension and excitement, so I allowed the first day to pass without doing anything. On the second day I waited until ten at night, knowing that he'd have stopped expecting me by then and would be off guard. I parked in the sleepy cul-de-sac a few houses up the street from his bungalow. The night was still; there was barely a sound. I tiptoed along the path and into his back garden. The key turned easily in the lock. Crawling on all fours, trying to control my breathing, certain the pounding of my heart must be audible, I crept to the hall and inched my way forward towards the living room door. I heard the television and saw John perched on his sofa, watching some late night detritus that didn't seem to hold his attention. The door was only open an inch but it was enough for me to watch him flick through the channels. He yawned, evidently disappointed that the evening had petered out without my appearance. He'd soon retire to his bed to dream of the morrow.

I made my way to the end of the hall and entered his bedroom through the open door, planning my ambush as I went. I pushed myself into a large walk-in wardrobe and hid amongst his ties. An hour seemed to pass. Proud of my stealthy entrance to his house, I now awaited only his arrival in the bedroom. However, I felt my own eyes closing. I joked to myself that he'd find me there the following morning sleeping between his ties and his shoes. But just as I was losing faith in my ability to stay awake I heard movement from the living room. Weary footsteps approached. Again my heart raced.

There was the flick of a switch and the room blazed with light. John had shuffled into the bedroom and was standing with his back to the wardrobe. I watched for one poetic moment, breathless with the sense of power. It was glorious to know I had complete control over what was about to follow. I revelled in his ignorance of my presence. But then, like a child pouncing on her presents on Christmas morning, I could contain my excitement no longer. I leapt from the wardrobe screaming: "Got You!"

He leapt into the air, his arms stretched high for what seemed an eternity, and he screamed. It was too much. I started laughing, partly with relief that I hadn't given this elderly man a heart attack, partly with sheer joy at my triumph. The initial snigger became a full-bellied guffaw and then I was lying on the bed, helpless with hilarity. Once he'd recovered and I'd managed to stop laughing, I played to his wishes. To begin with I tied him to his bed and left him there, helpless, before retiring to his spare room to sleep. In the morning I woke him with a breakfast of cornflakes, mustard and ketchup. I fed these to him while he was still tied up and threatened him with much worse if he resisted. Later he was tied to a chair in his study while I continued to torture his mind until he could take no more.

For a few hours, John had allowed himself to live out a fantasy, his needs being met non-judgmentally by a trusted Mistress, his inner self allowed to express itself as it needed. We'd become good friends and travelled a journey together.

*

Role-play isn't for everyone. It can require careful planning and boundless imagination. But for those wishing to live out their fantasies it can be an exciting route – and, if due care is taken, a safe route – toward a world without limits where dreams can be made real. It can be both exciting and hilarious. Of course it should be fun, as with all BDSM activities, but for the Dominatrix as well as the submissive it can also be deeply fulfilling. Many role-play games such as those with John have left me with precious memories.

Chapter 11

Five months had passed since my interview with the two police officers investigating Chris's death. My fear of red vans and envelopes was subsiding and a healing process was underway. But some ghosts refuse to rest in their graves. The cogs of bureaucracy are immune to emotion; they turn in time to the pushing of pens and the cold reality of the judicial process. One morning I had to sign for an official letter. I knew at once what it was, though until it was opened I clung to the hope that I was wrong.

I pulled the documents out of the A4 envelope and my heart seemed to stop and accelerate at the same time. The message in bold black type, "You are summoned to the inquest", was followed by warnings about what would happen if I failed to attend without good reason. I was given fourteen days to prepare for my part in the assassination of Chris's character. Sworn to tell the truth, I'd have to deliver the final word – with his family present. Its weight would fall across the shoulders of all who cared about him.

The shadow had returned to darken my life. There was no escape from what lay ahead. How can you prepare for the unknown, other than to expect anything and fear everything? Yin and yang raged once more. I tried to imagine the inquest process down to the finest detail. Where would I sit, what would the room look like, how would people view me? How would the grieving widow react to the presence of her husband's Mistress? Would I face consequences for nitrous oxide use? My imaginings began to eclipse the likely reality.

What had begun as a personal quest to discover the fate of a missing friend had stolen a year from me. Now I simply wanted the inquest to be over and my life to move on at last.

Predictably, the night before the inquest was spent in restless insomnia. I don't remember preparing for my appearance in court, nor do I recall my journey into the city. I was tired and numb, a mindless automaton. Unconscious pistons turned the wheels of necessity; my senses had retreated elsewhere.

Before I realised it I was standing in a long, slow queue snaking back from the courthouse entrance, cooled by the Arctic blast of a faulty air conditioner. Those attending a courthouse have to form a conga and wait patiently to be searched. Along the line, the fearful took their final breaths of freedom, eyes flitting to and fro. It was a long wait before I was led into the main building and treated for hypothermia. Then I discovered I was in the wrong place.

In my zombie-like state I'd wandered into the court of criminal justice.

*

At last I reached the correct building, joined another queue, and was searched and admitted. A board behind the reception desk listed the hearings for the day. Seeing Chris's name last on the board I went into the waiting room, relieved to see it empty. Despite my earlier navigational failure I was early. At the reception area I announced who I was.

"Ah," said the woman, "yes, just wait there."

She hurried away very quickly and then a heavy-set lady wearing courtroom garb trundled to my side. She introduced herself with a firm but friendly handshake, but her words bounced off my ears. I was too scared to take in what she said. I glanced around anxiously, knowing Chris's family might already be nearby. The inevitability of the coming storm surged in the pit of my stomach. Everybody was supposed to enter the courtroom together, but the authorities had been pre-warned about the situation so their plan was to keep me apart from the family.

"Come on in," said the robed lady. "There's no point in you meeting the family, risking unnecessary clashes."

She escorted me into the empty courtroom and I was relieved. No doubt their main concern was for the family, but they didn't want trouble so their arrangements were good for me, too.

A few people had said to me, "I bet the press will be there". Seemingly it's part of a reporter's job to sit in endless inquests waiting for something juicy, and this would indeed be juicy for them. The prospect of the inquest being reported in the papers and my being 'outed' as a Dominatrix was unthinkable; discretion is the most important rule for any woman in my profession. Thankfully, the press made no appearance. Perhaps the friendly policemen who liked the family so much had taken steps to keep them at bay.

"You'll be seated just to the left of the witness box," the robed lady continued. "The deceased's family will sit on the opposite side."

She then gave me a step by step guide to what was to follow. She ensured that her eyes never left mine, but many of her words were still drowned by the voices screaming in my head. At least I picked out a few salient instructions and questions.

"Like everyone in the court, you must stand when the judge enters," she said. "Will you be prepared to swear on the Bible that you'll tell the truth?"

She seemed relieved when I said, "Yes, of course". Perhaps she'd been under the common misconception that Dominatrixes drink blood, eat children for breakfast and are anarchists or witches, not normal women with good hearts and souls.

"The judge will ask you questions taken directly from your statement to the police," the lady told me. "Always answer precisely. Never elaborate beyond what you're asked." She paused, then murmured: "The family are aware of Chris's other life but they don't know any details about it, so please be as discreet as you can with your answers."

Her demeanour was officious but her voice was soft and rather kind. She rightly wished to protect everyone, mindful of the hurt an ill-judged word could cause. I was relieved to discover that a deal of thought had been given to the finer details of the situation.

"Thank you for finding ways of keeping me and the family apart before the proceedings start," I said.

"That's important. Your exit has been planned, too. The route has been mapped. The family will be kept occupied until after you've left."

The robed lady had answered my questions, including questions I hadn't asked. My heart was hammering in my chest, but I now knew what I faced and some of the uncertainty had been laid to rest. Once she was satisfied that her information had been digested, she swept from the room. A few moments later I heard her muffled voice from the other side of the door. I guessed she was giving instructions to the family.

I gazed around the empty courthouse and then heard a door open behind me. My heart shot to my feet, the blood drained from my muscles and the breath was sucked from my lungs. It was time. There was nowhere to hide. I kept my eyes resolutely forward.

A woman and two men representing Chris's family filed past me and took their seats. I felt their eyes burn into me. I was their nemesis, an object for their abhorrence, the cause of their pain. They knew nothing in detail about Chris's secret life, but I was the manifestation of it. They couldn't hate what they neither knew nor understood, but they could pack all their bitterness into a cold tight package and drop it at the only door available to them.

When they finally sat I allowed myself to search their faces, the faces of those whose lives had been so tragically touched. Chris's widow was flanked by his brother and his father. They both bore striking resemblances to the man I'd known. His father was an older version of him and the brother had the same eyes.

"It's much like looking at Chris again," I thought, determined not to start crying.

*

A few others had dribbled to their seats, but my attention was on the trio opposite. Then the judge entered the room and my wobbly legs hoisted me from my seat and just about managed to hold me upright. Kindly, he asked us all to be seated. He was a middle-aged man wearing a smart suit and, thankfully, no intimidating wig. He gazed around the room, welcomed us, made some introductions and went through his opening notes.

"The purpose of this inquest is to establish the events leading up to the sad death of a husband, father and friend," he reminded us. (The word 'father' shocked me. What was the judge talking about? I knew Chris had no children; he'd told me so!) "There will be no prosecution, allegations or accusations. Nor are we here to point any blame at anyone. Is this clear?"

Everyone nodded in acknowledgment. His voice was calm and respectful but his gaze was directed at each member of Chris's family. He seemed a little like a boxing referee at the start of a bout, establishing the rules before a glove could be laid. He understood the potential for sparks and was dampening the ground to prevent fire.

The judge now reiterated the words of the robed lady, explaining the procedure to everyone present.

"The police will give their evidence first, then the widow of the deceased will confirm some details, and then we shall hear from the witness."

The witness. Me. My mouth went dry and my body trembled. Then the opening statement concluded with a hammer blow; the first glove had punched before the bell had rung, a sharp jab to my stomach:

"At the end of the proceedings, the family will have an opportunity to pose questions to the witness."

Nobody had warned me about that. Perhaps they'd been right. Ignorance had been bliss.

The police were represented by a youthful fellow with flushed cheeks. He fidgeted as he took the stand and began to read from his notes. Before he'd mumbled his opening sentence the judge stopped him. Apparently this child in policeman's clothing had prepared his statement fastidiously, but the judge wished to hear only the facts, presented as highlights with no needless additions. The poor little officer started again.

"On the... the day concerned, I was called to the f...family home, where there had been a 999 call. Once the paramedics had... um... pronounced the man... ahem... dead, I examined the scene."

Slowly, his stuttering anxiety segued into new-found confidence. His stumbling words describing how Chris's body had been found portrayed a sad, horrific scene. It was all there, like a knife to the heart: the mask, the tank attached by tubes, even the state of the body, all laid bare to those who could listen. The officer concluded that there had been no suspicious circumstances and no third party had been involved. The case was closed and the police would pursue no further inquiries.

Then Chris's widow made the short walk to the stand. She was dressed informally, like the rest of her family. T-shirt and jeans seemed an odd choice, but perhaps reflected her state of mind. Her head remained bowed throughout her ordeal. She sat rather than struggling to stand. My mind spiralled into an abyss of fear, to a new level of anguish, as her torrent of antipathy surged about me and filled the room. I was certain that the percussive beating of my heart could be heard for miles. How much more difficult must it have been for her! I wished I could offer the sincere condolences I felt.

The judge confirmed some personal details and then moved on to the autopsy. At first he struggled with the technicalities of her husband's fetish, the words 'breath' and 'play' dragging across his tongue. She confirmed that while she hadn't known about the fetish, she'd been aware of a tank of nitrous oxide.

"I thought it was something he was using on his car," she muttered.

At last it was my turn to answer the judge's questions. A noose swung above my head. My legs would barely take my weight. Chairs scattered as I stumbled the short distance to the stand. I felt the eyes of everyone present piercing my body, watching my every move. My hands grasped the wooden barrier, my knuckles drained of blood. Nervous glue sealed my lips. I struggled to swear my oath. I rocked back into the chair and focussed on the judge, not wanting to meet the family's eyes.

The judge began by confirming that I was a professional Dominatrix and I'd known Chris for ten years. His eyes were scanning my statement, only occasionally looking up at me over his spectacles. Then he read out the first part of what I'd said during the police interview.

"Is it the case, as you told the police, that Chris had seen many girls for sexual services over the years?"

I said that Chris had told me so. The family gasped. The robed lady had asked me to be discreet, but nobody had asked the judge! He then moved on to the nitrous oxide.

"Yes," I confirmed, "Chris provided the gas for use in our sessions."

"Did he use it at other times, to your knowledge?"

"I believe he used it with other women."

Then the judge asked me to verify when Chris had started using the gas. I told him.

"Was he aware of its danger?"

"Chris was a man who always paid attention to detail," I replied. "He was fully aware of the danger."

I couldn't imagine how those words would affect Chris's family, but I was obliged to tell the truth. Thank goodness I hadn't been asked to describe details. I suspected that the danger of nitrous oxide use had been its greatest attraction for Chris, a rush of adrenalin that had ultimately cost him his life. However, I was allowed to keep that suspicion to myself.

"Were you aware," asked the judge, "that Chris used the gas when alone and at home?"

"No, I wasn't."

The judge shuffled his notes. I flushed with unwarranted guilt and moved to correct myself.

"Well, as I told the police, Chris said that on one occasion he'd taken a few breaths just to test a new bottle."

The judge was satisfied.

"I have no more questions for the witness," he said. "Do any members of the deceased's family wish to ask her anything?"

This was the moment I'd most been dreading. To my intense relief all the trio opposite me faced the floor and mumbled, "No". Never have two letters brought quite so much relief. I began to consider my exit. My blood started to flow again, pumping warmth to my limbs, rose tinging my pallid skin. Then five short words sliced through the silence, twisting my stomach. My ordeal still wasn't over.

"Why do you do it?"

The words were spat from the mouth of Chris's grieving father. I allowed my eyes to lock his. His face was full of anger and aggression. It all became too much for me to bear. I felt great sorrow for Chris's family, but he'd also been my friend and I hadn't been allowed to grieve for him publicly. I'd broken no law; my only crime was to have been a passenger on his journey. I understood that to many I represented the very thing that had robbed Chris of his life, but I wasn't responsible for his death. The fatigue of sleepless nights pulled me down toward the depths of my anger.

"I don't do it!" I was confused. What *had* the question meant? "I've never used nitrous oxide!"

"But I thought Chris took it when he was with you!"

The old man glanced at the judge, confusion lining his forehead. I looked at the judge, too. I didn't know what to answer. Anger was bursting from the old man's face but he chose to suppress whatever he'd been about to say. I could tell he'd promised not to have an outburst, though for a moment he hadn't been able to help himself. I understood. I'd expected anger, though not the rambling way it had been expressed.

However, this was becoming a hair-splitting exercise. It was true that Chris had taken the gas in my presence, but I'd only been there to ensure his safety. The judge ended the spiral of confusion by asking further questions that enabled me to clarify the matter. Then, after a brief pause, Chris's wife decided to speak.

"I have a question," she said.

"Oh, God," I thought. "Why?"

For me, this was the worst possible development. I wanted to be as discreet as the law would allow, protecting the family as far as possible, but now I faced a question from the widow while bound under oath to be truthful. A verbal tap-dance followed, sentences stumbling as they stepped on toes. First she asked a question that had already been answered. She struggled to arrange her words and was visibly upset. Finally, she asked:

"Why did Chris decide to use a tank rather than keeping to the smaller, safer, canisters?"

My words jumbled together as I battled to arrange them into sensible order. I knew why Chris had stopped using the canisters; he'd found them awkward and fiddly to use. But my mouth was no longer connected to my thoughts and I quickly became incoherent.

"Chris was obsessed and intrigued by the fixtures and fittings of the bottle, their valves and the different ways of taking the gas," I managed at last.

My answer had been delivered. For the moment I was saved. The widow and the rest of the family seemed satisfied; my explanation had reflected the man they'd known. But then the glove pounded my chin again, a right hook that reduced my mind to tatters. Chris's widow had finally come out punching and my back was on the ropes.

"What was Chris doing when he took the gas with you? Watching TV or something?"

The questions shocked me. "I'm a Dominatrix," I thought. "What do you suppose he was doing, or I was doing to him? Is it possible you have *no* idea?"

An image flashed through my mind of Chris tied down and vulnerable as I probed him with vibrators and passed an electric current through his manhood. This had been described graphically in my statement to the police, and the judge now perused it. I was under oath to tell the truth, the whole truth and nothing but the truth, even if it involved sex toys and CBT. And the question had come from Chris's widow!

She'd asked it out of naïveté, I realised, and I didn't want to spoil her innocence. This inquest was a bad enough experience for me, but I couldn't begin to imagine how she was feeling. She must have been going through Hell. All the family must. My eyes begged the judge for a merciful escape. I wanted to avoid answering because I knew what effect the truth would have. But the judge still had his head down. He was going through my statement at the speed of light, but that wasn't fast enough to help me. Then unplanned words snapped from my lips:

"Chris just liked the way it made him feel. He'd become giddy and it would make him laugh."

Now the judge got in on the act. At last he'd read the report properly.

"It's a high, isn't it?"

"Yes," I said, "though it only lasts for a few moments."

The judge now moved things along, suggesting it was time for the questioning to end. I believe if he'd read my interview report carefully to begin with, he wouldn't have offered the questioning time! I leaned back in my chair, satisfied I'd answered the most difficult of questions truthfully but without causing harm. Surely my ordeal was over at last. I looked out from the stand, longing for the comfort of home. But as I moved from the ropes and away to my corner, a glove poked again at my chin. After taking a breath, the widow said:

"I just have one more question."

"Bloody hell!" I thought.

"Did you ever come to my house?"

Until then she'd avoided eye contact, but her head was raised now, her sad eyes staring directly at me. I knew she feared my answer, but it was something she needed to ask. She must have had a hundred questions in her mind, but the one she'd voiced probably meant most to her. I expect the delay before I replied must have seemed like an age to her, and I could see she was holding her breath, but she had no reason to worry. I'd never been to Chris's house. I don't go to clients' homes; John was a very special exception, and he lived alone. I looked back at her, maintaining eye contact so she'd know my answer was genuine, and simply said:

"No."

She held my gaze for a moment and I knew she believed me. She turned away, nodded and finally took a breath. This was a massive relief to her.

"Well," I thought, "perhaps my presence here today has done some good."

And that, at last, was the end. My year-long ordeal had finally come to a close.

"I shall now give my verdict on this inquest," said the judge. "The witness is welcome to stay for this; or to leave if she so wishes."

I so wished. In any case, I thought the judge was politely asking me to go. I left the stand and made for the exit, avoiding the family as the robed lady had promised.

*

Chris will always be an important part of me. The moments we shared and the connection between us will remain in my heart. I could have done nothing to prevent his death; I'd played no part in it. He was obsessed by a fetish that demanded great care. He'd have taken nitrous oxide regardless of his sessions with me and nothing would have stopped him. I'd been able to keep him safe, regulating the use of the gas and keeping him from harm. I'd never dreamt he'd use the mask when alone; but he had, and now he was gone. Nevertheless I've asked the same questions many times over: What if I hadn't done the nitro with him? Was I partly to blame? If it hadn't been for the nitro play in my Chamber, would he have been on his bed that day trying out the new mask? In truth I'll never know.

My heart still goes out to his family, especially his widow, who'd clearly loved him deeply. She'd lost a husband and a friend; even worse, her past had been turned into an illusion.

Chris had been a charismatic gentleman with many attractive traits. It's true he'd had secrets, but he'd still been the man his family knew. They could and should cling to their good memories of him. I hope they will.

Chapter 12

A client from Birmingham with whom I'd become good friends asked me at the end of a session whether I wanted to go to see Peter Kay perform in Manchester the following evening. He had two tickets, but he'd split with his girlfriend so one ticket was going begging. Since he was a perfect gentleman I accepted and had a great evening. It was the first of many shows and concerts. Then he offered me the travel opportunity of a lifetime with the panache of an advertising agency:

"A week in New York, staying in the Ritz!" he promised. "You'll travel business class with all expenses paid! This is a VIP opportunity, Mistress! Among other delights you'll get to see the band *The Script* – and have a chance to hang out with the stars!"

What could I do? What would any fun-loving music lover with a travel bug do? I stayed at home to be with my dog. The bond between Charlie and me had become so strong I didn't think I could leave him for a week. He cried whenever he was separated from me, even for a few hours, not a doggy cry but a howl from the heart. He wouldn't touch food or water. I couldn't guarantee that this would change after a day, and if it didn't then he'd be dead within the week. Moreover, any sitter looking after him was driven mad within hours by his inability to do anything but stress out, usually followed by diarrhoea and vomiting. Most people don't understand this. They think I'm silly. "We know a lovely lady who'd take good care of him," they say. The truth is that I suffer just as much separation anxiety as Charlie does. The allure of New York wasn't enough.

That client and I went our separate ways when he acquired a girlfriend who didn't approve of 'Lucina'. I've lost several male friends because of women who feel threatened when they've no reason to be. It makes me sad.

Dog owners are a bit like newly-blessed parents; we become introverted, avoiding invitations in favour of taking care of our babies. To socialise means either answering awkward questions about why you can't be away for too long, or finding friends who don't mind your dog coming with you. While I grew accustomed to this way of life, I started to become bored; not with my life, not with those I love, and certainly not with Charlie, but with the lack of something new to challenge my need for adventure.

*

I've lived adventures throughout my adult life, always finding the next 'new thing' just as the last 'old thing' had outlived its use or lost its lustre. I needed something to push my buttons, something that would thrill and amuse me and not be a part of my usual routine. So I did what any self-respecting Dominatrix would do: I decided to learn how to fly. I don't mean that I threw myself from a window flapping my arms madly, though there have been days when I've been tempted. I mean I trained to be a pilot.

Once again the idea came from my friend Peter; and no, his surname isn't Pan. As you'll have gathered from earlier chapters, Peter has a habit of changing my life merely through the power of suggestion. For some time now, he and his wife have been my next door neighbours. Peter had been in the RAF as a young man and had flown jets. In his later life he'd flown microlights in Thailand. England was a little cold for open microlights so he considered flying the 'fixed wing' variety. We lived close to Barton Airfield in Trafford. They offered an hour in the air to give you a taster of what it would be like to fly yourself.

"Take a lesson and see whether you like it," said Peter. "I'll walk Charlie while you're gone."

"Most people wouldn't believe a professional Dominatrix could be intelligent enough to earn a pilot's licence."

"Maybe they wouldn't. That's the problem with stereotypes. There are blonde women who become top brain surgeons."

"I can hold my own intellectually," I said, "but I'm not brilliant enough to be a brain surgeon."

"You're not blonde, either."

As it turned out I took to flying like the proverbial duck to water, and since my first experience I've never looked back. Being up there among the clouds is both peaceful and exhilarating. I thought, "This is a place I could escape to on a regular basis". However, in no way was I prepared for everything involved in learning to fly. I imagined that training to be a pilot was an entirely practical matter, but the reality was very different. I had to study a myriad of subjects and become proficient in several disciplines.

Five examinations have to be passed before you can earn a pilot's licence. They progress from the very easy to the very difficult and the topics range from air law to knowing all parts of the engine. There's a general skills test (like a driving test but in the air), and then a general knowledge ground exam in which the instructor questions you for over an hour on everything you've learned. The questions are chosen at random so you have to be well prepared. In addition there's the radio licence, which involves a separate course and exam. We were only a small airfield, but I had to learn about the methods of other, larger, airports too, in case I had to land there one day or pass through or near their airspace. Barton is smack inside Manchester Airport airspace, so it's crucial for pilots to be able to identify where that space starts and ends by examining the lines on the aviation map and knowing the land. There are no signs on clouds saying 'No entry' or 'Diversion'.

The initial lessons were about controlling the aircraft. The instructor took off and landed, but out over safe hillsides I took over and performed the necessary manoeuvres. For me, the greatest fun came from handling stalls and emergency moves, which are required if the aircraft is put into difficulties by a gust of wind or stalled by the pilot. The instructor stalled the plane and I had to correct it. Of course a plane rapidly loses altitude as it stalls, which is exciting when you're only two thousand feet above the ground – though not as exciting as some of the other manoeuvres. My favourite was when the plane was put into a nose dive, facing down, plummeting towards the mountains, and the instructor said, "OK, correct". I loved those movements; so much so that I left the drop a little too long on one occasion and nearly gave the poor instructor a heart attack. I knew what I was doing was risky. I was challenging myself, as people do when they climb dangerous mountains or swim with sharks. But I should have thought more about the instructor.

"Lucina, you need to show a greater will to live," he said.

I worked my way through the flying schedule and the exams at the same time. Three out of the five exams are the same for all pilots, including helicopter and commercial pilots. I managed them all until it came to navigation. It took me a long time to get my head around aviation maps, but in the end I did it. The exam requires you to pinpoint coordinates and identify what's there. This can take ages as you trace your fingers across the huge map, and you don't have time in the exam, so I practised finding places over and over again until I could do it really quickly. You also had to plan your flying route using 'triangles of velocity'. I've done a thousand now. To become a pilot it's necessary to be able to calculate the direction of your flight and your fuel consumption according to wind direction and speed. I was very relieved once that exam was under my belt!

After all the manoeuvres had been learned it was time for me to learn to take off and land. Take-off is easy. I had my radio licence by then so I could tell the tower what I was doing. The aeroplane takes off at eighty miles an hour. This involves engine at full throttle, but the position of the nose determines the speed you reach: higher you go slower, lower you go faster. The take-off and landing practice follows a left hand circuit, so at one thousand feet altitude you turn left, then left again after a few hundred yards so you're 'downwind', all the time keeping in touch with the tower; then on to left base, eventually turning on to final. By this point your position is weather-dependent, but the aim is always to land at sixty or seventy miles per hour, avoiding all telegraph wires and talking to the tower at the same time.

To land, you only put the nose up for a few moments before the wheels hit the ground. If you leave it too long the nose could hit the grass; not long enough and you'll simply take off again, or if you weren't close enough to the ground you could stall two feet in the air, which would take out the undercarriage. I spent weeks and weeks going around this circuit, over and over again, until I was dreaming about what I was saying to the tower: 'taking off', 'downwind', 'on final to touch and go'. Sometimes I had a good session and felt I was getting the hang of it, but then the next session would be awful, as though I was just starting. It was disheartening at times but I plodded on. The problem is that no two landings are ever the same. It depends on the weather and who else is in the circuit. You have to be on the ball all the time. It was hard, but I was still flying, still in the air.

*

The time was approaching for my first solo flight. The prospect was exciting and nerve-racking. It had to happen, and I knew it could be any time; and one day, although the instructor said nothing, I knew the time had arrived. It was light and clear and there was no wind, perfect for a first solo. I took off doing all my usual checks and completed one circuit perfectly. On the way in on final, I was about to notify the tower I was 'on final to touch and go'.

"Tell them you're going to land," said the instructor.

"This is it!" I thought.

We pulled up alongside the tower and he notified them that his student was going to do her first final (solo circuit). My adrenalin level rose. He gave me a little pep talk about what to expect, such as saying the plane would be lighter without him on board, and then he got out.

Off I went round to take-off point. My legs would have been jelly if I'd been standing up. I lined up for take-off and announced to the tower I was ready. I looked at the empty seat beside me. I'd always had the security of a teacher there to correct any mistake. Now I was on my own. The tower confirmed I was clear for take-off.

I said, "Taking off". Throttle in full power. Off I went. As the plane hit full speed I raised the nose a little and I was off the ground. No going back now. I was flying on my own. The only way down was to land.

Completing the circuit, I approached final. I've never been as nervous in my life as I was then, looking at those numbers on the runway as I came in. All the mistakes I'd made during training, all the instructor's corrections, were going around in my head. My heart was trying to jump out of my chest. Yet I needed to keep a steady hand and eye.

"Don't land on the numbers," said a voice.

It was my own mind speaking. I flew just past the numbers at sixty miles per hour, raised the nose slightly as the plane neared the ground so the front wheel landed on the grass, and then the two back wheels. It was a little bumpy on that uneven surface, but the feeling of those wheels on the ground is one of the best I've had. That feeling never grows old.

*

I spent the next couple of sessions in the circuit on my own, learning to cope with windier weather and other aircraft. Pilots are like drivers; some think they know everything but they know very little. One day the weather was beautiful when I arrived.

"OK, Lucina," said the instructor. "Let's go out of the circuit. You've been in it enough lately."

This time he was with me but I did all the flying, including take-off and landing. We flew on what was called 'the triangle': a roughly thirty minute flight that took me up to Bolton over the M6, left towards Wigan, then down the 'low level corridor', a corridor through Manchester airspace where you're limited to a certain width and height. It was challenging, and again only known by the map, no signs.

Back at the airfield I was told to pull over and my instructor got out. "OK," he said, "off you go now and do it again, on your own."

"Really?"

"Yeah. Do a touch and go and repeat it if you want."

Exciting! I hadn't been out of the circuit on my own before. After a confident take-off and reaching one thousand feet I turned towards the hills of Bolton and told the tower I was leaving the circuit.

"I can hardly believe this," I thought as I flew over the hills. "Here I am, flying an aeroplane on my own!"

It seemed surreal, as though I might wake up any moment. It was amazing, just looking at the beautiful countryside and glistening lakes. It was peaceful and calming beyond belief. It still hadn't really sunk in that I was flying on my own, outside the familiar circuit.

"It had better sink in soon," I decided, "because I have to land this thing shortly."

I completed the triangle and headed back towards Barton airfield, but the excitement had made me a little disorientated. How far away was I? Going by my calculations I knew I must be close. Barton is a large field in the middle of dozens of other fields so it's hard to spot. I was beginning to panic a little when I saw the sunlight catching the little white dots that were planes in a line. Now I knew where I was. As I approached at two thousand feet, a large commercial plane heading into Manchester airport passed above me at five thousand feet; below me was the ground. Amazing feelings! I did a touch and go and then did the whole thing again.

*

After I'd shown up a few times to be told, "Hi Lucina, just take a plane, it's all fueled up", I was informed it was time to do my first solo landing away. I had to do two of those successfully to gain my licence.

The first was on a tiny airstrip called Ince, just past Wigan. It wasn't really an airstrip but a small field in the middle of hundreds of fields. They didn't have a radio, just a tannoy in a small shack, which was never answered. There was no circuit as such, so I had to make up my own. You had to be careful not to land too long as there wasn't enough room to stop so you'd end up in the bushes. However, it was difficult to land short enough as the hedge on approach was ten feet high. When I eventually found the airfield I think my wheels skimmed the top of that hedge as I went over, but I landed her beautifully. What an amazing feeling!

The second landing away was at Blackpool, which technically should have been much easier. Blackpool is easy to see: you just head towards the coast. You can't miss the sea from the air and you look out for the Tower. Before the Tower is the airport, which has a large tarmac runway. The tower at Blackpool airport is a lot more official than the Barton one. The tower at Barton only has control over you when you're on the ground, but Blackpool has control of you in the air, too. I set off confidently; I'd landed in the most difficult of places, Ince, so this would be easy.

On the way to Blackpool, however, the cloud came low so I had to drop my altitude. Everything was hazy. It was easy to become disorientated. I radioed to Barton to let them know I was changing frequency to Blackpool. Then I changed to Blackpool and notified them I was in their airspace. You have to tell them you are a student, so I did. Then the airport tower contacted me and gave me a load of coordinates to follow.

Although all the students fly to Blackpool airport, their air controllers aren't kind. They have no patience with students, and it shows. I asked the man in the tower to repeat his instruction more slowly and I confirmed I was a student. Again his instructions were rapid but this time I could just make them out. I repeated what I thought he wanted me to do and he seemed happy. However, I was now very flustered. A large airstrip should be easy to find, but it isn't easy at all when you're agitated. It turned out to be less difficult for me to find Warton. I announced I was downwind and a panicked voice cried:

"Go north immediately! You're attempting to land at Warton!"

"OMG," I thought, "they'll scramble jets to escort me away!"

Warton is a military base about three miles from Blackpool. Personally, I think it's easy to confuse it with Blackpool airport, especially when you're in a fluster. Military bases do not take kindly to unknown aircraft. If I hadn't diverted they *would* have scrambled two jets. The thought of two military jets flying alongside my little plane, both pointing at me to get out of the way, was hilarious... well, it was afterwards!

Eventually I did find Blackpool and did the worst landing ever, bumping along the runway; I wasn't accustomed to such fast tarmac. Ever since that day I've avoided Blackpool.

*

The training and the five examinations were hard work but the investment of time and effort was well worthwhile. Less than a year after my initial exploratory flying lesson I received my pilot's licence. However, I won't be taking a job with a commercial airline any time soon. My licence is for flying small light aircraft, not A380-800 jumbo jets. (Now there's an idea: a mile high club for BDSM! I wonder if Richard Branson sees it as a possible diversification for Virgin Airlines?)

Since achieving my licence I've had many glorious flights and created wonderful memories, including flying over my home town of Barrow and the hills and countryside I once cycled around and still love so much. There have been nail-biting moments such as having to land in a thunderstorm, but what never palls is simply being up there, away from the world, flying alongside big clouds and playing with the smaller ones. It always makes me feel privileged.

My constant companionship with Charlie and my occasional flying days are my two main methods of escape from day to day life and the demands of running a business. Flying an aeroplane and owning a Yorkshire terrier have one thing in common: you have to be in control of both the plane and the dog, and both of them can be rebellious. Landing the plane in the thunderstorm, and dealing with Charlie when he becomes a 'Yorkshire terror', are challenges; but how satisfying it is to meet those challenges without causing hurt or harm!

Yorkshire terriers were first bred in the mid-19th century as small dogs capable of catching vermin under the machines in the West Yorkshire factories and killing rats on board ship. Charlie is true to his breed: give him a toy that squeaks and he'll seize it between his little terrier jaws and murder it. I have to warn slaves in my Chamber: *whatever you do, don't squeak*, because Charlie is waiting in the lounge beside the dungeon. Unlike the plane, which sits at Barton airfield waiting patiently for me, Charlie demands my company full-time. He spends all five of my working days each week in my Chamber, taking walks with me or another Mistress in between clients.

What a difference he's made to my life. And what a difference flying has made, too!

Chapter 13

It's a fallacy to suppose that all subservients are men. Although most of the clients who visit my Chamber are male, this might say more about the disparate ways in which men and women deal with their sexuality than about gender difference in attitudes to submission. My experience suggests that men and women are equally likely to want domination, but men are far more likely to seek a professional service. Many of the men who seriously aspire to explore the length and depth of their subservience will at some point pay for domination. In contrast, women generally find it easier to establish opportunities for 'session time' without having to pay.

As if to prove the point, for the past few months I've been training a lifestyle slave who happens to be a woman. She's to be called Emma. Until recently, Emma had little knowledge of the BDSM scene.

"I only knew about it through the occasional dalliance with pornography," she said, "and through having fun with bondage games in the privacy of my bedroom."

The idea that an adult would willingly give themselves to the service of another had been alien to Emma's perception of the world. She'd found it impossible to believe. Then one day, sharing stories with her boyfriend, she was surprised to learn that he regularly visited a professional Dominatrix. Finding she was intrigued by this news, he suggested that the next time he visited his Mistress she should accompany him as a fellow-subservient.

They spent some time making plans. It's quite common for those of a submissive disposition to plan an early session down to the finest detail. The act of planning brings a strong sense of anticipation, which adds to the excitement; the drawback is that it can kill spontaneity. At length they determined to visit my Chamber and booked their session for the following Friday afternoon.

Even to this day, my slave Emma recounts past events and impressions with some amusement.

"Until I met you, Princess Lucina, I'd always imagined that BDSM activities had to be confined to the hours of darkness. The idea that I'd be attending a dungeon while the vampires were asleep seemed strange."

No doubt she felt more than a little apprehensive when she first dipped her toe into the sinuous tides of BDSM. Her innocence, her ignorance of the reality, had allowed her imagination to fill her mind with mysteries cloaked in shadow. Being uncertain about what would happen must have added to her excitement and seasoned it with fear.

*

It's easy to recall my first meeting with her, a fresh and somewhat naïve submissive lost in awe of her surroundings, not knowing what to expect. Of course I was eager to put my new slave through her paces while ensuring that the introduction would be a pleasurable first step on her journey.

"I found my induction more extreme than anything I'd imagined," she told me later, "but I enjoyed every moment of it."

I ensure that every new submissive feels at ease in my presence as soon as she or he arrives. This establishes a foundation of trust on which we can subsequently build. It ensured Emma's enjoyment, as it does all inexperienced slaves.

A professional Dominatrix understands that slaves just beginning their BDSM odyssey will be nervous. To become an integral part of a slave's adventure we have to be warm and understanding, not cold and heartless; so I don't set out to frighten anyone, new to the scene or otherwise. I'm dominant, and where possible I'll act upon instinct, but any journey proceeds step by step and it must begin from a position of comfort. When an artist stares at a blank canvas she has no way of knowing whether her next painting will be her finest, but to give it the best chance, the canvas has to rest securely on her easel, and her palette and brushes must be comfortably within reach. Domination is analogous to painting; every new submissive the Dominatrix meets provides an opportunity for perfect synergy, rewarding for both parties; but they have to start the right way.

Emma found her first encounter intoxicating. From the outset she sought to please me.

"It wasn't because I was frightened or anything, Princess Lucina, I just wanted to – well, *belong* to you."

Of course, any slave entering my dungeon becomes my property and is told so, and it's made clear that his or her only purpose is to serve me. But Emma submitted to me naturally. We were very well matched. I wasn't surprised when the days following our first session brought a shower of SMS text messages from my new-found friend. She'd bitten from the apple and now she wanted to taste more – not just the rest of that single fruit, but the entire bowl-full! She wanted to know more about BDSM and all it could offer her.

"I want to meet you again, please, Princess Lucina. Without my boyfriend this time."

I agreed. On the day scheduled for the session she arrived early, obviously excited. I knew she'd been apprehensive about a second meeting. When you create something perfect, you're tempted to preserve it with reverence rather than risk spoiling the memory. What had grabbed her attention during the first meeting? The intensity of the session, the atmosphere of the Chamber, the clothes I'd worn? By arriving early for our second meeting she caught me in jeans and blouse. All the feelings she'd experienced during our first session came flooding back, and in that moment she became certain of her needs.

Inevitably, a third session soon followed, and with it she crossed the Rubicon toward her destiny. From that day she's never looked back and she continues to develop as my slave. She's now been my property for six months and she reports almost daily in order to attend to her duties. She's expected to dress as I see fit and she's required to keep my Chamber spotless. She wears a collar with an inscription indicating that I own her. I didn't ask her to do that, but few gestures could highlight the veracity of her submission more clearly. She gives herself to me through choice, acting on her desires and fulfilling her needs. It's the ideal symbiotic relationship between Mistress and slave, nothing false or scripted, just two consenting adults sharing a journey without knowing quite where it will lead.

"I feel guilty when I displease you, Mistress," she's told me more than once. "What controls me isn't the fear that you'll be angry with me as the fear that I'll disappoint you."

Punishment is a cornerstone of slave training, but – as I said earlier when I described my slave Tony – few if any submissives truly enjoy it, contrary to popular belief. Punishment simply enables them to expunge guilt while reminding them of their duty. Perhaps it worked in a similar way for the flagellants of the Middle Ages. Some submissives are excited by the feeling of helplessness before an impending punishment, as happens in many forms of role-play, but that's not the same as enjoying the act itself. For many, it's the hope of praise and the fear of displeasure that generates their need to obey. It can induce a level of devotion seldom seen in human encounters, though it might be comparable to Stockholm Syndrome, in which hostages or kidnap victims develop an emotional rapport with their captors and even a love for them.

Each domination session provides motivation for the next, and the drama slowly builds to a zenith of self-knowledge and fulfilment. This adventure is driven by a need that crawls beneath every sinew and fills the heart with craving. There's no journey's end for either submissive or Dominatrix. For each mile taken there's always be another mile to travel, but once you're on the journey there's no going back. For Emma, the universe is a simple place: she lives by duty, my satisfaction her only purpose. This might seem alien, even perverse, to someone outside the BDSM world, but anyone who's active in the scene would say they consider themselves blessed. Theirs is a world of good fortune, built on trust and gilded with commitment to self-knowledge. They didn't choose to be submissive; it's a mental and emotional state, not a voluntary condition. Submissiveness can't be cured because it isn't an illness.

*

As I've mentioned, most of my family ties have been loose since my mother passed away, but there's one special exception: my eldest niece, Samantha. A bond was established between us when she was a baby and I took time off school, aged thirteen, to look after her. She's now married, lives a hundred miles away from me, has a full time job and is very happy, but the bond remains strong and we're in regular contact. Despite the many ways in which our lives have changed, one thing has remained constant: Sam knows she can turn to me for anything at any time. Even if she was in the wrong I'd stand by her and do all I could to make it right. It's called 'unconditional love'.

When I first dipped my toe into the world of domination she was one of the first people I told, knowing she'd find it funny and not be judgmental. Everyone in her office now knows me as 'Sam's auntie the Dominatrix', and there's a standard threat for anyone who steps out of line: "I'm going to get Sam's auntie to come in and sort you out!"

While I was living in my Manchester apartment, Sam found herself between boyfriends and came to stay with me for six weeks. She'd done some modelling during the previous few years and had twice borrowed my room to use for filming. One photographer would set up the camera and have her cane him in front of it. I once went in, just for giggles, and we caned him together. This recording went on 'clips for sale' or something of the kind, and years later people were still contacting me asking if they could session with 'that busty blonde Mistress'. Sam has a very dominant personality, which comes across instantly. With a body like Sam Fox, a face like Katherine Jenkins and the personality of Tyson Fury, she'd have been a natural Dominatrix. We did a few sessions together; one guy who'd seen the clip, for example, wanted to play out a scene with us both and we had a great laugh. However, Sam didn't like touching strangers' private parts, which you have to do in order to attach various torture devices, so she decided BDSM wasn't for her in the long term. Indeed, it isn't everyone's cup of tea.

Once, lacking access to a cell, I tied a client to a chair in the lounge with a gimp mask tight around his head and sat him in front of the telly to wait until I'd finished my session elsewhere. Sam sat on the sofa, not blinking an eyelid, and they spent two hours in each other's company. To this day we share fond memories of that incident.

"Why do so many men clients want to dress as women?" she once asked me. "Are they gay?"

"A lot of them are bi-curious," I said, "though definitely not gay. But there seem to be several reasons. None of us are good at explaining our motives, especially men. In our culture, they like to believe they're driven by single, simple purposes. It's one of the illusions we can help them dispel when they come to us."

"Come on, Loz, that's no answer! What are the 'several reasons'?"

"Well, for one thing, dressing as the opposite sex can fulfil a man's need to feel degraded. Yes, I know, it panders to their sexism, but at an emotional level not a mental one. Some want to be made to work as maidservants; they want to be degraded, not to feel feminine. Others find the touch of women's underwear alluring; the feeling of silky or lacy lingerie, or stockings. Fetish, in other words. But the two motives aren't mutually exclusive."

Her face showed no understanding. That didn't surprise me; it had taken me a while to come to terms with cross-dressing games.

"And that's it? Just dressing as a woman is enough because it makes them feel debased or fuels a fetish?"

I shrugged.

"For some it seems to, yes. But in several cases, dressing as a woman changes a slave's whole demeanour. His *character* becomes female." I hesitated. "Well, perhaps he becomes a male-fantasy female rather than a real woman; you know, a bisexually promiscuous harlot –"

She sniggered.

"I've met one or two bisexually promiscuous harlots who're *real* women."

"Me too," I agreed. "But no two slaves follow exactly the same journey. One might want you to subject him to strap-on play, another might want to be punished for being a whore… A few of them shave their legs and wear wigs and become expert at using cosmetics. They become *genuinely* feminine and want to be given a woman's name. Some have to be forced to dress as women, but some *choose* to do it for one of the aforementioned reasons."

She looked thoughtful.

"Using a strap-on with a slave would worry me," she said. "I'd be afraid of injuring him. And wouldn't it be better for him to play with another man?"

"If they were gay," I said, "why would they visit a Dominatrix? As for causing injury, there's no need to worry. It's just like any other sort of BDSM: you start small and gently, with something the submissive can tolerate easily, and you build up gradually to the bigger and more intense until you're pushing the limits."

It's one of life's great misconceptions that a man who likes something up the bum must have gay tendencies. It isn't true. Many clients who enjoy anal penetration, especially the ones I've just introduced to it, have to be reassured that it doesn't mean they're into cock. The male's back passage is an erogenous zone and contains the equivalent of the G spot; and done properly, prostate massage is very pleasurable for him. Relatively few women experience the same pleasure with anal play. Of course, the responsive slave *might* enjoy cock and want to be fucked by a man, but most of them don't. However, none of that matters when they're with me. They can fantasise about being fucked by half the Trojan army, or they can hate the prospect of a cock anywhere near them. The trick is to enjoy, not to question.

I told Sam about one client who'd travelled so far along the cross-dressing path that he finally confessed his fetish to his long-suffering wife, created a new personality with a new name and became a regular visitor to transvestite conventions. For some submissives, once the genie is out of the bottle it can't be put back in. The slave has plunged into a world he can't bear to leave.

"This was Clara, *alias* David3," I said. "David3 was high up in the education profession. He booked two hours with me every holiday. He enjoyed light pain, but it wasn't long before I realised humiliation was really his thing. I'd dress him in women's panties and make him stand in front of the large windows of my Manchester apartment, facing some new flats where builders were working. That was living dangerously, but we both loved it."

"And that was it?" said Sam. "Just wearing panties in full view of the builders?"

"Oh, no, it progressed from there."

I told her how I'd started to feminise David3 more and more until feminisation eventually dominated his sessions. He'd even turn up wearing bra and panties under his plain t-shirt and trousers, and sometimes I ordered him to wear the lingerie in his lectures. He loved that. "Our secret," I would say. I threatened to take pictures of him dressed as a woman and post them around his workplace for his students to laugh at. He loved those threats. Needless to say, it was his idea to introduce threats into the role play. I only include threats if they're requested; I don't do them lightly.

In one session I decided to go for it fully. So, mostly for my own amusement, I dressed him as a Mistress: one of my old PVC dresses, long boots, long PVC gloves and a dark wig. I allowed him to sit on the throne and then crop and flog imaginary clients. The way he copied me, the way he used the words I'd used on him so many times, made me laugh. I believe that was when he started to become Clara.

"It was the best session I had with him," I told Sam, "but after that day I didn't hear from him again. Holidays came and went without a word. It seemed odd, but these things happen. Unfortunately, if a client just disappears, I'm in no position to chase him up; I can only hope all's well."

The effort I'd invested in finding out why Chris had disappeared was unique; Chris was a highly valued friend, not 'just' a client. It was the only time I've tried to chase up a vanished slave.

Many years later, one of the Mistresses who used my Stockport Chamber did an outcall where she dressed a client up as a woman and they went out clothes shopping together. He told her he used to session with me and it was thanks to me he'd developed his 'alter ego', Clara. He messaged me later:

"My last session with You had such an impact on me that it changed my life for ever. I realised that 'being a woman' was something I really wanted in my life. I got a full wardrobe for Clara. I even 'came out' to my wife. She was less than pleased but she's let me explore my feminine side provided she has nothing to do with it. I go to transvestite conventions and parties now and I've truly come to life."

David3 attributed the liberation and expression of his Clara personality to me. You can guess how much that gratified me. It's wonderful to know that simply by doing your job you've had a beneficial, emancipating effect on someone's life.

*

Cross-dressing has many different motives, levels and outcomes. It's something a Dominatrix learns almost to expect of a new submissive, though of course not all of them want it; and when they do, the exact nature of the fantasy or fantasies has to be explored and as far as possible enacted.

Like most Dominatrixes I have a supply of women's underwear and shoes of different sizes, so that clients ranging from small slim bank clerks to eighteen-stone bricklayers can cross-dress comfortably in the Chamber and live out their dreams with my help. There's something both amusing and endearing about the eighteen-stone bricklayer mincing around the dungeon in lacy lingerie and high heels as his (or her) imagination is explored. But when a new slave expresses a wish to be either cross-dressed or feminised, or an urge to be forced into cross-dressing, I never make assumptions. Is this someone who wants to be a debased maidservant, or a bisexual harlot, or a 'real' woman, or just a man who needs to be punished for cross-dressing? Or is he (or she) something else entirely? It can take more than one session to learn enough detail about that individual's fantasy to pursue it to the requisite depths, but it's worth the investment of time and effort.

One thing that's important to me, as to any good Dominatrix, is that every client should feel comfortable enough in session to be able to relax and explore all the corners of their minds in a safe, secure place without facing any judgment.

Chapter 14

Certain events in life leave so deep an impression that you relive each moment of them again and again, retaining dimensions beneath the surface image. You remember what you wore that day, the feeling of rain on your skin, what you'd eaten for breakfast. Sometimes you'd rather forget it all, but you can't. It was such an event that thrust me into the dazzling beams of public attention in 2012 and set my business back for months or perhaps years.

The day started well enough. It was Halloween, a Tuesday, a little after ten, and a heavy mist pressed on my windows. I'd just finished my second cup of coffee, the warm bitter liquid biting at my senses as the caffeine eased into my blood. I was catching up with my appointments diary after my day at the dog sanctuary. I scrolled through a mountain of messages ranging from clients requesting appointments to the usual time-wasting spam. After I'd finished I'd be able to relax because I had no bookings that day. Tuesdays are to me as Mondays are to most people; they can be hectic. So a slow start to a Tuesday calls for a little mental celebration.

More coffee drained between my lips, lethargy pulled at my body and I sank into serenity. It was one of those moments when the simplest of pleasures seems like perfection, and I wanted it to last. Charlie gazed up from the comfort of a snuggled doze, his sleepy eyes half closed. The day was set calm before us and the park summoned us for a walk. I threw on some clothes and soon we were wandering the wooded paths, Charlie chasing ahead through autumnal gold mixed with carmine and grey.

*

Such perfection is fragile. A single event can shatter it into chaos and disaster. My impromptu day off had provided an opportunity to enjoy a walk with Charlie and I didn't want it to end. I was half way around the park, drifting wherever my feet chose to take me. However, a frozen mist hung and the air was bitter cold, as if heralding what was to come. My phone buzzed, an incessant wail, determined to split the silence and destroy the calm.

From time to time a Mistress can be blessed with a client whose needs lead him to a practical form of servitude. His skills are employed in whatever way the Mistress finds useful and he becomes a friend. Gary was just such a friend with skills, specifically carpentry skills, so I'd put him to work in my Chamber. Now he was on the phone, whispering.

Gary was in his sixties but a lifetime of sports had kept him fit. He'd formerly 'belonged' to another Mistress, who had once brought him to my apartment in Manchester. He never forgot me. Devoted slave though he was, he'd felt for some time she'd been neglecting him; he was running around after her for little return. So he was tempted to have his needs met elsewhere. As it happened he lived in Stockport, and when I moved there he approached me to ask if I could use him. Of course I could! Gary helped me build up the dungeon and in return I satisfied his needs, which were simple: he liked to be locked away with chains as restraints and a mask and gag. In the early years in Stockport it was mainly Gary and me in the Chamber, and I'd been known to have a few drinks with him at home. He also sat with Charlie sometimes when I needed to go out. I'd grown to trust him so much he had a set of keys for the dungeon.

"I've been getting on with the job, Lucina," (he'd been working on a 'fucking machine' – *his* crazy idea) "but a client's just appeared."

A client? Had I forgotten an appointment? Was this not a free day after all? One aspect of my work that I take very seriously is organisation. To let a client down goes against all I stand for, and I'd only cancel a session, especially at the last minute, if I had no other option. Clients often have to arrange windows of time between work and family commitments so they can meet me, so it's essential to be reliable. To keep them waiting can stress them and spoil the session in advance. Moreover, a slave's psychological build-up to a session can begin weeks beforehand so he needs me to be there as arranged.

"What's his name, Gary? What does he look like?"

"He's an oldish chap, says he's called Bernard. Seems nice enough. Gleam in his eye. He was a bit surprised to find me here!"

So *Bernard* had been knocking on the door! Bernard was an old man but he still had a passion for BDSM, particularly a hard caning. It can take a lot of courage for a submissive to make his first approach to a Dominatrix, but although Bernard had left it until late in life he'd embraced his needs perfectly. I loved and respected this. I also respected the fact that he remained sexually active despite his age and didn't give in to aches and pains. However, life hadn't been treating him well. He'd been seeing me on a monthly basis for seven years when his wife found some of our e-mail exchanges. It's a risk of the job. She sent me a threatening message:

"If you see Bernard again I'll go to the police and tell them you've been assaulting an old and ill man."

I don't usually react on impulse; better to sit back and let things sink in. So I didn't reply immediately. Then rage got the better of me. How dared she threaten me? I wasn't going to be intimidated! She must have been angry, maybe devastated, on discovering her husband's secret sessions, but she should have taken it up with him, not me. Despite my fury, my reply was polite:

"Everything I did with Bernard was consensual and I can prove it. They were legal acts and I have nothing to hide, so the police won't be interested. I asked him many times if there were any health issues I needed to be aware of and he assured me there were none. If you want to take things further, be my guest. I'll be happy to have this dragged through the mud in public if you are."

I heard nothing more from her.

*

I didn't know it at the time, but that Tuesday morning call from Gary was the fall of the first domino, starting a cascade that would escalate to disaster. All I knew then was that my calm mood had been shattered by an urgent need to get to the Chamber to meet a forgotten appointment. Before that I'd need to go home, shower, wash my hair and dress appropriately. It's unlikely that my casual look, straight from the park with my dog, would please Bernard or indeed any client.

Ransacking my memory as I rushed to make myself ready, I finally recalled that Bernard had e-mailed me two weeks previously to enquire about an appointment. I'd offered him a date and time but hadn't heard anything back so I'd assumed there was no arrangement; he hadn't confirmed.

"He says he's happy to wait for you," said Gary.

"Give him a cup of tea, Gary, and warm the place up. He's elderly and it's a bitterly cold day."

Showered and dressed, I started the twenty-minute drive to my Chamber. Have you ever noticed that traffic jams are at their worst when you can least afford them? My twenty minute drive dwindled into a slow crawl as the M60 coagulated to a car park. Gary had switched from tradesman to smiling host, keeping Bernard happy with an endless supply of steaming hot tea, but that didn't excuse my late arrival. I made another call to Gary: more steaming tea for Bernard and a change of route for me. This would add another thirty minutes to my journey time, but at least I'd be moving.

More dominos were falling. It seemed that Fate had wanted me to be close to my destination before it struck. Lucina is supposed to be in charge of the Fates, not the other way round, but the hierarchy had changed.

I passed the final road junction. My Chamber was almost in sight. Then my phone rang again. Gary's number flashed on the digital display.

"It's OK, Gary, please tell Bernard I'm nearly there. I'll see you in a couple of minutes."

Triumph! I'd been tested and not found wanting. The challenge had been met. Or so I thought. Gary's next words disabused me of the illusion.

"Lucina, I'm so sorry, but the Chamber's on fire!"

*

The final domino had fallen. What had begun with a phone call in the park had ended with news of a catastrophe.

"How, Gary? What's happened?"

At first I thought he was joking. It wouldn't be unlike Gary to carry out a prank. I didn't mind that side of him; I gave back as good as I got. But then he started apologising and knew from his tone that it wasn't a joke.

"I'm sorry. I'm really sorry. I was starting the heater when something exploded and burst into flames. I couldn't put it out! It's spreading everywhere!"

Because there was a limit to the electric power I could use in the unit without everything tripping, I'd installed a big fan heater powered by a large tank of propane. One of my clients who owned a garage had recommended this. It had proved ideal; heating in the cellar under the mill was essential if you wanted to avoid hypothermia. But the downside had now become evident.

Gary's words cut like a knife. My heart sank into my leather boots and my blood turned to ice. I'd imagined an accident with a candle, not a full scale inferno. But soon I could see the truth for myself. As I said earlier in this book, my Chamber is part of a much bigger building, a former mill, which houses several businesses. Their alarms had sounded and all their employees had poured out into the yard and the car park. The entire building had been evacuated. Smoke billowed from my Chamber door at the front of the mill into a spiralling pillar that reached the clouds. Two fire engines were dousing flames hidden from my view while the building's evacuees watched.

As I turned on to the street I saw Bernard walking with the stoop of an old man towards the bus station. The disappointment on his face made me want to stop and say how sorry I was, but I was needed elsewhere. There was nothing I could do but keep driving.

Expecting the propane and oxygen tanks in my Chamber to explode, and not wanting the mill to land on my car, I parked as far away as I could and wandered toward the crowd. Looking back, my priorities seem ridiculous; my car would have been the least of my worries if the mill had gone up into the air! Heads turned towards me and each huddle of faces stopped chattering as I approached. I could feel the eyes of everyone present pressing on me, staring. Not having had time to grab jackets and coats when the alarms sounded, they were trying to keep warm. I saw some of them elbowing their friends and pointing to me: "That's her, there she is." There was a wave of silence. I'd never felt so vulnerable; the villain of the piece was on a walk of shame to the scene of her crime.

It's easy to allow paranoia to drive our imaginations. In truth, I don't know what people were thinking that day, but given my isolation and the ghastly circumstances it was easy to imagine the worst. I'm sure there'd been rumours about the dungeon, though I'd been very discreet. Until then. Judgment becomes easier when you're happy to base it on a stereotype.

Another Mistress who works in my Chamber greeted me, her smile bringing a measure of comfort. I needed it. She walked through the crowd with me, so she'd be able to confirm the way people were reacting. I was and always will be grateful to her. Despite the many disasters that have befallen me over the years I've rarely ever needed anyone beside me in support, but on this occasion it made a real difference. That Mistress refused to leave my side for the rest of the day. Under such circumstances you learn much about yourself but even more about those close to you.

We walked towards the front of the building where Gary was chatting with the head fireman. His face was grey and troubled. He was in his overalls, which he wore when he was working. At least there was something to be grateful for: if he'd been wearing the usual chains he'd have been out there still wearing them.

All around us people were taking photos. The fire had become the most exciting thing to have happened since the last most exciting thing. Gary was terrified that one of the photos would end up in the paper. In fact, he was convinced the press had appeared. Would his wife now discover where he'd been? Would he be blamed for the fire?

"How the hell am I going to explain this one?" he kept saying.

I was a little taken aback that his home life was his exclusive concern when he'd just burnt down my business. "If you're that worried about being caught you shouldn't play away," I wanted to tell him. I'm sure he'd have been happy to clear off once the firemen had questioned him about the layout of the Chamber because he was glad to introduce me as the 'owner'.

"This is the lady you need to talk to," he said.

Very nice of him. However, he was going nowhere. He'd exited the building so quickly he'd left his clothes, keys and phone inside. The fireman nodded a greeting.

"Yes, I rent the premises in the cellar where the fire started," I told him.

"Anything dangerous in there? I mean, anything likely to make the fire spread further?"

"Tanks of nitrous oxide. And propane. And one oxygen tank just in the first doorway as you go in."

He summoned his colleagues and soon they were rushing to and fro with equipment, but he was furious.

"Think I'm happy sending my men into a place with substances like that on the loose?"

I hadn't realised how serious the implications were until then. I'd put lives at risk.

"I know," I said, and nodded.

Realising I was sincerely sorry he mellowed a little.

"Where's the back door to the cellar," he asked, "and how do I get to it?"

I led him to the back entrance of the building, through the reception and down the steps into the back of the large cellar. I could see my door with the shutter down at the end of the large open space. Gary hadn't opened it when he'd arrived at the Chamber. I could hear the hiss of static from the fireman's radio, followed by cackling and laughter as his colleagues searched through the premises. I didn't think too much of it at first; my mind was on my business being reduced to ashes. But then I noticed the fireman's face; he was smiling at me. It was a welcome gesture because he still seemed cross about the oxygen tank. But I've seen that look, the smirk and twinkle in the eye, on many faces over the years, including more faces of authority than I care to recall.

"What are they saying on the radio?" I asked.

"They've just realised what the place is!"

The comment was accompanied by a broad smile and a chuckle.

"Well," I thought, "I've brought some entertainment to the local fire service. Probably an education, too!"

Every cloud has its silver lining, although the silver might not benefit those most in need of it. Amidst the chaos of the burning building, with firemen battling the flames, a mobile café arrived. I'd never seen it before and I've never seen it since. The owner was an enterprising fellow. Someone had obviously tipped him off, and he did good trade. People queued for a hot drink. Away from the fire the day was terribly cold and my sides ached from shivering as well as misery. My pleasure in the gold of autumn had been driven away by the chaos and the bitter air. After the rosy calm of morning had come a freezing hell of turmoil.

At last the fire was extinguished.

"Faulty valve on the propane heater," the head fireman told me. "There's been a lot of damage, I'm afraid. You can't be allowed in there until the fire inspector gives permission."

The crowds filed away to their buildings as though they were leaving some grand sporting event. One by one they wandered off, stomachs full of hot chocolate, heads full of stories and phones full of photos. They'd remember the day with pleasure. I wouldn't. Soon the only people left beside me were those who were lending me support. Peter had joined them. I was grateful.

*

There was a particular reason for the smirks and twinkles, and once again Gary was at the back of it. About a month earlier I'd been drinking coffee with him after a session and looking at a present from a client: an A1 size photo he'd printed from my web site and had framed.

"Lovely thought, but I don't know what I'll do with it," I said.

Gary had one of his mad brainwaves.

"Get a large portrait of you seated on your throne and hang it in the lobby for everyone to see when they arrive!"

I stared in disbelief, amazed at how little he understood my character.

"Do you think I'm the queen?" I demanded.

Now, standing across the street with Peter beside me, watching the firemen pack away their gear, I saw three of them staring, nodding in my direction and nudging each other. I smiled at them and received huge grins in return.

"Look at those firemen smiling at me!" I said.

Peter laughed.

"Yes, they actually are!"

I wondered whether they'd recognised me, and if so how, but there was too much going on for me to give the matter much thought. It was only a week later, when there was light again in what was left of the Chamber, that I understood. Gary had put the client's gift, the A1 photo of me, beside the front door for everyone to see when they came in. He and I had always exchanged banter, and this was just another of his jokes to wind me up. He knew I wouldn't like it. (I'd always got my own back, though!)

"Bloody hell, Gary," I said later, "no wonder they all recognised me!"

"I wasn't expecting it to get quite so busy, was I?"

*

Of course the fire could have had far worse consequences. It's easy at such times to sink into the depths of misery and lose your sense of proportion. However, I realised I'd better let the mill manager, Andy, know what had happened. He'd always been good to me, but this would push his patience to the limit. How well I remembered him saying, "Do what you like, Lucina, just don't burn the place down".

In response to his happy greeting on the phone I said, "I'm so sorry, Andy, but I've burnt your building down."

He reacted just as I'd reacted to Gary's phone call earlier.

"What?" he chuckled.

"I've burnt down the unit. The firemen are just leaving. I'm sorry."

"OK," he said. "I'll come over."

Charlie had spent a lot of the day in the car– there'd been no alternative – but Gary went and sat with him as much as he could. Fortunately, Charlie was happy in the car and quite often stayed there. At home alone he'd be stressed and upset; in the car he was fine. He'd see in which direction I was going and then he'd sit on the back shelf and watch. At that time, people hadn't developed the habit of breaking into cars to steal dogs. That's changed, unfortunately. I hardly ever leave Charlie in the car nowadays.

*

"Nobody's been hurt, Gary and Bernard both escaped without injury and the fire was confined to your Chamber," said a rosy-faced WPC, her eyes dancing. There again was that little smirk and twinkle. I looked at her and, never one to let a disaster get in the way of a pretty face, wondered if she wanted a job. "We'll be taking no interest in the fire: no suspicious circumstances, nobody injured," she continued.

I realised I was returning the smirk and twinkle. Well, at least I wouldn't be heading to the police station. But I couldn't make light of the situation, as the various uniformed officers with their knowing looks were doing. Take a stereotype, mix in a healthy dollop of cliché, shake in a profession paid to be stern, and smirks and giggles will result. As the sun sank to give way to All Hallows the smoke hung thick about me. The ashen air drifted silver, lit by a waxing moon; the cruellest trick without a treat.

There comes a point when one can take no more. My body was ravaged by the cold and my mind was exhausted. The day had seemed endless, one awful moment leading to the next, a procession of calamities. Almost five hours had passed since the fire had started and the adrenalin had begun to wear off. So had my sense of humour and my capacity to view this awful situation lightly. I hadn't eaten or drunk all day since my morning cup of coffee. The icy mist that hung in the air thickened as darkness crept in and it was growing ever colder.

The fire inspector appeared, introduced himself and showed me his ID. I only glanced at it; I didn't doubt who he was, a very tall man with a serious face, there to do his job. He wanted to ask me questions. We weren't yet allowed into the Chamber so we stood at the top of the steps, shivering. My fingers and toes had lost all sensation. I could think of nothing but the predicament I was in and I wanted it all to be over.

"I just want to go home and recover," I said. "Today has battered me. I need to sit down and take stock." Preferably with a glass of wine.

But as we know, human compassion never oils the officious wheels of bureaucracy. The inspector had to interview me and Gary. He opened a large folder and started the questioning, beginning with all my personal details. I hadn't yet realised how serious a job he had. I thought he was just one more in the long line of people who seemed to have spent the day questioning me. For hours I'd been giving my details to one person after another and I'd had enough. I answered like a robot, sighing from time to time. It was obvious I was exhausted.

"Were you here when the fire started?" he asked.

"No."

He glared at me and with a very sharp authoritative voice snapped, "Well, where were you then?"

That woke me up. I realised he meant business. Among all the people who'd questioned me that day, this was the one who needed to be taken most seriously.

"I was on my way to the Chamber when I got the call from Gary."

"What was Gary was doing when the fire started?"

At every question he darted an intense look at me, trying to detect a lie. But how could I tell him that Gary was making a 'fucking machine'?

"I'm not sure," I temporised. "Some carpentry work, I think. He does all my maintenance."

He finished his questions and then said, "I need to speak to Gary. On his own."

I got Gary out of my car where he'd been hiding and he was duly interviewed. It was just as well he hadn't been able to leave earlier because this was now a legal matter, so they'd have been knocking on his door. Of course he had to give his name and address, which worried him greatly. How was he going to explain a letter dropping on the mat, or even an official visitor? However, the inspector's questions mainly concerned where he'd been and what he'd been doing when the fire started. Apart from the small lie about the 'fucking machine' we both told the complete truth. There was no reason to do otherwise.

I'm not sure it has a bearing on the case, but the 'fucking machine' still hasn't been finished.

*

At last I was asked to accompany the inspector, Mark, to survey the damage. After the official questions were over, Mark's expression softened a little. I could tell he was nobody's fool and well experienced in his work. He'd know if someone was lying and he knew I wasn't.

"Are you ready to see what's left of your Chamber?" His look was almost sympathetic.

"Yes, I am."

The Mistress who'd walked through the crowd with me was still by my side as we walked down the steps down into the belly of the monster, the charred remains of my Chamber. With no windows to supply natural light we had to rely on a torch. The air was heavy with the stench of smoke and my feet waded through rubble and icy water. I was surprised and grateful to discover that the lobby was mostly intact: the sofa, the towel unit and even the pictures hanging from the wall were unharmed, though they all stank of smoke. I glanced right, left, and through the open door to the lounge. Again, it seemed mostly undamaged. Everything was in its place.

We stumbled forward, the gloom devouring everything not revealed by the torch beam. As I've said, the room ahead had been divided into two dungeons, both used for sessions. The fire had started at the far end, the flames roaring across the ceiling and engulfing everything in their path. The damage was frightening: scarred walls, melted cables and the incinerated remains of equipment. One of my biggest problems has always been to keep the Chamber warm; cellars are notoriously cold places. Today, despite the weather outside, heat radiated from the blackened walls.

"It's like a sauna. Quite ironic," I thought, and chuckled to myself.

The air was thick with soot. Cables hung from the ceiling. Flotsam bobbed in the icy depths flooding the Chamber. Broken lights hung on wires. Furnishings had been gutted by the conflagration. There was devastation at every turn. This had been the front line of the battle, where the firefighters had met the blaze. I spied the tanks of nitrous oxide, so close to having been engulfed. To their immense credit, the firemen had saved them. I learned later that nitro wasn't explosive, but the tank of oxygen was, and it was right next to them! I had an old medical anaesthesia machine that mixed nitro with oxygen. I'd stopped using it after Chris died, indeed I'd stopped the use of such substances altogether, but I hadn't disposed of the oxygen bottle.

We waded on through a soup of floating sex toys. The inspector caught a large pink dildo in his torch beam. It was surreal, watching this big flesh-coloured item float by, sailing past our feet like a long lost friend. I glanced back at the other Mistress as the small but strong ray of torchlight followed the dildo as it passed. I knew what she was thinking, too. Again I chuckled to myself.

"Your rubber's melted," a fireman had told me earlier, grinning.

He'd been right. Some objects had been blown from their places while others had melted. A line of dildos that had stood to attention now drooped over the edge of their shelf.

At last the misery came to an end; we ejected ourselves from the devastation, our clothes reeking of smoke.

"I'll have to return tomorrow, Ms White," said Mark. "You must be here. My chief will join us."

I hoped the chief fire investigator would have a sense of humour.

As I drove home I began to reflect: this *could* have been so much worse! Had the gas canisters exploded, or had Gary and Bernard not been so quick to evacuate the premises, who knows what might have happened. Things can be replaced but people can't. Luckily, Gary had some fire training. He said he'd felt faint after one breath of smoke. He knew from experience that if he'd taken another he'd have passed out, so he made a rapid exit. I wondered: would I have got out as quickly? Wouldn't I have underestimated the effects of flames and smoke? I couldn't have left without Charlie, and it's highly likely I'd have tried to grab a few possessions, too.

Right then, I didn't think the Chamber would be rebuilt. I believed it was all over, not because of the work that would be needed but because I didn't think the fire department would allow me to open again. Only months earlier they'd shut down a Chamber not far from me, saying if there was a fire and clients were restrained the risk would be too high. The woman who ran that Chamber hadn't even suffered a fire, and here I was with a Chamber burned to ruins.

"Your insurance will cover you, surely," said one of my friends.

Ignorance is bliss indeed.

"If only," I replied. "No insurance company will give me cover because I'm a Dominatrix. I mean, *no* insurance company. Believe me, I've searched!"

No doubt the coming days would bring new challenges, but at that moment I needed to rest. I was so glad to get home, a familiar comforting environment where I could try to put the day's events to rest for a few hours. I opened a bottle of wine and cuddled up to Charlie, who was enviably oblivious of what had happened, and glad to be back with me after spending so long in the car alone.

Chapter 15

Mark rang me at eleven the following morning.
"Can you meet my boss and me at the Chamber sometime today?"
"Yes, of course."
"What would be the best time?"
"Any time," I laughed. "I'm not exactly busy with work at the moment!"

We arranged to meet at two in the afternoon. I arrived a little early and went down to the Chamber. The ashen stench filled my nostrils as I toured the wrecked rooms again, and the cold hit me. The two-inch river was gone, probably evaporated by the previous day's hot walls. There was no sign it had ever been there. But even the narrow beam of my torch and the faint light from the door, which I'd left open, showed enough of the damage to devastate me. Even if I left the door open for a week, I thought, the stench wouldn't clear. Everything I'd built hung by a thread. I'd lost my Chamber and perhaps my entire business. Would I be allowed to rebuild? *Could* I rebuild? Despair seemed to ooze from the rooms, their darkness threatening to consume all who approached.

"Hello, Lucina!"

Mark appeared at the door and introduced his boss, a smaller, rather stocky man with a warm smile and the inevitable smirk and glint in the eye. Mark seemed quite relaxed, which put me more at ease. We decided to convene in the Chamber lobby, one of the few undamaged areas. I couldn't nestle into the cushions of the white leather sofa in my lounge because it was now black with smoke. Eventually it would be thrown away along with the rest of the furniture. The two back rooms had been wrecked by the fire raging across the ceiling, but even though the flames had stopped short of the lobby the smoke had had its effect. There was also the water damage, and the floor was filthy with the residues of water and smoke. However, the larger play-room didn't seem as badly affected as I'd feared. It was a relief to see an old friend.

The two officers went into business mode with no further preamble. After another good look around and a few silent nods of agreement they stood in the lobby area with me. Mark pulled a set of forms from his folder.

"You'll be served with a prohibition order."

"What does that mean?"

"It means you can no longer conduct business here until certain breaches of Health and Safety regulations had been corrected."

They handed me a form to sign, then explained the prohibition and how much trouble I'd be in if I didn't comply.

"You must *not* use these premises for any work at all." Mark looked serious again. "Though you can use the lobby area if you want because it leads directly to the exit, so it's safe."

"I don't think I'll be doing much domination in here," I laughed, looking around.

My eyes eventually met theirs. I seemed to be the only one who found the idea funny. I asked the question that was most haunting me:

"Can I open again after I've complied with all the regulations?"

"Yes," said the chief investigator. "Once we're happy with everything you can continue your business."

What wonderful news! I couldn't believe it! Suddenly I had something to work for again.

"But let's be clear," said Mark, "you can't open until the prohibition is lifted, and we're the only ones who can lift it."

"No problem," I thought. Since I'd no electricity, heat or light, my equipment was ruined and my work space smelled like the world's worst barbecue, it was hardly a shock to learn I wouldn't be conducting business any time soon. When times are bad we always compare them with better times. We never stop to think of worse alternatives. However, the chief investigator's words had induced a great wave of relief. The prohibition notice provided a light at the end of the tunnel. Far from being terminal it brought structure and hope, a way to move forward, an end in sight.

"Tell me what needs to be done and I'll do it."

"First," said the chief investigator, "there will be a formal interview at the fire station. It will be recorded and it might lead to a prosecution. It would be advisable to hire a solicitor." Seeing the look on my face he added, "It's a small room with a large tape recorder. A bit like something out of *The Bill*." And he gave me a friendly little smile.

The wave of relief ebbed. My worry deepened. You know you're in trouble when you're advised to hire a solicitor. I was reminded of the interview with the two policemen in the build-up to Chris's inquest, imagining having to swap my leather corset for a stripy suit and my Chamber for a tiny room with bars. I had to ask the question at the forefront of my mind, daft as it sounded.

"Do you think I'll go to prison?"

My face must have been a picture because the two officers obviously warmed to the maiden in distress. Mark's laugh was sympathetic.

"No, that won't happen. The situation isn't so bad. Nobody was injured or died. If they had, you wouldn't be here talking to us now. You'll probably be fined, but nothing worse."

Again I was assured that the reality wouldn't be as bad as I'd imagined. There was still a cloud, but this time I might be able to capture the silver lining. When it's a straight choice between prison time and a fine, you don't hesitate to reach for the cheque book. (The law has changed since then. Nowadays, a breach of Health and Safety regulations can lead to jail time as well as an unlimited fine.)

"How big a fine?" I asked.

"The court will decide that, but the maximum is £2500 per offence."

I could find myself struggling with debt, but at least I'd be at liberty. If for one moment I'd considered the cost of repairing and re-equipping my Chamber, the prospect of the additional expense of a hefty fine could have tipped me over the edge. But at the time I didn't, and now I had some inkling of what had to be done. The cloud of uncertainty was lifting.

In some ways it didn't seem fair. I'd apparently broken the law but I hadn't done so knowingly or intentionally. Andy the manager had been in the Chamber many times, as had the area manager, and fire alarms and exits and so on had never been mentioned. No one had so much as hinted I was sitting in a death trap during the four years I'd run the Chamber. Nevertheless I was still responsible for the fire, even though I hadn't been there and the shutters had been down. Andy shared none of the responsibility.

When a thief steals from a house he makes a premeditated decision to break and enter. I'd done nothing comparable. But that wasn't the point. I was being naïve and ignorant. In the UK there are around 3500 classes of criminal offence, ranging from the obvious to the bizarre. A solicitor's office is lined with books, each referencing thousands of lines of legislation. In some cases, the law is so complex that entire teams of legal experts have to work together to resolve the tangle. With that in mind, it seems surprising that *ignorance is no defence* is a cornerstone of British law.

*

A few days later I arrived at the fire station. I was very nervous so I was grateful when Mark greeted me with a smile and a hand-shake; incredibly welcoming.

"Have you been in a fire station before?" he asked.

"No, I haven't."

"Would you like a tour?"

He showed me every room in the station and in each one the firemen greeted me with huge smiles and the all-too-familiar smirks and eye-twinkles. But seeing that I was determined to stand my ground despite my nervousness, Mark was doing his best to help. He was warm and kind and I believe he'd developed a soft spot for me, perhaps even a little respect.

I'd decided that as I would plead guilty to all the offences there'd be little point in hiring a solicitor. Since a solicitor is hired to argue your defence, why spend money when you have no defence and there's no argument to be made? I already faced a crippling financial burden and I wasn't going to add to it. My view was: if you're telling the truth, why worry? The truth now will still be the truth in a year's time. I didn't intend to try wriggling out of the situation with fancy words; I was in the wrong so I would face the music. Of course, subsequent events have taught me that solicitors are charged with the supremely important task of protecting us from ourselves.

Mark opened a door into the interview room, which contained a desk, four chairs and a recorder. On the other side of the desk sat his boss, who again greeted me with his biggest smile and shook my hand.

He was fiddling with the huge tape recording system and muttering about it being temperamental. Mark offered me a seat on the near side of the desk and then he sat next to his boss. He pointed to the empty seat beside me.

"That's for your legal representative. I see you haven't brought one."

"No. I don't see the point."

His smile seemed to say I was a very brave lady but also a little stupid.

They both confirmed that they'd set the tape recording and then proceeded to ask questions. I suddenly felt vulnerable without a solicitor. My mouth dried. I just wanted this to be over.

When we answer questions in such an environment, our answers will be made available to any future court hearing. That seems reasonable when the questions being asked are relevant to the offences alleged against you. But what if the questions are more personal and seem to have no bearing on your case? Does their lack of relevance ensure that they go no further than the walls of the interview room? The answer is *no*: anything you put on tape is admissible in court and can be used to assassinate your character.

My clever tactic was to tell the truth, the whole truth and nothing but the truth. After all, I thought, the law is designed to protect the innocent and I was guilty of nothing worse than ignorance. I hadn't realised that criminal prosecutions are driven by statistics. Those who make themselves easy targets by telling the truth are absorbed into the positive figures, which can be rolled out to prove that crime is being kept off our streets. In contrast, those who know the law and how to break it also know how to defend themselves when they're caught. So not only had my ignorance opened me to possible charges, it had also made me an easy target. Even the gentlemen questioning me stopped from time to time to ask if I'd like to rephrase an answer. A solicitor would have guided my words so my fate might have been different. Everything's easier in hindsight.

"What is the nature of your business?" they wanted to know. "What services do you provide?"

They were reasonable questions in principle, but I knew my answers might elicit bias in a magistrate.

"Why do you use nitrous oxide?" they persisted.

I explained about the brief loss of consciousness that excited some clients.

"If you used bondage on a client and then used the gas, would that client be able to escape in the event of a fire?"

Some clients enjoy extreme techniques of bondage, which I'm happy to provide. I had to think quickly so I could find an honest answer to this question that wouldn't incriminate me further.

"Regardless of the influence of any gas, a client who's tied up could always escape if he wanted or needed to," I said.

"Really?"

"The rings on the restraints are big enough to unclip if necessary."

Mark smiled. "Well, yes, I noticed that."

He'd taken everything in. He was a very observant man.

"Anyone can be released quickly," I added. "They might run on to the street naked or in a sissy outfit, but at least they'd be out."

Both my interviewers laughed. The image amused them. They might not have known that 'sissy' is the normal term in this context. Clients with such predilections like to be called 'sissies'.

I decided there and then that nitrous oxide would no longer be used in my Chamber, a decision I've upheld. Experience teaches us there can be folly in any assumption, and yet we make assumptions every day of our lives. All of us, even the Lucina of mythology, are helpless before the whims of Fate. We can't hope to prepare for every eventuality; yet if something unexpected happens we can be punished – because ignorance is no defense.

"I've had two encounters with nitro now. I'm going to quit while I'm ahead."

"Sensible, although it's legal to use it," agreed the chief investigator. "If it hadn't been legal we'd have thrown the book at you."

It can be argued that when you engage in any operation you should first check the rules of the game. But when the rules are so many and so complex that you need legal training to understand them, is it reasonable to expect any individual to know everything relevant? I'm not trying to minimise my culpability. I'd breached Health and Safety Law. But it's important to highlight that such mistakes are all too easy to make. Surely the law should prosecute those who damage society on purpose, not those who inadvertently fall foul of a system overburdened with legislation?

I could only hope that should fire again lap at the walls of my Chamber and oblige one of my slaves to escape naked (though free from bonds), the unclothed body of a ninety kilogram male running down a Manchester high street wouldn't cause too many traffic accidents or heart attacks.

*

My interview finally ended. I left the fire station with another warm hand-shake from Mark.

"Let me know when the work's been completed," he said. "If you need any advice or guidance, just tell me."

The grey mizzle of a dying season hung heavy in the cold Pennine air. It matched my mood. They'd told me I wouldn't hear whether I was to be prosecuted until at least the New Year, so I decided to throw myself wholeheartedly into rebuilding my Chamber. I had a couple of meetings with Andy the manager.

"I asked the area manager if we could extend you two months rent-free while you're not working," he told me, "but he said 'No'."

Well, it was good of him to have tried.

The most pressing task was to restore electricity to all parts of the building. The cable ran from the electricity cupboard right around the huge basement before entering my unit. This cable had burned only in my Chamber, but the fire inspectors insisted I must replace the whole length.

"None of the outside wire was damaged," I said. "I could get a breaker put in."

"No, we want the whole thing doing."

Early quotations left me feeling helpless before the cruel tides of commercial exploitation. The approach to Christmas was apparently the busiest time for every electrician in Stockport. Who'd have known? Electricians were in such high demand that they expected financial reimbursement on a par with brain surgeons and astronauts. In the end my friend Phil, a retired electrician, came to my rescue.

"Don't worry, Lucina, I'll do it at cost."

His advancing years meant he'd be slow, but I was in no position to dictate. However, did he have a certificate to show the work would be done by a commercial electrician, not a residential one?

"Oh, yes, I had to have certificates. It was my job, you know."

I handed over five hundred pounds for the purchase of cable, agreeing to pay the rest of what I owed him when he'd finished. Mark had taken pity on me, occasionally calling to check on progress and help me wade through the reams of legislation that governed fire safety in buildings used for commercial purposes. Everything was starting to come together. The sun had broken through the heavy black clouds. But this was going to be a long journey.

I gave Phil the keys to the Chamber so he and his son could get on with the job. At first they were there every day, and after a few days I went to take a look. Progress was painfully slow, but the Chamber was starting to look more like its old self. They'd restored the electricity supply so the premises could now be seen, and they'd swept up the dirt, broken glass and plastic so it looked a lot better. The hanging fluorescent lights had been replaced with new ones and the wires were tidy. I had light; the walls were no longer coated in soot. Maybe there was an end to the tunnel of misery. However, now I could see the damage in all its glory.

When I'd first looked at the place after the fire, much of the equipment on hooks half way up the walls seemed to have survived. Sadly, it hadn't. The leather gags and strap-on harnesses hadn't burned but they'd been baked as hard as nails, and anything containing metal was corroding because of the water. I took a bin liner and started to throw away my favourite toys one after the other.

During the following two weeks, Phil and his son replaced the long wire around the basement, but their presence had become more sporadic. I'd turn up to find nobody there. When I rang them I'd be told, "We were in for an hour this morning but we've had to go and fix a bathroom light". This wasn't good. There was still a lot of work to do, and at the present rate of progress I'd be closed for a year. I felt helpless.

About three weeks after the work had begun, Mike popped round to help me with the latest door-wedge of reconstituted rain forest, sorting the necessary rules from the irrelevant ones. You'd never guess how many Health and Safety regulations there are until you see them all written down. In this age of the paperless office and genuine concern for the plight of the planet, it's worrying that so much paper is wasted in the name of ensuring that ignorance can be no defence. However, I didn't have to meet all the regulations. Many were reserved for much bigger businesses. With the guidance of my now friendly fire inspector I was able to separate the wheat from the chaff and direct my efforts accordingly.

One of the 'breaches of Health and Safety' I'd committed was not having a Fire Risk Assessment. This was required by law for all new businesses.

"Be careful with it," Mark warned. "Fire risk assessment firms aren't regulated and some of them charge way over the odds."

He gave me a list of four assessors he knew were good. I made an appointment. Two retired fire-fighters arrived and looked around. Clearly uncomfortable about being in a dungeon, they were extremely rude. They called me out behind the Chamber into an area where the fire exit light had gone out.

"This isn't my property," I explained. "It belongs to the management."

They kept saying it was illegal. I kept repeating my answer. Eventually they left saying, "This isn't your concern". A few days later I received an e-mail with their full report. It was huge! Doors should swing this way, not that; signs were needed for fire assembly points… it went on and on. Mind-boggled, I sent the report to Mark to ask if this was all correct. He printed it off, highlighted the areas he wanted to be completed, and brought it to my Chamber the following day. His help was invaluable.

"If they tell you that you need a fire risk certificate," he said, "ignore them. You don't need one."

*

Progress with the restoration remained slow but we were moving forward so I'd every reason to feel hope. But as I've said before, the darkest moments come when you're least prepared. One day, which started like any other, Phil was due in the Chamber. When I spoke to him on the phone that morning I said: "I'll be down later. The fire inspector is going to call with some papers for me."

There was a pause, and then Phil had said, "OK, I'll see you later."

I arrived at the Chamber and opened the door to see Phil's son coming out carrying boxes of tools and looking sheepish. He said "Hi", but put his head down and avoided eye contact.

"Odd," I thought, "but never mind."

The Chamber was in darkness again. I supposed Phil had turned off the electricity to work on something. I went in and saw him beside my electric unit, scampering down his ladder although he was quite overweight. He was flustered, flushed, sweating and a little breathless.

"What's going on?" I asked.

He leapt from his ladder and started to rip the cable from the walls. All the work he'd done in the previous three weeks was undone in moments. I remember thinking that if he'd worked as quickly to install my cable as he did when he pulled it down I might already have been back in business. Now here I was, in a darkened Chamber once again and without the power even to make a cup of tea. Despair swallowed me whole.

"What on earth -?"

"Thing is, Lucina, my certificate's only for domestic premises, not commercial."

"And you've only just discovered that, have you?"

"No, but… Well, I'd have told you when I'd finished. But with that fire officer coming round, I reckoned I was making a mistake. I got cold feet."

I couldn't believe this! He'd lied when I'd asked him about certification. To this day I'm not sure why. He said he'd wanted to help but hadn't counted on a fire inspector paying such close attention. Maybe he'd just wanted the money. Either way, he'd stripped everything he'd done and disconnected everything too. Then he scuttled out of the Chamber as if his arse was on fire.

Perhaps it was just as well; the work wouldn't have passed the scrutiny of Mark, who would do everything by the book despite his efforts to be friendly and helpful. However, here I was, back to square one, my Chamber once again cold and dark. I can usually find some amusement in events, but right then I'd lost my sense of fun. Andy called to see how I was getting on and I'm afraid he got the brunt of it.

"That's it," I told him. "I've had enough. I'm giving in. I'm quitting the unit."

"You're still under contract with me, Lucina."

"Seriously? That's the least of my worries!"

He said nothing more.

I called Gary.

"Phil's walked out and left me," I said. "It's over, Gary. I can't do this any more."

Gary isn't the best at dealing with fraught women, but he did quite well on that occasion and suggested a coffee. We couldn't have made one in the Chamber unless he'd brought a camping stove so we went to the local cafe. Over a plate of chips, I said:

"I don't know what to do. Time's getting on and I'm hardly any nearer to getting the Chamber back together."

It was fast approaching Christmas and every electrician was fully booked. If I couldn't find somebody to rewire the Chamber soon my business would sink without trace. In any business, the longer you're unable to provide for your customers' needs, the likelier they are to go elsewhere. Money was draining from my account and I could do nothing to replenish it.

Gary put his head down.

"I know an electrician who's commercially qualified," he said. "He has his own business and deals with huge contracts."

"Why didn't you mention him before?" I demanded.

"The problem is," explained Gary, "he's my best friend and I don't like to divulge the BDSM side of my life to anyone." He looked up at me. "If you're desperate, though, I'll have a word."

"I'm desperate!" I said.

Gary called Paul there and then and sheepishly told him about me and the premises. Paul didn't so much as blink.

"I'll pop round immediately," he said.

He came and had the power connected within twenty minutes, so at least I had heating and light again. Then he looked around.

"It'll cost about two thousand to put this to rights," he said.

"That's OK," I said.

"It's Christmas, so I won't be able to do the work myself" (Christmas again!), "but I'll get my lads in. It'll pump up the price, but if you need it doing fast, it'll happen."

I agreed. I did need it done quickly!

"If it's going to be over two thousand," he went on, "I'll tell you, and I'll try to get in to do some of the work myself."

Paul started on the task but everything was now going wrong. Every time we painted the Chamber the walls would become dust-covered and need to be painted again. Somebody would promise a delivery and the delivery wouldn't arrive. It was as though no matter which way I turned I was being battered by misfortune, debacle and mishap. Hope was dying. It was hard to continue.

Whenever I could I had Charlie with me, and he was always a comfort. Even when the Chamber was being painted and cleaned out he was there, as long as it was safe for him. Occasionally he'd stay in the car while I was sorting out lighting or somesuch, until it was safe for him to be back down there. When the Chamber was hazardous for him for long periods, Peter and his wife looked after him for me.

*

One evening around that time I returned home to find that thieves had prised a window wide open and my apartment was freezing cold. It's hard to describe your feelings when you discover you've been burgled. This was the last straw. I was exhausted from the weeks of hard work in the Chamber and the emotional stress. The chain of misfortunes had become a morass in which I now found myself drowning. The thief had only stolen two laptops and a watch, but he'd stripped me of my sense of security and violated my privacy. Even though I always try to be positive, at that point I had no energy left. I sat with my head in my hands and cried.

Burglary isn't so much a crime against possession as a trespass into the victim's soul. Stolen property can be replaced, but the injury to the soul is for life. From that night on, even the smallest sound startled me into a fear that grew out of all proportion. I was no longer comfortable in my ground floor apartment.

Anger welled up in me. It wasn't fair that Fate had chosen to batter me again. Were I a slave and Fate my Mistress, I'd have been screaming for mercy by that stage. I'd had enough. Yet I had to do *something*! I noticed the flat on the top (third) floor had come up for rent so I asked if I could view it. It was an amazing flat with patio doors leading on to a small balcony with huge trees in view. I loved it and took it straight away. However, on top of everything that was happening with my Chamber, I now had the added stress of moving Charlie and myself into a new home. My life seemed to have slid from fiasco to calamity.

The law is designed to protect our privacy and wellbeing against those who seek to abuse it. Theft is a premeditated crime for which ignorance can't be considered as even a shred of mitigation. Yet such crimes are often punished more leniently than those where the perpetrator hadn't known they were committing an offence – as in my case.

Somehow, though, I *had* to keep going.

Chapter 16

All the work on the Chamber had been completed but the smell lingered. Smoke clings everywhere. All the furniture had to be thrown out and replaced. Everything had to be washed and scrubbed over and over again and the walls and floors painted. But even months later, a faint whiff of smoke would greet us as we entered a room. Where had it come from?

Once the electricians' work was finished I supposed I could start work again, so I messaged Mark to ask if he'd inspect the premises. He came the following day. I had the biggest smile on my face as he entered because the place was spotless and freshly painted, with gleaming new fire alarms and exit signs and shiny new fire extinguishers at every exit. Mark looked around with his usual diligence.

"You've done really well, Lucina."

Even a Dominatrix loves the occasional pat on the head!

"You might have done a little *too* well." Mark smiled. "Make sure those ultra-sensitive alarms don't go off by mistake and give us a false call-out. You could end up with another prohibition!"

My smile faded, but then he went on: "I'm happy to lift the prohibition we put on you seven weeks ago. You can start working again whenever you want."

I don't often congratulate myself but I'll never forget the feeling those words gave me! If I could have grabbed hold of myself and waltzed around the room I'd have done so. But fond as Mark had become of me, he probably wouldn't have been up for a dance. On the day of the fire I'd looked into the darkness and thought it was the end, but despite all the setbacks then and since, hard work had brought me through it and once again I had a functional Chamber, one hundred percent legal and, more importantly, safe.

"The fire might have done me a favour," I thought.

As Mark departed he gave me a final piece of advice: "Remember, you don't need a fire risk certificate. I'm happy with everything. That's all that matters."

Sure enough, a few weeks later a lady from the Fire Risk Team called.

"Has all the work recommended in the report been done?" she asked.

"Yes, it has."

"Good. Well, our two men will be in your area tomorrow. If they could pop in and approve the work they'll be able to issue a fire risk certificate. It will only cost you two hundred pounds."

"I don't need a certificate," I said.

"Oh, I think you do, Ms White."

I grinned and told her about my conversation with Mark.

"Stockport's head fire inspector told me I don't need one, and since he was happy, that's the end of the matter."

"Oh." She paused. "I'll have a word with our two men and get back to you."

I never heard from her again.

*

A few mornings after Mark's visit I arrived at the Chamber to be greeted by Gary.

"Paul's dropped off your invoice for the work," he said, "and you're not going to like it."

"Why?"

"It's over five thousand pounds."

I thought it was one of Gary's little jokes. But he handed me a large envelope, which I ripped open, and there it was: the final invoice for the electrical work. Five thousand five hundred pounds. No wonder Paul had left the Chamber in a hurry before I'd arrived. He'd promised to tell me if the bill was going to exceed two thousand, but he hadn't.

"When life has you on the ropes," I muttered, "it likes to keep you there."

However, I understood why the bill was so enormous: a decision had been made to rewire the Chamber completely after two days of trying and failing to rescue the existing cable. It had been necessary and the work had been completed to the highest standard, complying fully with Health and Safety regulations. Also, much more power could now be supplied to the unit, so I'd had large industrial heaters fitted to the walls. Paul's invoice was itemised down to the last screw, and all the fittings had been supplied at cost. Moreover, he agreed I could pay the bill in monthly instalments of five hundred pounds, which I could afford now I was earning again.

It seemed the page had turned and a ghastly chapter was closed. As the days ran into weeks and the weeks into months, I'd still heard nothing about a possible prosecution. January and February came and went without a summons. I was working, self-sufficient and paying my bills. I had a lot of debts to meet, not only to Paul the electrician but also to people who'd lent me money, and I had to replace the ruined dungeon equipment bit by bit. Nevertheless I was starting to get back on my feet. For the first time in what seemed an eternity I felt I'd taken back control and was able to live again. After all that had happened with Chris and the inquest I knew that legal wheels grind slowly, but after twelve months of anxious waiting it seemed my luck might have changed. A full year had passed and I hadn't heard from the courts. I could celebrate the thirty-first of October that year in a rejuvenated Chamber.

"Have they decided to drop it?" I thought. "I'm not sure how these things work, but surely now, after a year, I can relax."

I should have known better after the Chris case. I should have known that as soon as I start to relax, the shit hits the fan. The fickle hand of Fate grips its knife firmly and knows how to strike when your guard is down.

I walked to the outside door of my flat to answer the buzzer.

"Ms White?" said the postman.

I said "Yes" and he thrust a large envelope into my hands.

"Please sign," he said.

He seemed to be in a hurry. I signed, and he couldn't get away quickly enough. I was bemused, but I understood his anxiety later. I'm sure he'd had many such envelopes thrown back at him. I still wasn't certain what the envelope contained, but the awful feeling in the pit of my stomach told me it wasn't good news.

I went upstairs and opened the envelope in comfort. It was brimming with photos, together with a transcript of my statement and a summons to court.

"OMG, I don't believe it!" I thought.

My attention was mainly on the first page of the documents, the summons. It gave the date for my court appearance. It had taken a year for the authorities to inform me of my impending fate, but my appearance in court was scheduled *for the following week*. They said I'd need a solicitor. So my first priority was to hire one and I had little time to do it.

Although ignorance is no defence, the British legal system doesn't reward honesty. It was difficult not to feel angry about the judicial process. Throughout that terrible year I'd cooperated fully with the investigation, acted on every instruction down to the finest detail and met every challenge. Yet my only crime had been a naivety that's probably shared by millions. Now I was to be punished further, the emotional and financial stresses of the preceding months presumably considered insufficient for rehabilitation. The Crown Prosecution Service had an easy target.

*

My solicitor seemed confident; he knew the law and was authoritative in reciting it. If he performed for the magistrate as he rehearsed in his posh office in central Manchester, where I sat watching him scan documents and wondering whether I'd be charged for the coffee, I could be confident of receiving a fair trial. He seemed to want to do all of the talking, so I let him.

This was different from the anticipation of Chris's inquest, when uncertainty had fed the wraith of fear so it haunted mind and soul. This time I knew what I faced. I knew the charges stacked against me and the fines they'd entail. It was merely a matter of waiting to confirm what I already knew, rather like opening an umbrella and waiting for the rain.

"You're looking at a hefty fine plus all court costs," the solicitor informed me, "but I'm sure they'll take account of your compliance with everything required of you, and that's the angle I'll go for. And you're right: being so honest has made you an easy target. They won't need to put any effort into the case."

Mark knew better than anyone how hard I'd worked to comply with the law. During the past year he'd been promoted and transferred to another station, but I found him. His voice on the phone was friendly and he sounded happy to hear from me.

"What can I do for you, Lucina?"

"I've been summoned to court. This week."

"You're joking! After a year?" he gasped, and then sighed.

"Could you put in a good word for me, Mark?"

"I don't know if I'll be allowed to, Lucina." He sighed again. "Let me call Stockport fire station and I'll get back to you."

He returned my call within the hour.

"Sorry, Lucina, they won't let me say anything in your favour. I didn't really stand a chance."

On the day of the hearing I woke with self-absorbed apathy. My body was drained of vitality. It was as if all my care was for the morrow and none for that day. It's hard to muster enthusiasm for an event you wish to end before it's started. After all, I knew I was due to appear in court and I'd be fined; hardly the ingredients of a great day out. I gazed into the mirror, trying to summon the energy to make myself ready. I longed for the simple kind of day that I love: walking Charlie, whipping a client, feeling happy and carefree.

I decided to leave Fate to its own devices. If its plan were to beat me, I wouldn't give it the satisfaction of making any effort to fight it. I wasn't going to brood about what I couldn't change. I certainly wouldn't dress for the occasion, though I did decide to wear a suit. The magistrate would have little interest in my grooming or my taste in fashion, so why waste my time? As I showered I wondered whether to wash my hair. At the time I had long hair that cascaded down my back, so any woman will understand my dilemma: *is it looking greasy, can I get away with it?* Usually, if you decide not to wash it, it will look fine as you step outside but within an hour it will seem to grow greasier by the moment. If a dungeon session or other desirable event had been in prospect I wouldn't have chanced it, but this was court so I decided not to bother. That decision would come back to bite me on the bum.

My preparation for the day in court therefore consisted of an unhurried breakfast and a walk with my ever-faithful dog. "Should I pursue anything other than pleasure under these circumstances?" I asked. Charlie wagged. He seemed to agree.

*

As you might expect, a magistrate's court isn't the happiest place in which to spend your time and it doesn't overflow with charm. Awaiting my hearing I sat outside the courtroom surrounded by the misery of criminal minds, people about to suffer the confiscation of liberty. I was in a hall of thieves, sitting where prisoners had been condemned. It was a formal place full of quiet hustle and bustle: soft voices, worried faces, shoes squeaking on the polished floor. It wasn't like the inquest, when I'd suffered the stress of facing the more-or-less unknown although I hadn't been on trial. This time I knew what I faced, and I was *the accused*.

In our green gardens and quiet streets, we think of a courthouse as a place where those guilty of premeditated crimes suffer the might of the law so the innocent are protected. But the law has no definite shade; it isn't black, nor is it white. Should I be tried as a thief, or given care by those who knew better? I deserved neither. I was a casualty of ignorance. I only hoped, as I still hope, for a fair society. We must try to be all we can be as we tread the path of life, but if we insist on being honest we must beware of those seeking easy targets. Let me say it again: I've never knowingly broken the law, yet my treatment has at times been harsher than what falls on those who steal laptops from empty flats. In truth, the law isn't always driven by a need to protect: it can be energised by bureaucrats seeking to fill quotas. Crime is a statistical element of a flow chart used to win political elections. We're all just numbers.

"I believe we're the last ones in," said my solicitor, pointing to the relevant courtroom. "I'll see you in there," he added, and disappeared.

My moment of justice was approaching. My nerves had finally started to tingle. I already knew my fate: I'd have my wrists slapped, and like any good citizen I'd smile and say sorry for my 'crimes'. But a degree of anxiety was now added to the growing anger fuelled by my predicament.

Moments before my case was due to be heard, a young woman burst from the court. She wasn't particularly well dressed and I wondered what small misdemeanour had caused her to be summoned there. Tears flooded from her eyes and her hysterical ramblings echoed round the now almost-empty hall. There's probably no ideal preparation for a hearing before a magistrate, but if there were it wouldn't include the ravings of a distraught woman. She seemed broken, crying and sobbing. Nevertheless, her appearance strengthened my resolve.

"However they try to degrade or intimidate me, they won't see me act like that!" I decided. "I won't cry or shout. These people in posh suits and ties won't see any weakness in me. After all, I've seen too many of their type with their pants down, being spanked."

*

My turn arrived and I was ushered into the court. The room was surprisingly large. The dock was surrounded by bullet-proof glass with small holes punched in it. It seems that those guilty of ignorance are so dangerous that the magistrate must be protected by a secure barrier.

The court was almost empty. A bored magistrate slumped in his large chair at one end, propped up by his minions, yawning, exhausted, and showing no interest in anything around him. I supposed he wanted to go home for dinner. At the back of the court sat a couple of scruffy journalists, the quality of their attire matching the rags for which they bent the truth.

My solicitor, the indomitable lion, sat to one side. His confident command of all legal precedents was to be my lance and his truth my shield. He'd be my champion and I would leave the court victorious. My knight was accompanied by a praying mantis hired by the prosecution to enhance the CPS statistics for Stockport. I had no fear of this beastly fiend. My gallant hero would stride to my defence and she would be vanquished.

The magistrate stirred momentarily, bringing relief to all who'd feared that he'd slipped from this world to join the angels in the Court of Heaven. The charges were read and I was asked how I would plead.

"Guilty."

As I watched these official people from behind the bullet-proof glass and said "Guilty", my legs became a little weak and I felt emotion welling up inside me. All the anticipation had come to a head and I was suddenly overwhelmed. Tears pricked my eyes. Then I remembered the woman who'd left the hearing before mine.

"Come on, Lucina," I thought. "You can do this." I took a deep breath, dispelled any thought of tears, straightened my back and thought, "Right, bring it on".

In the eyes of the law I had no defence, but while I was at the mercy of the court I had the protection of my knightly master of law. Forward he would surely march, his armour gleaming, this man of steel with words that would pierce all who stood before him. But it was there, in that moment, amidst the dust and debris of British judicial proceedings, that I finally discovered the true folly of my actions a year earlier.

The praying mantis was amazing. If ever I needed a prosecution lawyer I'd know where to go! Her strong voice ensured that nothing was missed in ensuring my demise. Every element of the statement I'd innocently tendered to the fire inspectors now tumbled in venomous spittle from the lips of the attacking prosecution. No stone was left unturned in the assassination of my character. Apparently my profession as a Dominatrix had played a role in my criminal actions. Could such a woman, wallowing in such a dark place so remote from normality, be allowed upon our streets? The mantis's speech took twenty minutes. Even I grew bored of hearing what a naughty girl I'd been.

I'd entered this theatre of lunacy expecting a fair and balanced hearing. Moreover, I'd anticipated that any verdict would take account of the suffering my ignorance had already incurred and be duly balanced. Instead, my profession was to cast me into the pit and ensure I received no mercy from the law. This wasn't a trial but a sacrifice. I was to be offered to the cold god of statistical representation. My fate would not be in vain; those who walked the streets of Stockport could rest assured that, statistically speaking, crime was being washed from our community. As the praying mantis devoured the last few morsels of my defence, the journalists awoke and started to scribble in their notebooks. One of them started whispering into his mobile. The magistrate finally woke from his slumber, screaming for all phones to be switched off. It was reassuring to find that the court could focus on such a priority. It was even more reassuring to discover that the magistrate was *still* alive.

I had much to say in return but of course I wasn't allowed to speak. I was paying my solicitor seven hundred pounds to do it for me. He stood up, a tall man but now stooping, and I swear he looked out of his depth. His body language told me I was already doomed. Continually looking down at his papers, nervously stroking his tie, he mumbled something about my compliance with the rules and how much I'd had to spend during the past year and this should be taken into consideration. He never looked up and he carried no conviction. He finished after five minutes.

"That can't be it!" I thought. "He's going to stand up again, right?"

I wanted to shout out the truth. Then the praying mantis stood again and asked if she could add something.

"Indeed, Ms White complied with the fire service's requirements and assisted them in their investigation all the way."

She said this with far more passion than my solicitor had contrived. If only she'd been on my side! Perhaps Mark had exerted some influence after all. I was glad now I hadn't taken a solicitor to the fire station interview. The empty chair beside me had been more useful.

*

The court held a short recess to decide whether it was to be the lions or the noose. I sat and fiddled nervously, wondering when the last execution had been held in Stockport. After all, my ignorance was serious enough, but it was now known that I was also a Dominatrix. The court had grounds for at least a hanging. However, there was always the hope that the magistrate would fall back to sleep before delivering his verdict.

As the sentence was read, I stood in the dock and stared straight at the magistrate, unwilling to show an ounce of emotion. It was to be a fine of eight thousand pounds, which would include costs. I would also need to find another seven hundred pounds for my solicitor, though I wondered why.

As I left, the magistrate finally displayed an impressive talent for stringing words into two whole sentences.

"You may pay your fine in monthly instalments. However, I urge you to pay as much as you can afford."

I later read on a chip paper, which had started life as a parody of the news, that the court had ordered me to get a job that would pay more money. The reporters had been almost asleep until the words 'professional Dominatrix' were spoken, whereupon no two people had ever been seen to move so quickly. They'd grabbed pen and paper from their pockets and scribbled so rapidly I swear I'd seen smoke rising. But they hadn't been prepared, and swiftly as they wrote they couldn't capture all the information as it was being read out. In any case the magistrate was mumbling so inaudibly that I wondered whether he'd suffered a stroke, those beside him too dull to notice, and the journalists were at the back of the courtroom. Perhaps they hadn't deliberately misled their readers; they'd just invented things to fill in the gaps.

Of course, the case being over, my knight of the law recovered his confidence and urged me to launch an appeal. His opinion was that the sentence was too harsh and had been intended more as an example to others than as a fair and balanced fine. "If you'd run a hairdressing salon the fine would have been half as much." But having been pilloried as a Dominatrix I was glad to have escaped with my life. Nothing good could come of an appeal. I wanted it all to be over. After everything that had happened with Chris, the inquest, the fire and now this court hearing, to invite further upheaval was unthinkable. I'd hold my head high, take my punishment (oh, the irony!) and get on with my life. It was almost comical as the solicitor and I stood by the exit door. He shook my hand, said "Good luck", and was gone. I saw his back as the door closed behind him and he disappeared to the left in a puff of smoke.

It didn't take long to discover his reason for haste. I left the court while the door was still swinging behind my solicitor, but I went to the right. Then there they were, the two reporters shouting questions at me and two photographers with the largest lenses I've ever seen pointing into my face. They ran ahead and then crouched, snapping a few shots before rushing forward for a change of angle.

"Now that's going to be a close-up," I thought.

More than any other time in my life, I was filled with inconsolable regret at not having taken the time to wash my hair. I walked past my car and onwards, not wishing to be photographed climbing behind the wheel. I could already imagine the headline: *Evil Dominatrix Can Afford a Car While Being Guilty of Ignorance!*

The scruffy photographer kept asking me for a quotation, and I amused myself by saying, "No comment", as in the films.

"If you give me a comment we'll use a good photo," he said, "but if you don't we'll pick the worst."

*

That night I went to bed knowing that my 'worst' photo would soon adorn the Stockport Express, which would be enough to 'out' me. In a profession that relies so much on discretion, I feared that such pictures would tell all of Stockport about me and this would spell an end to my business. When I awoke I found dozens of voicemails and texts on my phone, which was unusual. One text was from Sam and I went straight to it. "Loz," it said, "you're in the *Sun*!"

The other messages demonstrated that I was featured not only in the *Sun* but also in nearly every national daily in Britain. My image could also be seen online, courtesy of newsfeeds that flooded the web and spread from country to country. From Bombay to Tel Aviv and New York to Kuala Lumpur, the world was waking to the shocking news that I'd gone to court without washing my hair. Life is about experiences, and this was an experience! I put the covers back over my head.

"Charlie, we're not getting up today," I joked.

My world lay shattered in words scribbled black on cheap recycled paper. Headlines that stretched the truth to a point of blatant lies screamed their version of the facts to all who were gullible enough to believe them. From tales of a sex dungeon to the Mistress of a sex fetish club, the media stirred a pot of half-truths and bumbled facts with no consideration for accuracy or decency. In our society we believe what we read because it's come from the media. Sadly, to accept that journalism is governed by moral values is an illusion. You can't trust the press. The world it reports is nothing more than smoke and mirrors. For two days I was inundated with messages telling me all the places where my photo appeared. At one point, I had front page coverage in the *Metro* and on page two of the *Daily Mail*. That amused me.

"Is this really top news?" I thought.

This hostile reporting, I supposed, would harm my business and all I'd worked for. To their credit, the *Daily Mirror* reported with reasonable accuracy, even taking some care to describe the intricacies of BDSM. But to those for whom the scene is a lifestyle, most of the headlines printed about my case were nails in the coffin. They reiterated a false, worn-out cliché. On that same day, Oscar Pistorius, a convicted murderer, only made page three.

My letterbox was filled with offers of interviews. I was invited to appear on the Jeremy Kyle show and asked to go on *This Morning*. Were my actions really worthy of such coverage, or do we live in a world where the priority is to fan the flames of scandal because it's more interesting than *real* news?

However, once I recovered from the shock I wasn't devastated. My world wasn't in tatters. I sat with my morning coffee and thought.

"I can either let this stress me out or simply see the funny side," I decided.

I was a little miffed that they called my Chamber a 'sex dungeon'. The word 'sex' hadn't been mentioned in court. I'm a Dominatrix; I don't offer sexual services! But I refused to let their nonsense get to me. BDSM is an art to which we're born. The dynamic that forms between Mistress and slave transcends the cliché and rests in a place beyond description, a place of trust and loving care, not tarnished by acts of gratuitous sexual relief. The reality of BDSM is light-years from the stereotypical comedy sketch involving whips and chains, a false image fed by ignorance and fuelled by the media with no regard for those involved, or for the truth. We're real people with feelings; we have families and we have friends. When such lies are printed about me they affect my life and the lives of all those I love. Fortunately, everyone in the scene was equally annoyed by the misrepresentations and I received a lot of positive feedback.

*

The events of that year taught me a lot about the country in which I live and the bureaucratic machine that governs its laws. But I also learned that I'm strong and surrounded by wonderful people. Those whom the media sought to tarnish are the very same people who gave me my strength. I will forever be grateful for the financial, moral and emotional support of the people with whom I share the wonderful world of BDSM. It was they who rallied to my cause, and they who helped me through my trials.

I pity those who're blind to the reality of the world in which we live, because ours is a far better place for those who value integrity and honour. During the witch-hunt that followed my trial, local newspaper reporters toured the companies and families that work and live around my Chamber. Their hope was to find hostility toward my profession. To their frustration, they found none. I'd made friends with some of my neighbours so they had nothing bad to say about me, but others whom I hardly knew said nothing negative either.

"She keeps herself to herself," they said. "She doesn't do any harm." (Apart from causing the odd fire, I thought.)

I know and understand the nature of the press so I wasn't surprised by their actions, but the intensity of their interest amazed me. They only really annoyed me when they printed a photo of the front door to the Chamber, which is quite discreet. That could have put our safety at risk. But could they be expected to care?

I may be ignorant but I know the value of truth, honesty and decency. The law might punish me for that, and the media had already done so, but I'll never change.

Chapter 17

Restoring my business after these disasters was a priority, but so was the need to find relief in other aspects of my life. It's not enough to say that I have a love of dogs and a passion for elephants. That would be true, but animals, like humans, have distinct and indeed unique characters. For instance, no two dogs are the same; each has its specific behavioural traits. When we spend prolonged periods with any animal we become exposed to its personality and the resulting familiarity breeds not contempt but growing fondness. I'm naturally drawn to all manner of beasts, from elephants in the jungle to dogs playing Frisbee in the park. I'm in continual quest of animal company. Many animals love unconditionally, forgiving cruelty without question and wishing only for our love. They become part of us, an extension to our families and deserving recipients of our affection.

"Isn't there a conflict," a friend asked me, "between working as a Dominatrix and caring for animals?"

"Given the intensity of my work as a Mistress," I said, "my time with animals is an essential release. And no, there's no conflict. To be an effective Dominatrix you need to be understanding and caring, just as you must when you look after animals."

As Peter might have warned my friend, don't be misled by stereotypes!

"But those two sides of your life have to be kept apart, surely?"

"Oh, of course," I agreed. "I don't suppose many clients would find me appealing if I attended my Chamber dressed in jeans and wellingtons. And imagine the stir I'd cause if I walked my dog in the park wearing a leather corset and high-heeled thigh-length boots!"

The point is worth repeating: in an act of domination, provided it's handled properly, two individual personalities share a symbiotic experience that can only be achieved with care, compassion and trust. Their minds fit together like jigsaw pieces. When I'm in session I care deeply for the wishes and needs and emotions of those under my power, though I don't suffer fools and I'm never shy of making my feelings known. If I lose faith in someone I lose patience with them. However, if trust and honesty are given then my patience is unlimited. Trust is everything. The encounter becomes part of a journey in which each party addresses the other's needs. My compassion for animals reflects and balances the emotions I feel as a Mistress. You don't have to have four legs and a tail in order for me to love you. But animals just accept me for the love I give, while some people – not my clients, I hasten to add – label me with a stereotype, just as the inquiring friend had risked doing.

*

More than once in this book I've mentioned my regular Monday dog-rescue work. This is how it started.

One day while I was out in my car I came upon a small sign offering directions to an 'Animal Sanctuary'. With some excitement, I turned from the main road to follow a small lane along a canal. After a while I drew up beside a cottage with small grounds housing a cattery, kennels and an area dedicated to rabbits. I alighted and wandered along the short path to Reception. I knew before the door opened that this place would play an important part in my life.

"Do you have any openings for volunteers?" I asked.

"Oh, yes, we always want more volunteers!"

The receptionist produced a simple application form. I was asked my name, age, contact details and previous experience of working with animals. Then came the key question: "Why do you want to volunteer at this sanctuary?"

"It will give me a chance to make a difference," I said, "by helping animals that have been abandoned or abused. I'm eager to start."

Moments later it was done. My application was accepted.

*

Ever since making the transition to professional Dominatrix I've understood the importance of having time for myself. It's hard to convey just how demanding my role can be and how much of me is given in its practice. The job can be exciting and it's deeply rewarding, but the pressures on my time and emotional energy can be immense. Submissives can be as demanding as little boys being led around a toyshop. My dedication can lead to me giving time to clients outside of sessions. It can result in a seven day week.

Therefore, I now devote two days a week to my own pursuits. Sunday is my day of rest, a time to shelter from the demands of my profession and to lose myself in hobbies such as flying and enjoying time with Charlie. Monday is my animal sanctuary day. Ever since the moment of that first application I've dedicated the beginning of every week to the service of my four-legged friends.

My work at a dog sanctuary has often been a guiding light to my soul, just as my time spent with elephants added so much to my life. It can be hard working with animals, seeing their suffering at first hand. People imagine I'm sadistic because of my profession. Convention portrays the Dominatrix as cruel. However, the cruelty perpetrated by my fellow humans is beyond my comprehension. Why would anyone deliberately harm an animal? No, I don't want an answer. I don't wish to understand people who perform such horrible acts.

I'm afraid the vile acts of cruelty I've witnessed over the years have poisoned my view of humanity. It's hard to feel anything other than anger when you're faced with such misery in creatures that need and deserve our protection and care. In a world that cries out for love and compassion we're surrounded by selfishness and greed. The sad fact is that money, and the craving for more of it, is often at the root of the cruellest acts.

Animal cruelty is a problem that stretches to the four corners of the Earth. Working with animals is hard but rewarding. Your greatest efforts sometimes seem to pale into insignificance, but if you can make even the smallest change to an animal's life it can bring love where there had been none. I'm a realist; I know I can't end the cruelty that's all around us. As individuals we can't change the world. Nevertheless our efforts make a difference, and I believe we all have a responsibility to do whatever we can. I've cried many tears over the things I've seen, but if each tear had wings it would carry my love to the animals that need it and bring comfort to them.

*

My first day as a volunteer was marked with torrential rain and my clothes were sopping wet before my duties had even begun.

There were only enough kennels for about ten dogs, their claustrophobic dimensions bleak in the damp greyness that swallowed everything around me. To one side, a small paddock stretched to the boundary of the sanctuary's grounds, providing space to play with the dogs when they were released from the cold walls of their enclosures. It wasn't long before I was cleaning kennels, walking dogs and playing fetch in the paddock. At times it was hard to say who was having more fun, me or the dogs. While the work was sometimes hard it was always enjoyable and rewarding.

My fellow volunteers were very friendly. It's easy to fit in when you're surrounded by those who share your interests. As always, the only awkward moments arose from questions about my job.

"What do you do for a living, Lucina?"

How should I answer? I never want to mislead people, but announcing that you're a professional Dominatrix might not be the best approach to making friends and establishing good working relationships. The problem is that when you're forced to be economical with the truth it becomes harder to be honest later.

"I'm a qualified beauty therapist," I temporised.

It was true, of course, and it solved the problem. It's more relaxing to answer questions about cosmetics while you sip coffee than to field a barrage of enquiries about spanking and black leather.

It wasn't long before I was befriended by a lady called Jess, a Trustee of the sanctuary. She could be described as highly regimented, in other words bossy, but she was also hard-working and gave herself completely to the job. She'd never ask anything of a volunteer that she wasn't willing to do herself. During the school holidays the team was supplemented by a small army of young and enthusiastic labourers, all being ordered this way and that by Sergeant Major Jess.

Mondays became the highlight of my week. Soon I was joining Jess as she opened the doors at seven in the morning and I wouldn't leave until eight in the evening. I loved being the first to arrive and the last to leave because it gave me time alone with the dogs. Twelve hours or more in the kennels passed in a blink. By the time I returned home I was exhausted and I often felt stiff the next morning. Tuesday was probably the best day to visit my Chamber for a spanking because my arms still ached from Monday! Charlie either went with me to the sanctuary or stayed with Peter or his wife for the day.

The dogs were walked twice each day, once in the morning and once in the afternoon. Many of the volunteers liked to walk the dogs in groups. For them it was a means of recreation, a chance to swap news and gossip while giving time to the animals. In contrast, I preferred to take advantage of the beautiful countryside surrounding the sanctuary, walking my dogs alone in the green splendour of Nature. It recalled my childhood bicycle rides to the Lakes.

It wasn't unusual for me to spend much of the Festive Season caring for the animals at the sanctuary. Every ounce of love I gave to them was returned with interest. Some were simply being re-homed, perhaps after an owner had died or the animal had inexplicably been abandoned, but there were also cases of neglect or abuse. There was sadness in all those cases, but it was balanced by the joy of seeing a dog respond to love, care and attention, or being found a wonderful new home.

There was no better feeling than when dogs returned with their new owners for a visit. Seeing them happy and surrounded by love reminded me of why I gave – and continue to give – so much of myself to this cause. Every animal that graduated from the cold grey of the sanctuary kennels to the loving arms of new owners was literally a life saved.

Some dogs proved difficult to care for. Lives of suffering at the hands of abusive owners had made them aggressive. Not surprisingly, most volunteers avoided such dogs, so they were often left in the kennels. A lot of volunteers wanted a nice stroll with an easy dog, which of course is fine, and some simply weren't strong enough to handle large dogs that had developed nervous aggression.

Nervous aggression tended to worsen over time. When the suffering animals saw another dog on a walk they'd want to attack. It seemed some of them could never be rehomed because nobody wants a dog that looks as though it wants to rip your head off as soon as it sees you. The ones that *were* rehomed usually went to volunteers who'd fallen for them. In fact, it was the animals suffering nervous aggression that needed the most love and attention. One large German Shepherd called Elsa went to a friend of mine, and she behaved perfectly once she had a stable home and was loved. Others were similar: they were off their heads, but their aggression ceased as soon as they knew they were safe. I drew enormous satisfaction from the time I spent with dogs that would otherwise have been overlooked. Nothing is more rewarding than enhancing the quality of life of an animal that has previously known only pain and suffering.

Over the years I've grown particularly fond of several animals at the sanctuary, as you might expect. It's impossible to remain detached. Many dogs have found their way into my heart. But one in particular stands out. His name was Leo.

*

I'd worked at the dog sanctuary for around two years when I first met Leo. He was a handsome animal, a black, golden and tan cross between a German Shepherd and a Rottweiler. He was two years old and the only life he'd known was that of a guard dog. He'd never seen the outside world, chased a ball or had a cuddle, so it was no surprise that he was nervous and untrusting. He hadn't been abandoned, but his owner had become exasperated by his continual loud barking, so Leo found himself in the sanctuary. I'd always supposed that being a guard dog involved loud barking. Surely a silent guard dog wouldn't be much use?

Leo wasn't much different from many other dogs at the sanctuary. His nervous aggression was a consequence of the life he'd led. The first time I tried to approach his kennel he flung himself at the bars, barking and snarling at me. Animal lover though I am, the experience should have ended my attempts to interact with him. Once a dog has indicated that it wants you for lunch, it's sensible to maintain a safe distance. But I persisted.

I can't remember the first time I entered Leo's kennel, or – given the result of my first attempt – why I tried. But I found the courage, and it was beginning of a friendship that will always live in my heart. Of course Rome wasn't built in a day, and Leo didn't become a cute cuddly teddy bear from the moment I entered his kennel. In the early days, the hardest task was taking him for walks. He was always so tense that the slightest provocation would send him into frenzy. Men were a particular worry for him. God only knows what had happened in his young life, but if he saw a man in a high-vis jacket he'd lose it and be desperate to get away.

As you can imagine, Leo was unpopular. Most helpers considered him unapproachable and regarded his nervous aggression as savagery. Few ventured close to his kennel; when they did, he met them with a snarl. Usually he was left in his kennel until after the other dogs had been walked. This allowed me the opportunity to work with him alone.

Before each walk we spent time playing in the paddock to burn off some of his energy and teach him to relax and have fun. He took surprisingly quickly to playing, especially when a football was involved. He was a gifted player. If he'd been born with only two feet he'd have earned millions in the Premier League. It was heartening to watch him learning to be happy and becoming a little more like a normal dog. Sometimes we'd almost forgo the walk so he could play longer in the paddock, or rest on the grass while I fussed him.

"He isn't a savage beast," I told my fellow-volunteers. "He's a fun-loving animal with a beautiful soul and boundless playfulness."

They weren't convinced, but he seemed content when he was with me, and I was always sad when I had to return him to his kennel. No matter how rough his playtime became, he never tried to hurt me. He was always gentle with me. The more we played, the closer we grew and the more he came out of his shell. Our play-fighting seemed to bond us.

As Leo grew calmer, other volunteers became interested in spending time with him, but by then he only wanted to be with me. As soon as I appeared, no matter what he was doing or who he was with, his eyes would light up and he would run to me. It's wonderful to win any dog's confidence and trust, but to gain it from a rescue dog like Leo was incredible. I became very attached to him.

"I have to stay until everyone else has left," I explained, "so I can enjoy quality time with my friend."

During the day the sanctuary was noisy with dogs barking and people moving around, which unsettled Leo. He changed once the kennels had fallen quiet and everyone had gone home. He cuddled into me, draping himself across my legs while I stroked his back. I believe this was his first-ever experience of affection and he revelled in it. It was hard to leave him, especially in cold winter weather. I always ensured he had a treat as a parting gift, but it was still difficult to close the door on him.

For two years our friendship blossomed. It would never be easy to find a home for Leo. He responded badly to many different things, from men to traffic, so it would be well-nigh impossible to find someone with the experience and patience needed to care for him. Despite my bond with him, there was no way I could have handled him at home. He was a big dog and aggressive toward strangers. So he remained in the sanctuary.

*

Around that time, the landscape began to shift in the world of dog rescues. A few people had been attacked in sanctuaries around the UK and several kennels had been sued as a result. The administration of most of these charity-run organisations is controlled by Trustees, most of whom never interact with the animals; Jess was an exception. The Trustees would be responsible if the sanctuary was sued, and the fines and legal expenses could cost them their homes. So the law had been changed. New Health and Safety regulations brought an end to my quiet evenings with Leo in his kennel and undermined our relationship. Dogs aren't like people: they love unconditionally, but they don't always understand what's happening around them. On many evenings that summer I drove away from the sanctuary with tears in my eyes, passing Leo in the paddock and knowing he was waiting for his friend. He must have felt confused, but there was nothing I could do about it.

The mood around us was darkening. Volunteers are the life blood of an animal sanctuary. They take care of the animals, so they were hardest hit by the lack of common sense of the new laws. Frustration and anger were growing. One dog, a huge but lovable Rottweiler, was re-homed to a family. He had the gentlest of hearts, but two weeks later he was returned: a child had accidentally stepped on him and he'd nipped at her foot. It was a reflex, and no injury was caused, but the dog was immediately put to sleep. Why would you adopt a rescue Rottweiler if you have a young family, and why would you be surprised if it reacted to being trodden on? Such incidents became frequent, dogs being sent to their deaths because they'd been inappropriately re-homed. I began to fear for Leo.

One morning I took a call from Jess. From the moment I answered the phone I knew something was wrong.

"The sanctuary's employed an animal behaviourist," she said.

"What for? First I've heard of it."

"First any of us have heard of it. It seems we need a behaviourist to decide which dogs are so dangerous they'll have to be destroyed."

Leo. What about Leo?

"That's right against the purpose of the sanctuary!" I was angry as well as afraid. "This expert will assess the most vulnerable dogs and the most dangerous, so the ones most in need of care and love will be condemned."

"I know," said Jess. "That's what we're all saying."

"How long has the behaviourist spent in the kennels?"

"Oh, almost two hours."

"One hundred and twenty minutes?" I couldn't believe my ears. "And what decision -?"

"Two dogs are to be euthanised." Jess sighed. "Yes, I know. It didn't take this expert long to achieve greater insight than the entire group of volunteers who've devoted themselves to the upkeep of the sanctuary for months or years and know all the dogs personally."

I hardly dared ask which two dogs were condemned, but Jess assured me Leo wasn't one of them.

"We're told that Leo can be distracted from his aggression by food, so he's safe."

One of the two who'd received the death penalty was called Poppy. Like Leo, Poppy suffered from nervous aggression, but she was beginning to respond to the volunteers' care. If anything, she'd progressed further than Leo. A fair judgment based on behaviour would have condemned Leo, not Poppy. But the *expert* had devoted *nearly two hours* to the assessment, so who could argue? I make no apology for sarcasm. Animals that had been entrusted to our protection were to be slaughtered in the name of Health and Safety. This wasn't my first or last experience of ridiculous bureaucracy, but perhaps it was the bitterest.

Not long afterwards, it was decided that the kennels would be closed as soon as the few remaining dogs had been homed. Meanwhile, because of the potential liability, volunteers would no longer be permitted to attend. Which Dickens character was it who said, "The Law is an ass"?

A rug had been pulled from under my feet. I'd come to rely on my Monday escape and especially on my time with Leo. What hope was there of a good home for him? He'd surely suffer the same fate as poor Poppy. Now he was alone, a prisoner in his kennel and doubtless suffering. It was bad enough for me to know this, but to realise that he couldn't understand made it worse.

*

Over the next couple of months I struggled to come to terms with what had happened. Sadness and frustration filled me. One evening I went on one of my long walks through the woods. I have my ups and downs like everyone else, though I've never suffered from clinical depression. However, this was the closest I'd been. I couldn't shake off the thought that Leo must have felt I'd let him down.

Then I met up with Jess.

"I have a plan," she said. "We can save Leo."

My heart leapt.

"Tell me!"

"My friend Pat Senior has cared for dogs for more than thirty-five years," said Jess. "A friend of hers, Mandy, has excellent kennels in Chester and she intends to have Leo sent there."

Pat Senior threw her full weight behind our cause. At first the sanctuary didn't want to release Leo. The official story was that they were getting a behaviourist to train him so they could try to re-home him, but Jess confided that the real plan was to wait until all the outrage had died down, then they'd put him to sleep. There was no behaviourist; in fact, Leo was now locked in his kennel round the clock, day after day.

"How long has he got?" I asked.

"They're planning to give him six weeks," said Jess.

Apparently it makes more sense to release a Rottweiler into a family with a young child than it does to transfer a dog to a professional kennels. But Pat was insistent, and with the promise that Leo *would* receive care from a behaviourist, the deal was agreed. As soon as I could I went to Chester to visit my old friend and I was delighted by what I found. Leo's new home was in the beautiful green Cheshire countryside, quiet and secluded. Mandy the owner was efficient and his kennel was warm and cosy, with a run that allowed him to see outside. It was everything I could have hoped for, and more. Mandy and Pat were friends so the situation seemed positive.

At first, Leo didn't seem to know me. He was shaken by all he'd been through and was probably overwhelmed by the move. I ignored his aggression and entered his kennel. He soon remembered me and his anger segued into joy. From that day forward, a trip to Chester every Monday to spend the day with Leo became a part of my routine. The countryside afforded magnificent walks and the isolation was perfect. There was an enclosed field for Leo to practise his football skills and his kennel was quite pleasant to sit in. That was a fabulous summer. At last I had hope for Leo, and he was housed in comfort.

Of course, for every up on life's rollercoaster there's a down. A meeting had been called by the behaviourist who'd been seeing Leo, and at that meeting I finally met the woman to whom I owed Leo's safety. In her sixties, Pat Senior was small but she blazed with determination. As she took her seat alongside me and a few other people from Leo's old sanctuary, I was glad she was on our side.

Given what had happened at the sanctuary, what followed shouldn't have surprised me. This thin beanpole of a behaviourist had been asked to assess Leo on the basis that he suffered from aggression brought on by his fear of men, traffic and crowds; so as a part of her investigation she'd taken him to a shopping centre, a busy street and a park. Everything that Leo most feared abounded in those places, so he'd become scared and responded aggressively. Now the beanpole was judging Leo without having bothered to see him at his best. She lectured us as though she were a teacher and we were children.

"Leo may not be re-homed with men or other dogs, or in a busy place," she concluded.

"What a brilliant insight!" I thought. "If you don't like curry, don't eat in an Indian restaurant."

The beanpole brought nothing to the meeting except arrogance.

"The work we'd have to put into him to bring him round might be more than we're willing to do, so we should think about putting him down," she said.

She'd reckoned without Pat.

"Put him down?" Pat jumped to her feet. "I've had over thirty-five years of experience with dogs and I've never put a healthy dog to sleep in my life!"

An argument ensued between Pat and Mandy, which became personal. We'd learned that Mandy hadn't used all the money I'd given her for the behaviourist *on* the behaviourist. There was tension because the alleged two months proved only to be six weeks. The build-up to the argument between those two friends was painful to watch, like a car crash; you know it's about to happen but there's nothing you can do to stop it. There was no resolving the animosity between them. The argument ended with Pat walking out, the rest of us being thrown out, and Leo once again being stuck in kennels that I wasn't allowed to visit.

*

During the following two weeks, Jess, Pat and I racked our brains for ideas about rescuing Leo. Then Pat had an inspiration. At the end of her road was a boarding kennels run by her acquaintance Jean, who had twenty-five years' experience with dogs. It was time to hatch plans for the Great Escape. Pat was the officer in charge, ably assisted by Jean; I was the eager private, keen to do her bit but yet to see battle. I soon received my orders and set out to implement them by contacting Mandy to inquire about Leo.

"It's hopeless," said Mandy. "I've tried to pass him on to other kennels but nobody wants an aggressive dog. But after that meeting a fortnight ago I know there'll be a backlash if I have him put down."

Mandy didn't want Leo staying with her any longer, but she couldn't rehome him or pass him on to another sanctuary because of his aggression. And she knew that if she'd put him to sleep, Pat and I would have had her hanged, drawn and quartered. She was stuck with a dog she could do nothing with.

"Yes," I agreed, "there would be backlash. But if there's no other alternative I'll take him myself. You know he's fine with me."

She hesitated. She wasn't happy with the idea but she couldn't see an alternative.

"I know how close you are to Leo," she said at last, "so I'll release him to you – but *nobody* else. You're to keep him yourself. He is *not* to go to Pat!"

Her response seemed to be more about power than care for Leo, but naturally I agreed. Phase One of the Great Escape Plan was completed. Then I phoned Pat.

"Right, Lucina," she said, "You take Leo from the kennels and we'll get him into Jean's kennels for the time being while we work with him."

"OK, Pat. Can we do it? Can we rehabilitate him?"

"We're going to have a damned good try!"

Phase Two. I went to Chester with renewed hope and Leo was delighted to see his old friend and be broken out of jail. He leapt into my car without a second thought. I drove him to Pat's house in a green-belt district of Bolton and together we took him for a walk before delivering him to Jean's kennels. Boarding kennels weren't our first choice, but Jean gave us a good weekly price for keeping him there. His new home wasn't as plush as the one he'd just left, but it wouldn't be permanent. And at least I could now see him.

I settled him in before I left. It was heart-wrenching that this vulnerable soul was being forced to go through yet another change. Yet despite the barking from the other dogs he seemed calm, as if my presence soothed him. Pat and I knew he hated being in kennels, but this was our last chance with him. If we couldn't help him this time, the only kindness left would be to have him put down. As my eyes met Leo's I made a promise:

"One way or another, Leo, I swear you'll never have to stay in kennels again after this."

To this day I remember the look he gave me. I'm sure he knew what I meant, right down to his soul. It is one of my greatest joys that I was able to keep that promise.

Six weeks of hard work lay ahead, but we agreed Leo was worth it. The first part of Pat's strategy was to help him to feel trusted.

"We ditch the muzzle and lengthen his lead," she decided. "You can't truss a dog up and restrict it like that. If you expect the worst from a dog, that's exactly what you'll get!"

He responded immediately, showing slightly less aggression on his walks. This was only the first step on a long road, but in showing Leo trust we were making progress. At times it was difficult to say which of us was in greater need of Pat's training: Leo needed my help, but I needed to be shown how best to help him.

From that day forth I walked Leo three times a week, often taking him for miles. Gradually I started to introduce him to busier places while allowing him to walk on a longer lead. There were some splendid walks near Pat's house, coincidentally the land over which I regularly flew: rolling hills, lakes and ponds. He no longer showed nervous aggression but became more and more like a normal dog. He enjoyed his walks, sniffing at things of interest, exploring everything in his path. There were tricky moments, especially to begin with; both Pat and her husband Charles were bitten. But we were committed to the cause and refused to yield to setbacks.

The next step was to introduce Leo to other dogs, starting with just one and then progressing to more. He was nervous, but it gradually became easier until it was second nature. I'd learned to be less stressed around him and he fed on my newfound confidence. We were like a team in training and we were starting to see results. Pat treated Leo just as she would any other animal and he responded favourably.

At last the day arrived to introduce Leo to Pat's house and the twenty-two dogs of all shapes and sizes that lived there. To begin with he was terrified, dropping to the floor, unwilling to move. But with time and encouragement, each visit brought more success. In the end he'd venture into the yard behind the house of his own volition and was happy with the other dogs around him. It was an amazing breakthrough, incredible to watch. Over the weeks, Leo spent more and more time at Pat's house until he had no reason to leave. At last he was free of kennels and had a home of his own, a life he could enjoy rather than endure.

One day Pat took in a puppy that had been abandoned, a little black Staffie with bits of white on his paws and chest. It seemed he'd been hit over the head and as a result he was obviously brain-damaged. When Leo first saw him he was curious and wouldn't stop following him around. His fascination became more like protection, and he took to standing over the pup to ensure he never got hurt. He was more like a mother to him; amazing to see. Eventually, Pat found a good home for the little dog and Leo was quite sad. What a turn-around, though, for a once aggressive dog.

For the next four years I travelled to Pat's every Monday and took Leo out into the country. We liked to walk through farms and across meadows. He'd taken a real shine to playing in water. It was much easier for me, knowing how well he was cared for. I rejoiced in the life he now had. Seeing how far he'd come, I couldn't have been prouder. We'd shared a memorable journey and together we'd learned to adapt.

He grew to love Pat and Charles, but when I was visiting it was as if nobody else existed. He followed me everywhere. If I went out he waited beside the door for my return. I'd stuck by him through thick and thin and he loved me for it. We'd become best friends for life.

*

Towards the end of 2014 Leo became ill and slowed down. You always hope at such times, but deep down you know better. The blood tests proved what I already knew: my friend would be gone before Christmas. Yet even when he became very ill, he still lit up when I visited. I took him in my car to visit his favourite places and did all I could to ensure he still had a chance to play in the water.

In the end he went peacefully. I'm glad he knew he was loved. He held a special place in my heart, and when he died he took part of me with him. Sometimes there's a bond that can't be replaced. Leo was more than a dog; he was a friend, loyal and true. I'll always miss him.

Chapter 18

Life is a rollercoaster. I've used the metaphor before; it's a cliché, but it's true. Every time you attain the heady heights of success you're sent plunging downward to some new calamity, knuckles white and heart racing. I sometimes think the author of life's book of mysteries has a warped sense of humour. Couldn't the writing be made a bit less dramatic from time to time?

It was a day much like any other in my Chamber. One of the Mistresses who sometimes rents the dungeon was warming the bottom of a client. Rhythmical slaps echoed from the cold stone of the Chamber walls, counterpointed by occasional groans. BDSM can be many things but it's seldom quiet, and noise carries from even the lightest spanking.

Meanwhile, I was pottering around reception next door to the dungeon, daydreaming and carefree. My mind sailed far from the damp grey Manchester day to a walk in the woods, and then to the Thai jungle and my beloved elephants. The stress of business, the pain of losing the closest of friends, and even the fire, were left far behind. I prepared to swim with the elephants in the river, the water warmed by the tropical summer. It was perfection. The winter in my heart was thawed.

After the papers had kindly published a photo of the entrance to the Chamber I'd become cautious about answering knocks on the door, but on this occasion the second knock was accompanied by a familiar voice. (Since then I've had a camera fitted for safety reasons.)

"It's me, Lucina. Tony."

Tony was the caretaker of the mill, not my submissive client with the same name, and like Andy the manager he'd taken a liking to me.

"You give me less bother than any of the others around here," he told me. Tony was in his sixties and appeared dazed and slow-moving, but he always got jobs done, and always to a high standard. He was garrulous, so I had to avoid chatting to him if I was in a hurry, but he was invariably good-natured and considerate. Sometimes he knocked on the door to tell me there was post for me to collect in Reception or that he'd found some item he thought I might be able to use, such as an old chair to tie slaves to or a piece of foam that could be turned into a kneeling mat.

Today he'd come to tell me about a visitor. An official-looking woman had asked where I could be found and he'd said, "Oh, yes, I know where she is, I'll show you". (Thanks, Tony!) So when I opened the door it was to see Tony standing on the threshold with a fresh-faced young woman, her demeanour innocent and agreeable.

"There she is," said Tony, and disappeared.

Meanwhile, the gentle spanking in the dungeon had segued into noisier punishment. Obviously my colleague's client had been a naughty boy. My visitor's eyes dilated. She blushed.

"Good morning. Can I help you?" I asked.

"Er... Lucina White?"

"Yes?"

Thwack went the sound from the dungeon.

"I... Oh dear... I'm Patricia Hodges. I'm from the Council."

The client's response to the *thwack* was half-groan, half-yelp. What was Mistress using, cane, crop or flogger? Cane, by the sound of it. More to the point, what did Patricia Hodges want with me? If she'd been a client she wouldn't have announced she was from the Council.

Thwack, thwack. This time the client's response was more yelp than groan. Ms Hodges lifted her hand to her mouth, trying to stifle laughter. Her blush deepened. Glaring at her and wondering to what depths the rollercoaster was about to plunge me this time, I wanted the ground to open under my feet. Whatever her business, the noises from the dungeon weren't making things easy for either her or me.

"Please sit down," I invited. "What do the Council want?"

She perched on the edge of the sofa, tense as a fiddle string.

"I'm afraid it's come to light that you don't have the correct planning permission, Ms White."

"Planning permission?"

Why should I need planning permission to fill an old cellar with a few bits of equipment? I didn't wish to build a house or extend one, or plonk a supermarket on green belt land. I wondered whether I should have obtained planning permission before admitting some of my more obese clients to the Chamber. I've met large gentlemen who oughtn't to be allowed inside some buildings without planning permission because of the risk of structural damage. But that probably wasn't what Patricia had in mind.

"You have to have planning permission for any premises when there's been a change in use," she explained.

Thwack! Hmm. It sounded as though Mistress was now using a different weapon. A flogger, if I wasn't mistaken.

"No, please, mercy!" cried a male voice from the dungeon.

I wanted to utter the same plea. Even turning a dusty old cellar into a BDSM parlour required planning permission, did it? What bureaucratic swamp was sucking me into its murky depths this time? It had been a wretched few years and Patricia was bringing me yet more bad news. She reacted to the expression on my face like the proverbial rabbit in headlights. I wondered whether she'd have enjoyed being strapped to my St Andrew's cross. However, she seemed a nice young woman.

"There – there won't be any prejudice against your – er – profession," she assured me. "You're not breaking any laws, so you'll get a fair hearing."

The phrase that sprang to mind here was *non sequitur*. I'd never knowingly broken any law. I'd never harmed or defrauded anyone. However, the magistrate's court hearing after the fire had scarred my memory. My tax returns were honest and I always paid what was due, though despite my entitlement as a United Kingdom citizen to professional assistance with my accounts, an accountant had dropped me from his list *because of the work I did*. If he'd dropped me because of my sexual orientation or the colour of my skin there'd have been a public outcry, but because I was a Dominatrix there was silence. I'd also had a bank close my account for the same reason; and as I said earlier, no insurance company would give me cover. If I'd run a strip club or opened a 'massage parlour', which as everyone knows is a euphemism for a brothel, almost any insurance company would have offered me a policy. This is the kind of prejudice that drives the BDSM scene underground. Yet here was Patricia, assuring me that because I hadn't broken the law I'd get a fair unbiased hearing. Amazingly, and despite all my experience, I believed her. She was warm and friendly.

"You're not in trouble for not applying for planning permission, but we didn't know you were here until we saw you in the papers," she said.

"I contacted the Council when I first opened here," I said, "to make them aware of the premises and to apply for my business rates discount."

She shook her head. "Different department. Your application will be judged on – er – well..."

Thwack, thwack, thwack!

"Yeeeoowww!"

The client was enjoying himself. Probably Mistress was, too. I wasn't.

"Yes? My application will be judged on what?"

"Er – well, such things as the hours you work, how much parking you use, the noise your premises generate..."

Thwack, thwack!

"Noooo! Mercy, Mistress, please!"

I wished the Mistress would gag that client or inflict a quieter torture. Both Patricia and I were trying to pretend that the background noise wasn't happening and neither of us mentioned it, but neither of us could help smirking.

"Nothing to do with the fact that my profession is part of the sex industry?" I prompted.

"Oh, no, no, certainly –"

There was an even louder *thwack* followed by a shrill scream from the dungeon. I thought Patricia was about to faint. In the event, she collected herself admirably.

"I'll send a form for you to complete and return to the planning office. There's no reason why you'd be turned down, but if – er – if there are any problems I'll let you know."

Under the circumstances she'd held herself together very well and maintained her professional manner throughout. Now, perhaps relieved that I hadn't used her bottom for target practice, she scurried away and left me with yet another crisis to solve. Once again, it seemed, I was guilty of breaking rules I hadn't known existed. How many laws do each of us innocently break every day? We don't know, do we? We're too busy being ignorant.

*

The promised form arrived with its myriad of questions, so detailed and complex that it was hard to see how anyone could provide all of the information requested. It asked not only for all the details about my unit but also for the whole building! I wondered at the need for so much red tape. Andy came down to the Chamber one afternoon to help. It took us two hours to go over all the questions. Even he was scratching his head at some of them.

"I'm going to have to see if I can find the blueprint to answer that one!"

Why can't the powers that be make things more comprehensible? The Council were surprisingly helpful, though. They guided me through the sections I needed to complete and identified the ones that could be binned, so with time and after more than a little frustration I managed to submit my application (together with the hefty fee). The rollercoaster had climbed again; another crisis over. I could sit back and return to my Thai jungle daydream.

Or so I thought. I should have known better. Fate always delivers the biggest kicks when you're on the floor and struggling to get back on your feet.

Weeks passed after I'd submitted the application before I heard anything. I'd been told it would be quite straightforward. I guessed they were busy, but the silence seemed ominous. I knew something was wrong.

Patricia's voice on the phone was nervous. Her muddled pile of words conveyed her message before she'd achieved any sort of coherence. One single seven-letter word said it all: *problem*. I could almost hear her blushing again.

Of course, it was all quite simple. The first rule of bureaucracy is: never make a decision if you can find a reason not to. The second rule is: if you can't find a reason, pass the buck. Unable to find a reason in my case, the planning committee had passed it to the councillors, who might now refer it to the planning office. Apparently, although it's politically incorrect to show discrimination, it isn't good for one's career to grant permission for a disused cellar to be turned into a *dungeon*. Instead, one should refuse to allow a straightforward planning application where all criteria have been met. I was tempted to ask whether Patricia's superiors knew how to spell 'hypocrisy'.

Her tone was sympathetic. She seemed aware of the hypocrisy. I could tell she'd rather not have to give me this information. But I struggled to get my head around what she was saying.

"So I'm not being given planning permission, am I?"

"It hasn't been granted right now. It's been passed on. The trouble is, Lucina," she continued, "there's one councillor who doesn't want you there."

Then she openly admitted the Council's duplicity. She didn't mince her words and even though they weren't what I wanted to hear I appreciated her honesty. I sighed, very disheartened.

"What happens next?" I asked. "Should I expect a load of legal jargon penalising my profession – without, of course, showing discrimination? Numerous forms to complete? Long waits? Lots of opportunities for the tabloid press to feast on my latest misfortune?"

"No, no more forms," Patricia assured me. "We just have to post a notice outside your... your Chamber giving notification of your planned – er – refurbishment, and then the Council will ask neighbouring residents and companies if they have any objections."

"I see. And if they do object?"

"Well, if there are more than four objections, the case will be referred to the planning office. I'll come to your Chamber when it suits you and explain in full."

She duly visited, no longer nervous, and there were no dungeon noises in the background this time. She happily accepted a coffee.

"As I told you, Lucina," she said, "the planning committee didn't want to make the decision so they passed your application on to the councillors. If there are more than four negative responses from the neighbours, the councillors can refuse planning permission on those grounds alone. Actually, 'neighbours' can include anyone resident in Stockport."

It was an easy way out for them, I supposed. If any four people living anywhere in Stockport, even miles away from my Chamber, decided they didn't want me there, they could object. Did that seem fair?

"But I thought the committee weren't allowed to turn me down purely because of what I do, only if I'm committing a public nuisance," I argued.

"Doing it this way they can," she said, still very sympathetic.

"How long will the neighbours be given to lodge their objections?"

"Twenty-eight days."

It wasn't just the possibility of objections from 'neighbours', it seemed. If just one councillor wished to scupper my business, he could go a long way towards doing so. Despite all I'd been through to rebuild after the fire, I might be forced to move and start again because one gentleman at the Council had taken exception to my presence in the business park and would move heaven and earth to have me removed. Of course, no harm had befallen the moral fibre of my small corner of Greater Manchester during the years he hadn't known about me, but I was no longer out of sight and therefore not out of mind.

"The problem the Council have," Patricia repeated, "is that you haven't done anything wrong. You comply with all the regulations and there's no obvious reason for refusing your application on the basis of anything you're doing. If you're refused permission for the change of use of your premises without a good reason, you can appeal. The appeal goes to a completely separate body, independent of Stockport. If you win the appeal, the Council will have to pay you compensation. So they have to be very careful, Lucina."

I could read between the lines of that assurance. The only way the Council could beat me was to stir up public opinion against me. Sure enough, within hours of Patricia's visit, the *Manchester Evening News* had learned that their favourite Dominatrix was having a few planning issues, so it was their duty to inform the world. *Dominatrix Applies for Planning Permission*, it said, once again using the awful court picture I'd grown to hate so much.

Throughout the twenty-eight day consultation period that followed I was subjected to relentless media attention: newsflashes on BBC Radio Two, coverage in a host of local and national newspapers, and so on. The Council also ensured my loss of privacy by publishing my home address on their website, which I understood was common practice. Wonderful, when I'd already been pestered by a stalker and had my previous flat burgled! However, when I contacted a lady from the planning office and explained my situation to her and how dangerous it could be to make my address public, she understood immediately and said she'd take it off. Within fifteen minutes my address was gone. So despite their infuriating bureaucracy, the Council behaved decently. Curiously, however, I discovered from the planning permission page on the Council website that the only application for change of use from the entire mill, apart from mine, had been to widen the gates!

Nevertheless, the barrage of requests for press interviews continued. There were impromptu photo opportunities and another invitation to appear on the Jeremy Kyle show, which once again I declined. The crystal waters of my Thai river daydream were tainted with blood and filled with the flashing teeth of sharks.

*

Even this dark cloud had the proverbial silver lining. My business was booming thanks to the free blanket advertising provided by the national dailies. One letter to the Council, which Patricia kindly shared with me, had come from a gentleman who, having learned of my services from the press coverage, would now make an appointment to visit me. And the twenty-eight days of consultation elicited not a single complaint about my business. Indeed, while my planning application was under review, many neighbouring companies and residents openly championed me. The general view was that if I paid my taxes and operated within the law I should be left alone to grow my business. I was, and remain, very grateful for their support.

I was told that Council representatives had been up and down the street knocking on doors, going into several units.

"Do you know what goes on over there?" they'd asked.

Much to their surprise, they discovered that everyone knew and no-one cared. Nobody had a bad word to say. Residents in nearby houses who hadn't known about me didn't care either. All the effort to stir up dirt against me failed.

"It was the topic of conversation in my local pub the other night," one client told me. "I couldn't admit I knew you or that I'd been in the dungeon, but all the chatter was positive. *Who'd have known there was a dungeon there? But you know what? Good for her. Let her get on with it. What's the big deal with things like that these days? What's all the fuss about?'* It was great!"

I was a little surprised by my own feelings and how my attitude had changed, but it was a case of straws and camels' backs. I'd tried for years to be discreet. I'd held my hands up when I was in the wrong. I'd admitted my responsibility for the fire. I'd been discriminated against by my accountant, the banks and the insurance companies. Now I was being discriminated against by the Council. I'd had enough! If my planning application was turned down I'd appeal and I'd fight it right to the top. I'd no longer apologise for what I do and who I am.

In the words of my accountant, "We simply don't understand your business enough, Lucina". *Their* ignorance, *their* discrimination against us, is seemingly acceptable! Is it any surprise that most Mistresses stay under the radar to avoid all the legal barriers and hassles? The BDSM world is vast. Those who take part in it aren't freaks. Most are good honest taxpayers, yet we're branded as some kind of untouchables. The branders, the stereotypers, are wrong. We're not bad, dangerous people. Enough! I had my war paint on, my thigh-high boots set, and I was ready.

"If it's a fight you want," I decided, "it's a fight you'll get! Why should I always get a raw deal because of my business? I'm here, so accept me. If you don't, I won't go away quietly, and certainly not without a fight!"

In the end, there was no fight. The councillor who'd attempted to have me referred to the planning office missed his own deadline to do so. He did lodge an objection but it was one day too late. Even Patricia found that amusing. Should his tardiness have earned him an appointment in my Chamber? Maybe he'd already paid me a visit, having germinated a new fantasy through reflecting on my occupation. It's a cliché, but often true, that those who protest most are those with most to hide. If you're out there, Mr Councillor – you know who you are – please feel free to call me if you'd like to be taught the error of your ways.

*

In December I received a phone call from the planning office. Patricia was on holiday. The caller sounded like the lady who'd taken my address off the website.

"Just to tell you, Lucina, your planning permission has been passed. Basically," she continued, "the councillors couldn't find any reason not to grant it so they passed it back to us and we've granted everything for you now. A letter's been sent to you but you won't get it until New Year. I wanted to give you peace of mind so you can relax over Christmas".

She hadn't needed to make that call. I thought it was a lovely gesture and appreciated it. Indeed, everyone on the Council I dealt with had been more than helpful. I'm sure they have their own red tape to deal with and I doubt if they like it any more than the rest of us do.

In fact, the letter arrived a few days before Christmas. Both the Health and Safety and Environmental Health departments had passed my application and there hadn't been a single objection to my business. My application had also been assessed by a gentleman whose purpose was to determine whether a business brings any economic advantage to any given area. In his judgment I'd made a substantial financial investment, converting a disused and shabby cellar into a working business environment.

Fate sometimes plays a hand that at first seems cruel but later proves beneficial. Had I not had the fire in my Chamber I wouldn't have made such a big investment. Furthermore, I would probably have failed to obey the Council's Health and Safety rules so my planning application could legitimately have been refused. Of course, when my planning permission finally arrived early in January, not a single newspaper ran the story. Consider: which headline would sell more papers, *Dominatrix Seeks Planning Permission for Seedy Sex Den* or *Successful Businesswoman Gets Planning Permission for New Premises*?

We learn from all life's experiences. The leaking of the news about my planning application had taught me a valuable lesson about advertising. Having been highlighted so often for the wrong reasons, I now wanted the world to know about my victory. As I said, my attitude had changed. It's amazing how much attention a single innocuous tweet can draw if it's tagged to the right people. Just tagging the *Manchester Evening News* into the tweet had the right effect, but even I was surprised by the mass of the response. Of course, the *M.E.N.* chose to use 'that' picture again, but with a small difference: this time I didn't look as though I was chewing a wasp. They selected one where I had a little grin. (Still with bad hair, though.) Even more surprising were the kind and supportive comments to the press by the Council. According to the published reports I'd gone from being a potential danger to local business to being, and I quote, *just what the area needs*;

or, as the *Daily Telegraph* put it, "She is good for the local economy". I was also heartened by the many e-mails I received from others in the BDSM scene. It was wonderful how many like-minded souls came together to support my cause during my difficulties. We promote the virtue of being neighbourly and helping others. The actions of those within the scene who rallied to my defence indicate that they're decent people with strong moral values.

The publicity that my Dominatrix activities earned will have been worthwhile if encourages greater understanding of those seeking to meet their genuine need for submission. For me, it remains an honour to be able to help meet such needs.

Chapter 19

I've always loved wolves, but who doesn't? From my earliest memories to the present day they've been special for me. Their eyes and the sound of their howls have enchanted me for as long as I can remember. There's something primeval about these most enigmatic of creatures, their allure enhanced by their places in Native American and European folklore. They're powerful animals, revered for their beauty and venerated for their spiritual presence, but they're dangerous and their gaze can pierce you to the core. There's something different, perhaps alien, about them. To the Norse, the wolf was adulated to the point of apotheosis. Japanese farmers left gifts of leftover food near dens in order to thank the wolves for protecting their crops. Turks and Mongols believed wolves to be their ancestors. Greeks and Romans associated them with the sun god Apollo or Phoebus. Interestingly, studies conducted in 1993 revealed a mere 0.2% genetic divergence between the grey wolf and the domestic dog. The domestic dog was accordingly reclassified as a subspecies of the grey wolf instead of a species in its own right.

There are those who think it right to persecute these magnificent beasts. *Little Red Riding Hood* and the *Three Little Pigs* are just two of the many tales that portray the wolf as a villain and a creature to fear. In the Bible, the wolf symbolises greed and destruction. Tolstoy and Chekhov wrote of wolves attacking livestock and people. Dante presented them as servants of the Devil. In England, wolves were culled to extinction; by the reign of Henry VIII they'd been wiped from the landscape, never to reappear. In many older cartoon films for children, especially Disney films, they were portrayed as bloodthirsty, which made the children afraid of them. Sometimes seen as pests, feared as predators and often misunderstood, wolves have not always been dealt the kindest of hands. From Christian condemnation of them as evil to hunters who kill them in their thousands for trophies or to sell their skins, the persecution of wolves is another example of human greed and stupidity. Wolves are family-orientated and kill only for food, protection or territory. When they mate they mate for life. If one of the pair dies it is very rare for the other to find a new mate. They simply grieve for the rest of their lives.

Nevertheless, despite every human attempt to wipe them off the face of the Earth, their numbers are recovering. I've always taken a keen interest in conservation and have watched with excitement as efforts to support populations of wolves have succeeded around the world. In Yellowstone Park, wolves have been reintroduced to the wild and are once again thriving, their population growing. People are encouraged to visit and learn about the animals, but they're prohibited from interacting directly with them. The wolves must be enabled to live and breed as wild animals and retain their natural mistrust of humans. There are similar projects in other parts of the globe, each doing its part to ensure this wonderful animal does not become another relic in a dusty museum. However, there are difficulties. For example, the scheme to reintroduce wolves to a remote part of the Scottish Highlands was side-lined when angry farmers declared they'd shoot the animals on sight.

*

I respect the policy that people shouldn't be permitted direct interaction with wolves and I agree with it, but it makes it hard to experience them in a personal way, which was my dream. However, some sanctuaries offer a dispensation. In Mexico, some interaction is permitted. Even there, great care is taken to ensure the animals' protection. Volunteers must serve a month's probation, building fences and digging ditches, before coming even close to a wolf. They have to show their commitment before they're trusted. I agree unreservedly with that policy. The prospect of two months in Mexico seemed irresistible, but my responsibilities made it impractical. Tempted though I was, it would have been financially challenging – and because I had Charlie, impossible. (At that time, Charlie had been in my life for two months.)

However, searching through the internet one evening for wolf sanctuaries and conservation, I found a website for a small sanctuary in Ontario, USA. The heading grabbed my attention: 'One of the only sanctuaries in the world where you can touch a wolf'. I was fascinated. I checked to ensure the sanctuary was genuine and legal, and thought, "This is for me". So I e-mailed them. A very good friend was happy to look after Charlie for me while I was away.

"I'm travelling from England. Where's the nearest hotel?"

You'd expect such an organisation to be flooded with enquiries and their rooms booked for months ahead. In fact, the sanctuary didn't offer accommodation; only day visits were offered. Moreover, I discovered that they never reply to e-mails and hardly ever answer their telephone. They had no Wifi, being in the middle of the desert, so their e-mails were picked up by a relative who lived miles away. I phoned, but reception was awful and neither of us could make out what the other was saying. I later learned that their cell phone was carried around in the back pocket of a very large lady who seldom answered it. The sanctuary isn't run as a business; it's a passion to be shared with those with a genuine interest.

Having received no confirmation e-mail, not even certain that the place existed, I decided to go anyway and booked my travel tickets. At least I hadn't had to pay the sanctuary in advance. At worst I'd have a holiday in America and an adventure I could recount in old age. At best I'd fulfil a lifelong dream and interact with a wolf before returning to the UK. In either event I'd be doing it on my own. It was exciting.

*

Indeed, just planning the trip was exciting. I'd never been to America on my own so it was a huge adventure. I had to check I had all the correct papers, visas etc. The attack on the Twin Towers was still a vivid memory so security had become very strict and intense. I flew the long haul to Atlanta airport and had to go through massive checks. Then there was a train ride to another terminal, which was huge and extremely busy. Fortunately, I'd allowed myself lots of time, so once I'd found my departure gate I could go for a coffee. You'd think my accent would have blended into insignificance in such a big international airport, but an amazing number of people were interested and asked where I was from.

When my flight was called I went through the departure gate and on to a much smaller plane. This flight would only be a couple of hours. As I took my seat I heard a 'meow' and looked round: there was a woman with a cat on her knee, and another woman carrying a dog. "This is fantastic!" I smiled. I hadn't known that some internal flights in America allow passengers to carry pets.

By the time the plane landed and I collected my bags it was 10 p.m. local time and I was very tired. I'd decided to hire a car. I was a little nervous because I'd never driven in the USA before, but I'd ensured the car had a sat nav. When I picked up my keys from the rental office, the woman serving me acted as though she'd never heard an English accent before. She was even more fascinated than the people who'd quizzed me at Atlanta airport.

Off I went. The motel I'd booked was only a couple of miles away and luckily the journey was all on the highway. Even luckier for me, it wasn't busy, so the wrong manoeuvres I made through driving on the unaccustomed side of the road caused no harm. I loved the excitement, doing all this on my own.

Ontario is surrounded by mountains, not far from the Nevada desert. My motel wasn't grand but it was only a place to rest my head for the night. I went into the tiny reception, where an oldish guy sat with sleepy eyes. I don't think he'd been busy because he didn't look stimulated. He gave me my keys and directions to my room on the 2nd floor of a tiny block. I made my way up. It was pitch black, no lights at all, and as I went to open the door I felt vulnerable. I made sure all of my doors were secured that night. The place made me uneasy. It seemed like the Bates Motel.

The next morning I rose early, had my shower and went for breakfast, filled with renewed excitement and determination to meet a wolf. I'd slept surprisingly soundly considering the unsettling accommodation. The sun was shining and the air was mild, though crisp and fresh. I drove to the highway from Ontario and looked up at the hills glistening around me, taking in the small businesses and shops as I drove down the street. People's lives in different parts of the world fascinate me. They're an integral part of every adventure.

This was unfamiliar territory, where tomatoes are tomate-ohs, basil is baze-il, and don't even get me started on the rest. As for directions I'd been given in my very scant communications from the wolf sanctuary, they were clear if a little odd. I was told to follow the highway until I passed a certain junction. This was easy; my car's sat-nav proved invaluable. After that it became trickier. I must follow a narrow road until I came to a large cactus, then look for a sign to Sun Valley, where I should turn left. I'm not good at directions at the best of times, but this was exciting. If I got lost I'd have to go back to the Bates Motel.

I live and work in the rain-drenched urban bustle of Greater Manchester. You don't find much in the way of desert and cacti in the busy streets of Stockport, though in northern England we too have our particular twists on the English language. Anyway, I proceeded from small town *Hicksville* into the sweltering heat of the desert guided only by faith. But when Fate wishes you success, nothing can bar your way. There, before me, I was amazed to see a large cactus. Actually, it was the only cactus around. It stood out like a huge green man with upturned arms. Just after it was the sign to Sun Valley. I couldn't believe it! I turned left on to the tiny dirt track and followed signs to the sanctuary. At times I wondered whether I was still on the road or had deviated from it and was now heading to nowhere, but Fate continued to smile and I reached my destination.

*

My host greeted me, a mad but likeable lady whose genes were half (or less) white and half (or more) Native American. She'd never met anyone from England before and was astonished that I'd travelled so far *just* to see a wolf. She had been awaiting my arrival keenly. I'm sure I seemed as foreign to her as this great land and its people did to me.

"This is Lucina and she is from England," she said, proud to have a visitor from so far away.

The wolf sanctuary was a plot of sand amidst the endless expanse of desert. My host resided in a large trailer. She shared it with every cat in the State. These animals had all been rescued from dog-baiting rings and cared for with the tireless generosity that characterised her. Having spent the previous night in a motel from a horror movie, I was now to be wedged into a tiny caravan a short distance from my host's trailer and her feline herd. It didn't matter; jetlag had taken hold so I could have slept in a cage with a bear. When you start to doze and dream while you're still walking to your bed, it matters not where you fall to slumber! A long hot soak in a whirlpool spa before luxuriating between delicate sheets of Egyptian cotton with my head upon a pillow of down would have been nice, but I knew it wasn't going to happen. Tiny though it was, with its small bed fitted into the kitchen area, my caravan had its own toilet and I was comfortable. I like being cosy. "Yes," I thought, "this will do me for a few nights." Most importantly, I was close to the wolves. I was probably sleeping about twenty feet from the nearest one.

The wolves were dotted around the trailers, all housed in tailor-made compounds of various sizes. Two full-time staff lived and worked at the sanctuary, assisting my host in a range of tasks. I'd always assumed that a sanctuary such as this must be focussed on protecting animals that would otherwise have been hunted, not on top predators. I was to learn that wolves were also victims of persecution here.

Believe it or not, it's common in these parts for wolf pups to be stolen from the wild and sold as guard dogs. They're tied to the outside of a trailer, fed scraps and given no opportunity to socialise. Some fully-grown wolves in the sanctuary had such histories; previously, they'd known little other than the cruelty of life in seclusion. Wolves are highly social in the wild, usually living in packs of up to eleven animals, so those forced into a solitary existence have no opportunity to develop the traits chacteristic of their species. It would have been a bad idea for me to come face to face with such animals, powerful adult wolves with full sets of teeth and little idea of how to behave around people. I don't mean they're likely to disguise themselves as your favourite grandmother and devour girls wearing red cloaks, but they could easily jump on you or take a playful bite at your extremities, and neither option would be pleasant. Wolves play rough and don't understand how fragile humans are. Even those animals stolen as pups and forced into lives of solitary servitude can still behave as instinct dictates, not as 'man's best friend'. So it wasn't possible to interact directly with some of them. However, it was permissible with others, though always with care.

Each day I sat beside the fence of one of the compounds getting to know the animals. If wolves lay close enough to the perimeter I'd do the same, poking my hand through the wire fencing and stroking them while they slept. Sitting outside the enclosure and being so close to a wolf, even with bars, was amazing. As they became used to me, one in particular would come to lie beside the fence as close to me as she could. I lay beside her with only the thin mesh between us and stroked her tummy or the back of her neck. We trusted each other.

I'll never forget the first time I came face to face with a wolf without a fence between us. It was in a large compound housing three huge white wolves. Of course, like the angler telling of former glories, I've sensed those animals growing larger in my memory as time has passed. Nevertheless, when you're up close and very personal with a mass of fur, teeth and muscle, you can be forgiven for losing some perspective.

I didn't make this journey alone; my host entered the compound with me. Before I entered, she said:

"Go sit on those logs at the far end of the enclosure and wait for the wolves to come to you. If they do, be submissive." (Irony again!) "The difference between making a friend and losing a hand is subtle. If you pat a wolf on top of the head it's likely to end badly. Tickle it under the chin and all will be well."

Suddenly I was vulnerable. There was no fence to protect me. My host was close at hand, but she couldn't have done much if things had gone wrong. One of the three wolves approached and for a moment I had some sense of what it would be like to be prey. Under those circumstances you have to trust that the wolf will take a liking to you. I've always believed that a wolf looks deeper than we can, into your heart and soul, and knows who you are; just as I'd felt with the elephants in Thailand. I knew they'd taken dislikes to some people in the past, but I thought the best option was to relax and be myself. They'd know how much love I felt for them.

Indeed, the animal seemed more inquisitive than aggressive and within moments it was sniffing at my clothes. Not wishing to lose an arm, I broke the habit of a lifetime and submitted to this beautiful beast. Moments later I received a very wet kiss. The wolf stroked its huge wet tongue across my face as a sign of affection.

*

I spent a wonderful week at the sanctuary. During that time I came to know many of the wolves. In one pen were three naughty pups. They hadn't yet been socialised but were entirely approachable. They loved visits from people and loved still more to play practical jokes. While one acted as a decoy, distracting you from the front, the other two would sneak up behind and bite playfully at your bottom. Each day ended with my tired head lying gently on a pillow. About five o'clock on the following morning a chorus of howls would rise, penetrating my dreams before I woke and realised the sound was real. To hear a wolf pack serenading the rising sun is truly spiritual. There's something magical about it. It was a glorious way to be wakened. I felt at one with Nature. "You can keep your five star hotels," I thought. "I wouldn't have swapped this for the world." I rose before anyone else to say, "Good morning", and the wolves always looked so happy to see me.

In one of the largest pens lived a big alpha male accompanied by an equally big female. People weren't generally permitted to enter this enclosure, but an exception was to be made for me. What an honour! The owner had become fond of me and let me get away with things that other visitors might not.

"You have a bond with the wolves," she said, "and they feel the same. You have a certain way with them."

"It's no big secret," I thought, "I simply love them. What they feel for me in return is love."

It's hard to explain the mixture of emotions that take hold at such times: excitement fuelled my nervous energy while fear hid in the shadows. These were huge animals, two hundred and fifty pounds of pure muscle wrapped in fur and equipped with teeth. Their warnings had to be respected.

"The male's very protective of his mate," my host told me. "When you enter, let them come to you. Always ensure that you stay lower than the female. If there's any sign of trouble, back away, but don't run. And don't turn your back on the animals."

That's easier said than done when you have hundreds of pounds of concentrated predator bearing down on you. A growl could mean that the wolf wished to be fussed, but could equally mean it was planning the dinner menu. I wouldn't be waiting around to find out!

My briefing over, I stepped through the gate and stood next to a rather large platform. My heart was pounding so loudly I feared the wolves would hear. After only a moment the female jumped on to the platform and stood looking down at me. Had she decided to attack I doubt whether I'd have survived. Instead, she pushed her huge white head into my neck and began to rub against me. It was a moment of complete perfection. I'd been accepted by this mighty animal and the affection she was showing was the greatest honour.

This ritual continued for around ten minutes while her mate slowly circled us. Eventually he too jumped on to the platform. He stood next to her for a few moments looking at me and then started to bare his teeth and growl. At times like that you can bond with an animal. I felt wholly at ease with both wolves; nothing inside me said that his growl was a warning. I would happily have stayed right where I was to see what happened. However, it was not to be. I didn't feel threatened, but my host took the growl and bared teeth as a sign.

"Time for you to leave, Lucina."

I could hear the panic in her voice so I didn't argue. I backed slowly from the pen, my heart racing and my mind filled with memories that will last a lifetime: nights in the caravan, a week spent in the enchanting company of wolves. They are extraordinary animals, each with its own personality. They can be gentle, sometimes even playful, and they can look right into your soul.

When I drove away from the sanctuary, I left a little of my heart in the desert. I returned to the small motel that night as it was growing dark. I found myself stuck in traffic: crowds of people leaving Las Vegas on a Sunday evening after a weekend break. It reminded me of returning from Cumbria on a Sunday and being stuck in Blackpool traffic, though on a much larger scale.

The motel wasn't as sinister this time. I was missing the wolves too much to care. When the plane took off the following day, my heart broke a little.

The memories of that week will never fade. One of the main reasons I haven't been back is that I know it would become harder and harder to leave if I did. As with the elephants, I'd reach a point where I wouldn't go home again. Nevertheless, I hope that one day I'll have a chance to repeat the experience. In the meantime I have Charlie; who is, after all, a subspecies of wolf.

I don't get to see wolves every week, but I still devote Mondays to working with rescue dogs; specifically, the ones Pat continues to house. She's growing older but her dedication to the cause of combating animal cruelty remains undiminished, and her experience, know-how and strong character make her a guide and an inspiration for other dog-lovers. My Monday visits to Pat's establishment are always a spiritual uplift and they recharge my emotional batteries. The following five days focus on my varied array of submissive clients and their different and sometimes surprising needs. I need that uplift and recharge so that I'm able to satisfy their wants – and mine – as fully as they deserve. But the memory of the wolf sanctuary in Ontario will remain with me for the rest of my life.

Chapter 20

As I've said, the BDSM scene is incredibly diverse and for each Dominatrix-slave pair the intensity tends to increase with experience. The more the need is fed, the stronger it becomes. Every thrill leads to the next. Boundaries are made clear and are never broken, though as session follows session and the relationship between Dominatrix and submissive deepens, those boundaries are stretched. It's part of the continuing process of exploration.

Almost every BDSM session is governed by rules to ensure that what takes place is sane, consensual and addresses the slave's needs. It's normal practice to agree a safe word, to be used when the slave reaches his/her limits in whatever activity is taking place. The safe word is necessary because begging and pleading with Mistress to stop can be integral to the session, part of the fun, and will be ignored – or provoke more intense treatment. However, uttered just once, the safe word ends the current activity. Then we move on to something else.

Nevertheless there are extreme areas of the BDSM scene where safe words aren't used. There are players who have ventured so far into their inner beings that they no longer find thrills when they're curbed by rules and agreed limits. A submissive can give himself to the whim of his Mistress within the safe confines of such limits, knowing the general path of the session in advance; he can stop it at any time. But remove those boundaries, take away his right to stop what is being done, and the submissive becomes *truly* a slave to the Mistress's wishes. It's a tightrope walk across a ravine without the comfort of a safety net! As for the Mistress, she can experience power within the prearranged boundaries of any BDSM encounter, but if the boundaries are lifted so she can conduct herself in any way she pleases, she can taste *absolute* power. It lures as a candle flame lures a moth.

BDSM encounters of this kind are called *edge play*. Both parties are fully aware of the risks and consensually choose to participate in activities that could cause harm. This is as far from the social principles and ethics we value as can ever be reached within a BDSM setting. However, for those who find themselves driven to climb higher, jump further and dive deeper, it's a place of honesty where they can be completely themselves, helpless in the face of total loss of liberty.

The activities commonly attempted during edge play include *breath play*, the act of allowing another to control one's breathing, as Chris did with me. I only ever tighten the noose if the slave is in the kneeling position; I like to push boundaries but I have limits; but the genuine risk to life enhances the excitement for some players. Complete trust is absolutely essential for any type of breath play and such activities can only be attempted when you have an established connection with the slave.

There's no greater test of the bond between Mistress and slave than an edge play scenario. There's no room for error; the danger is real and present. Few Dominatrixes and submissives are willing to participate in it, but those who do can become addicted. Edge play is so far removed from the pre-arranged script of a role-play scenario that it's hard to reconcile them both with the single label 'BDSM'. What those two extremes of the continuum have in common is that neither is suitable for the inexperienced, but both are means by which the slave can attain total submission and the Mistress total domination.

"It's crazy!" said one novice Dominatrix. "Can you imagine somebody begging to be hanged by the neck not knowing how it'll end?"

It's surprising how many people have 'execution' fantasies. Sometimes I'm asked to do something so extreme in this area that I have to say "No".

"It isn't common," I said, "but there are people who'll gladly place their lives in your hands in order to prove their ultimate trust."

What begins as a noose placed about one's neck can lead eventually to the rope being tightened. Like all types of BDSM session, edge play evolves. The tightening noose can lead to suspension and the subservient losing consciousness. A Dominatrix who participates in such acts feeds the irrational, frightening appetite of her inner animal. Personally, I've never taken part in suspension or pushed someone into losing consciousness, though I've been asked many times to do it. I always operate within safe and consensual limits. Pushing the boundaries is essential as the Dominatrix-submissive relationship evolves, but I never go too far. Nevertheless, I don't believe I have the right to sit in judgment on regular edge players any more than I have the right to judge people from other cultures. Like the seemingly liberated people of Thailand and the relatively inhibited people of Britain, edge players are what they are, born with individual needs that decades of conditioning have shaped. It's important for them to find Mistresses who'll meet their requirements.

Long experience has made me more willing to entertain the more extreme flavours of BDSM with the right submissives. I understand the dangers involved and how they feed my craving, but it's not something I undertake lightly and wouldn't even consider with a submissive I didn't know well.

*

Chris's main choice of BDSM activity, CBT (cock and ball torture), can involve anything from very light teasing to eye-watering brutality, normally with the full consent of the submissive. The male genitals are of course sensitive and extremely susceptible to pain. The use of pegs and candle wax as well as the light application of a paddle or whip can be stimulating for the recipient, but more extreme measures are called for in some cases. Those of a squeamish disposition should look away now.

CBT can be taken to an extreme beyond any level of endurance I'd imagined when I was training to be a Dominatrix. Pins, needles, nails, even screws can be used to penetrate the epidermis of the scrotum or the skin of the groin area. The heel of a stiletto, bricks, and even body weight can be applied directly to the genitals, causing excruciating pain. Needless to say, this extreme kind of CBT requires great care and can only be attempted when it's the express wish of the subservient.

One of my regular clients, who came to be called 'Brick Man', challenged the extremes to which CBT could be taken to such an extent that it was no longer possible to hurt him enough to satisfy his needs.

"Please, Princess Lucina," he begged, "place that rack under my balls, put a brick on them and then stand on the brick."

I was seriously afraid of causing lasting injury. To begin with I trod lightly on the brick, but that wasn't enough, so I pressed harder. In the end I stood on the brick so that my whole weight (plus that of the brick) was crushing his genitals.

"There, slave, how much is that hurting?"

"I can feel it, Mistress, but there's no pain."

Men reading this vignette will probably have tears streaming from their eyes, but I suspect that Brick Man's sensory nerves weren't wired in the same way as they are in most males. I'm happy to report that Brick Man wasn't irreparably injured by my attentions, though his genitals were swollen and inflamed for some time afterwards. I never did find a way of inflicting pain on his most delicate bits, though at his request I kept trying.

Ken was another edge-play aficionado with a penchant for CBT. I led him into my dungeon with the usual preamble and made him strip.

"Very well, slave Ken," I demanded when he was naked, "what would you like me to do to you?"

"Ball-nailing, please, Mistress," he said.

This is a dangerous game, but I know how to do it so it isn't life-threatening or seriously injurious.

"Has it been done to you before, slave?"

"Yes, Mistress, but not for eighteen months."

"On that bed, on your back."

I tied him to the bed, a narrow four-poster structure covered with red leather, and forced his legs apart. Then I laid a strip of wood across his genitals and nailed it to him, using a light hammer to drive each nail into place. It's safe enough if you know how to avoid large veins and major nerves, but there's no doubt it's excruciatingly painful. Ken screamed with pleasure. His screams were louder when I took the nails out again. Removing the attachments is more painful than driving them in because the nerves carrying pain sensations are already jangling.

Screws, it seems, are even more agonising than nails in this game, though it's still known as 'ball-nailing'. One of the other Mistresses who works in my Chamber particularly enjoys the use of screws; especially removing them.

*

For readers whose stomachs proved strong enough (or not strong enough) to tolerate the preceding paragraphs, the following passage will come as a relief. However, it might surprise you, if you're not part of the BDSM world, to learn that effective edge play can be psychological rather than physical, involving little pain or even no pain at all. The key ingredient in many sessions of this kind is the *anticipation* of pain, and even of injury or mutilation. If the submissive thinks there's even a slight chance that the pain will really happen, his anxiety can become feverish. Some slaves delight in this. For them, anticipation is the better part of suffering.

As always, the success of a session depends on a coordination or collaboration of ideas and needs between the two consenting adults involved, Dominatrix and slave. The symbiosis that characterises a successful relationship is as essential in edge play, physical or psychological, as in any other area of BDSM.

"No Mistress has ever managed to scare me," said David4.

It was only David4's third visit to my Chamber, but he'd already made his interest in psychological edge play evident. His bold statement was an obvious and deliberate challenge, and I never refuse such challenges. I'd discovered during his previous two sessions with me that he could endure extremes of pain, but he was now about to learn that words can be mightier than the whip.

"I have two vials here," I said, showing him the sealed glass containers. "One of them contains ordinary tap water. The other contains concentrated acetic acid, the stuff you can use for burning warts away. Now lie down."

He did as I ordered and I strapped him to the bed so he was immobilised, his challenge still ringing in my ears. Then I applied a tiny drop of the acid to his arm. A small burn immediately appeared on the skin. Despite his impressive pain tolerance he winced and clenched his teeth.

"Now," I said, "let's see what effect half the contents of this vial will have on your cock and balls. I'll save the other half until your genitals have been burned off like warts and then I'll drip it into your eyes."

Comedians say that the efficacy of a joke depends on the way you tell it. The same is true of a psychological edge-play threat: it's the way you tell it. And I know how to tell it effectively. David4 was less than half convinced that I'd do what I'd threatened. "Surely," he must have thought, "Princess Lucina wouldn't cause criminal injury to a client… but nevertheless, just suppose…" This man who'd never been scared by a Mistress was suddenly in a blind panic, struggling against his bonds. He could have saved his energy. If I tie up a slave so he can't escape, his struggles will be in vain (though I could get him out swiftly if there were a fire!).

Out of his line of vision, of course, I swapped the vials. He'd probably supposed I would do so but he'd no way of knowing that I had. So when the first drops trickled from the small glass container on to his genitalia, he screamed in expectation of life-changing mutilation. I've never seen a man's penis shrink so quickly and dramatically. There's no doubt he *felt* the pain he'd anticipated. He screamed again when the remaining drops dribbled into his eyes, and only then did he discover that he'd been tricked.

"You see, David," I smiled, "it's the power of the mind, not physical strength, that unlocks the vulnerability of the submissive."

He was impressed, and subsequently returned for more sessions. I never used the same game again with him, though. Edge play of that kind can only work once with a particular submissive.

*

Castration fantasies aren't common, but any Dominatrix is likely to have occasional clients who imagine having their testicles or penis (or both) removed. One of my slaves researched the nature and causes of such fantasies and shared his thoughts with me.

"It's interesting, isn't it, Princess Lucina, that when men think of being neutered they mostly imagine having their balls removed, but when women talk about neutering men they mostly think about cutting their cocks off. Obvious reasons for the difference, I suppose."

I supposed he was right.

He told me he'd read a scientific paper based on a survey of men interested in castration. About fifteen percent of the survey subjects had already been neutered: not a fantasy in those cases, but a genuine wish to be made into eunuchs – on which they'd acted. Among the remainder, many simply wanted to be free of sexual urges, but roughly a third of the respondents sought a 'cosmetic' change because they found their genitals ugly, and another third found castration fantasies sexually arousing. Most (though not all) of the castration fantasists who are likely to visit a Dominatrix belong to the last category: the thought of being castrated arouses them.

"There's a big website devoted to castration fantasists," my client told me, "called the Eunuch Archive. Some of the stories on there are *very* imaginative, though the writing is pretty lame in most cases."

I wondered why some men develop fantasies of that kind. What makes them into 'castration seekers'? According to the experts, so my client told me, the main factors are childhood abuse (including the threat of castration); homosexuality; seeing animals being castrated; and religious condemnation of sexuality. The experts have researched the topic so they know what they're talking about. However, I've met castration fantasists, including the client who told me about this research, whose imaginations haven't been shaped by *any* of those factors. They weren't abused as children, they're heterosexual, they haven't watched vets neutering animals, and they don't have religious hang-ups. In other words, they have castration fantasies that the experts haven't explained.

But that doesn't matter; a castration-fantasy client blindfolded and strapped to the St Andrew's cross can suffer a mind-blowing blend of arousal and terror when he hears knives being sharpened and feels cold steel against his scrotum. Once again, psychological edge play trumps the physical variety!

*

Many years ago I had a client called Paul who over a period of two years became a good friend. During that time we had sessions at least once per week. With Paul I indulged in a kind of edge play that I knew would appeal to him. It was a game I would never play with anyone else, but it was possible with him because we were friends and knew each other well.

"Could we try a bit of edge play this time?" he asked one Friday evening, his usual appointment time.

After a minute's thought I came up with an idea.

"I wonder whether that would be going too far?" I asked myself, chuckling. "Oh well, let's go for it anyway!"

I tied Paul to a chair very securely, so there was no way of escape, and I took his phone out of his pocket.

"What's your pass code?" I demanded.

He told me, quite happily.

"Right. You have three choices," I said. "I'm going to phone one of the following people, and you'll have to decide which one: Sandy, the girl you're trying to date; your Dad; or your friend Rob. I believe Rob is gay and knows almost everything about your life except your BDSM activities."

He didn't believe me, and he laughed, but in this business you should never make an idle threat. If you say you're going to do something you have to do it, otherwise whatever you do in the future will mean nothing.

"I'm not choosing," he decided.

I gave him two more chances, and when he still refused to choose I said, "OK then, I'll choose. I'll call Sandy."

I knew Sandy would be the one he'd least want to know where he was. I started to make the call.

"No!" he screamed. "Call Rob!"

So I did. I put the phone to Paul's ear and let him speak.

"Errrr... Hello, Rob," he said.

I could hear Rob sounding rather bemused and asking, "What's up?"

"Er – nothing, just wanted to say 'Hi'."

"OK," said Rob. "Are you drunk?"

When I hung up I could hardly stop laughing; but no harm had been done, none at all. I would never play this game with a client who wasn't a good friend, and I'd never do anything to cause problems in anyone's personal life, friend or otherwise. But my trick on Paul had been such fun!

*

By definition, edge play is conducted without boundaries, limits, or protections such as safe words. Nevertheless there are rules or at least guidelines that players should follow if they're going to be sensible. First, there must be genuine, unconstrained consent on the part of both Dominatrix and submissive. Second, it should only be attempted if the two parties already know and trust each other. Third, it is not for the inexperienced slave and certainly not for the inexperienced Mistress.

Edge play can be the culmination of a series of increasingly intense sessions between slave and Dominatrix, the ultimate in exploration of needs, and – if it's done correctly and effectively – a method for leading the slave into 'sub space' and giving the Mistress the ultimate high. As I've said before, regular meetings between Dominatrix and submissive involve a gradual stretching of boundaries and limits. The logical conclusion of such stretching is the removal of boundaries and limits altogether.

I understand all this, and I'm experienced enough to provide edge play without significant risk of injury to the submissive. Nevertheless, it's not something I attempt without a lot of thought or without ensuring that the slave is ready and willing to take the chance. Even then, I much prefer the psychological to the physical kind of edge play.

*

Edge play and role-play games can be seen as 'extreme' facets of BDSM. 'Middle of the road' facets often involve some kind of humiliation.

A standard way to humiliate male slaves is by 'penile degradation', commonly known as 'small penis humiliation', SPH for short. This hinges on the fashion for measuring an individual's masculinity by the size of his penis. Machismo is socially important among young males so they worry about *size*. In this form of humiliation, the man is made to feel that his penis is inadequate, an object of mockery, laughter and contempt. He is thereby degraded to a level far below the alpha male, making him fit only for enslavement and, in many cases, feminisation.

Patrick was a devotee of SPH, though his take on the theme was very much his own.

"Please, Princess Lucina, I need to be made to confess to my failure with my wife and reveal details about her sex life."

"I see. Are you *willing* to make that confession and reveal those details?"

"No, Mistress. I find it too embarrassing to talk about."

It's surprising how persuasive the judicious use of crop, cane, paddle, strap, whip and flogger can be in an interrogation setting. Some fifteen or twenty minutes of persistent questioning accompanied by increasing pain were needed to break slave Patrick's resistance. Then he sobbed out his tale of inadequacy. According to his 'confession', his wife had said: "Size isn't important, provided it's big enough; but yours isn't. And even a small one can be enjoyable, if it stands up properly; but yours doesn't." In Patrick's fantasy, his penis would have been too small to touch the sides of an average vagina even if it were capable of full erection, which it wasn't, and it oozed a few tiny drops of ejaculate after just ten seconds of contact. He then described the degradation of being made to watch for forty minutes while his wife made riotous and ecstatic love with her boyfriend, and having to lick them both clean when they'd finished.

In reality, Patrick's penis was of average size and capable of normal erections, and he and his wife seemed to enjoy a happy sex life. But his need for humiliation and mockery transcended that reality, and my task was to help him meet the need by means of 'forced confession'.

Not all SPH enthusiasts have fantasies like Patrick's, though I've met several with broadly similar ones. Some have hardly any explicit fantasy; they simply want the Mistress – or, better, several Mistresses – to laugh at them and tell them they're not men at all. In some cases this can lead to some kind of feminisation and cross-dressing. In a few cases it's associated with a castration fantasy. For many submissives it proves sexually arousing. There's no limit to human variety.

*

The predilection for anal penetration is more common than you might suppose. It's tempting to assume that submissives who visit a Dominatrix with this particular need are homosexual, but this is seldom if ever the case. As I pointed out to my niece when she was considering a career in domination and we discussed cross-dressing, a person predisposed to same-sex intercourse is unlikely to visit somebody of the opposite gender to be dominated.

So what, you might ask, is the appeal of anal penetration? One possibility is that the taboo on penetration of this part of the body makes it alluring. Another possibility, perhaps more obvious, is that there are sensitive erogenous zones around the anus and stimulation of them (done correctly) can be very sensual. There's a third option: people who've been on the receiving end of anal penetration describe it as more than a physical invasion; it's a *violation* that induces a mixture of positive and negative emotions, so it becomes a true act of submission. No doubt any client who seeks an anal penetration session is driven by his own personal blend of those three possibilities, plus others I haven't identified.

Some individuals prefer to be made helpless before being entered; others submit willingly. Ingress is usually achieved using either an artificial strap-on penis or a vibrating dildo, though you can use any implement that's safe. Arnie, a regular visitor to my Chamber, likes to experiment with various objects and utensils, some of them organic:

"I've a couple of carrots, Mistress, and a parsnip. Oh, and a courgette…"

It is surprising just how far anal sphincters can expand, and no less surprising how far some people will go to fill the orifice and what they'll use for the purpose. I'm certain that if adult acts were permitted on *Britain's Got Talent*, Arnie would be a winner!

*

SPH, adult baby play and anal penetration are fairly common 'middle of the road' scenarios in BDSM, though no submissive should be pigeonholed; each is a distinct individual requiring the Dominatrix to address his or her specific needs. However, some clients have needs and fantasies that are *truly* unique. Even other Mistresses find my descriptions difficult to believe.

David5 was a regular visitor to my Chamber.

"I'd like to sit naked on your whipping bench, please, Princess Lucina," he begged, "so I can play my guitar and sing before I'm punished."

"I've heard of hostile audiences," I said, "but you're the first performer I've met who actively seeks one!"

Geoff had a fetish for cagoule jackets. He liked to dress in rubber trousers and a cagoule, properly fastened, and then to wear a second cagoule backwards so it covered his face.

"Please will you wear similar clothes yourself, Princess Lucina?" he sometimes asked.

The second cagoule probably signified that Geoff liked his own idiosyncratic version of breath play. I've never met anyone else with a cagoule fetish, though rubber trousers aren't unique to him. There were times in session with Geoff when he was head to toe in cagoules and I would also be wearing an oversized cagoule with the hood up. I had to laugh at myself. Whatever people imagine a Dominatrix might look like, it probably isn't that!

Luke was another enthusiast for unusual sessions. He loved to be laughed at and would do anything to provoke a genuine laugh from his Mistress. I'd put some disco music on and he'd dance around the room to show me how he tried to attract girls in a night-club. One of his party tricks was to stand on his head and sing 'How much is that doggy in the window'. When it came to the 'woof woof' part he'd shake his willy as if he was wagging a tail. Tears of laughter rolled from my eyes.

A more common fetish is sploshing. This is where slaves become aroused by having food thrown at them or rubbed on them, or being made to roll around in it. One Mistress had such a client whom we called 'Foodie'. Foodie loved to be covered in food, but it had to be particular foods in a particular order: syrup first, then Rice Krispies, then eggs, then cream. Sometimes he wore tights and wanted to have beans put down the front. He loved the feeling of having the food rubbed all over him, in his face and into his hair. He'd turn up with three large gateaux, again being very particular about the ones he bought. The first two would be pushed into his face during the session. (Everyone should try this. There's something slapstick but rewarding about pushing a large cream cake into someone's face.) The final gateaux had to be a big white one. It was put on the floor and he'd mount it, having sex with the cake to finish the session.

Where did that fetish come from? Who knows? But if he enjoyed himself, who cares? Unfortunately, I had to call a halt to sessions with Foodie. He blocked my shower with the eggs.

*

There's no upper age limit to those who participate in the BDSM scene, no barrier of race, colour or creed. My regular visitor Brian is well into his eighties and still displays such a voracious hunger for the cane that it can't be satisfied. Brian is a wonderful gentleman who belongs to a bygone era when values were different. He's from the time of Benny Hill, a time of pinched bottoms and cheeky but innocent erotica. He knows nothing of political correctness; he's happy to remain unspoiled and uncorrupted by progress. That said, he's the only man alive who can get away with squeezing my bum. I'd never tolerate such behaviour from a younger man, but with Brian it feels complimentary.

*

What about the lives of these many and varied clients outside the confines of my Chamber? Several of them are married, but not all their partners have an inclination towards BDSM. If those wearing the gold wedding band can't explore their needs in the arms of their loved one, where else can they go? In some cases, the services that I and other Mistresses provide help to keep such marriages intact, rather than threatening them with the appearance of infidelity. But they might not help in all cases.

In an ideal world, a submissive would marry somebody with complementary interests; but then, in an ideal world, we'd promote freedom and individuality. Perhaps if submissives felt more comfortable about voicing their needs openly, they might find more appropriate matches. However, you can't choose the person with whom you'll bond for life solely on the basis of a shared interest in BDSM. Love often chooses for us, with little consideration of the fine print. In the end, those with a craving to pursue some facet of BDSM must balance the urgency of their needs against commitment to their chosen partner. Sadly, this can lead to a choice between guilt and frustration, and a path that might eventually end in unhappiness.

I'd like to believe that such cases are the exception rather than the rule.

Chapter 21

Not long after the planning-permission episode with the Council I received an e-mail from a production company in London. The media attention I'd received had interested them and they were keen to make a documentary film about my life as a Dominatrix. They'd already approached Channel 4 with the idea and the response had seemed positive, so now they wanted my opinion.

I still retain something of my childhood shyness and reticence. I'm never comfortable under the spotlight. I don't like being centre of attention with all eyes on me. I'm more than happy to sit quietly at the back of the room listening to what's being said and taking it all in. So I had no wish to be on TV. Nevertheless, the proposal appealed to me for two main reasons.

First, I'd had so much negative publicity that I thought it was time for a positive slant on my profession. If I accepted the offer I could at last have *My* say. I'd gone through a lot during the previous few years; events had blown my discretion to the four winds. There had been so much exposure of my work that I now had nothing to hide. On the contrary, my business set-up was now fully legal, everyone knew about it, and I was proud to work in BDSM. Therefore, I thought, making a good documentary would be liberating.

Second, the documentary would enable me to have a proper rant about how difficult it is to be legal and above board in the BDSM scene. I also wanted to show the viewers something of my world and to demonstrate that the clients who visit my Chamber are nice, intelligent men and women, not a shady collection of perverted weirdos as many people seem to imagine. A documentary would provide the perfect platform for me to promote the truth. As I've already said in this book, my business bank account had been closed, my accountant had dropped me, and I'd been caricatured in the papers at every turn – simply because of the work I do. It's much the same for any Mistress who finds herself 'outed'.

*

I exchanged a couple of e-mails with Amy, who worked for the production team.

"Can I come to Stockport to have a chat with you and also a look around the premises?" she asked.

I agreed. One glorious summer afternoon I picked Amy up from the station in Manchester and we drove to Stockport. Right from the outset I felt I couldn't trust her as I'd have wished. There was no rapport. She wore far too many layers of clothes for such a blistering hot day, and she seemed uncomfortable not only with me but also, oddly, with herself. Nevertheless she was pleasant enough, and as we drove to the premises we chatted about my work and the types of clients I had.

When we got to the Chamber I opened up and we went inside. She wasn't much taken with Charlie, which didn't improve my feelings about her. People react in many different ways the first time they enter the dungeon and some of their responses are amusing. Some just stand there, acting as though there's nothing unusual at all. Some are fascinated and can't take enough of it in. A few, such as new clients, are like kids in a sweet shop. Others seem deeply uncomfortable. Unfortunately, Amy was in the 'uncomfortable' bracket. Her body language conveyed severe awkwardness. I got the feeling that if she could have left there and then, she'd have done so.

"This isn't going well," I thought.

We sat and chatted over a coffee and the initial questions were predictable; "How did you become a Mistress?" ... "What's the strangest session you've ever done?" ... Then other questions followed that I considered intrusive: "How much do you make in a week?" ... "What's your yearly turnover?"

I started to talk about the dogs and my rescue work. "Will you be interested in showing that side of my life, for the contrast?"

"No," she said. "Nobody will be interested in that side of your life, just the domination with the fetishes, the slaves and so on. Will any other Mistresses be interested in being featured?"

"It's possible," I said, starting to find the documentary proposal less and less attractive. "I'd have to ask."

Then she inquired about slaves who could be involved. Of course, that was a reasonable question.

"I could probably find slaves who wouldn't mind being filmed," I said, "but they'd have to be masked all the time."

"Oh, no, my boss won't like that. They'll have to have their faces showing."

I looked at her in disbelief.

"It would be *impossible* to find a slave who'd be willing to be outed on national television."

But she didn't seem to understand. I got the feeling there was a lot about my world that she didn't understand, or even want to try to understand. Then she started to talk in more detail about what they'd be looking for, and what she said confirmed my suspicions.

"We'll be following you around for two weeks with a camera, and everything will have to be fetish based," she said, "like going shopping in Tesco in your Dom gear, and taking the rubbish out in your Dom gear."

I laughed.

"That isn't something I'd ever do."

"It doesn't matter," she replied. "It's just for TV."

This wasn't what I wanted at all! From the outset there had been a risk that the proposed documentary would come across as just another seedy interview on Channel 4, but now this had become a real worry. The production team seemed to want to sensationalise everything without portraying the reality. Nevertheless, Amy seemed happy with the results of her trip to Stockport and went back to London with positive reports to her colleagues. Over the weeks that followed I was bombarded with e-mails asking if I'd found any slaves who were happy not to wear a mask, whether I'd given any thought to shopping in my thigh-high boots while carrying a whip… Amy was pushy. I wasn't at all comfortable.

However, although the production team remained excited, Channel 4 lost interest in the project, saying they'd shown too many adult documentaries recently. Maybe this proposal could be taken up again at a later time, they suggested. They'd get back in touch.

They didn't. I was honestly relieved.

*

Fast forward to July, 2018: an e-mail appeared in my inbox from a different production company. This e-mail wasn't addressed only to me; it had also been sent to other Mistresses around the country. The company had broadcast a series entitled 'The Sex Business' on Channel 5 a year earlier and they'd been commissioned to do another such series of three episodes, one to be about domination. I watched some of the first series and thought it had been done well, so I sent a positive reply to their e-mail. A quick chat on the phone led to a visit from Christina, a trendy-looking assistant producer from London. When Christina arrived she didn't raise an eyebrow at the Chamber.

"I've seen many dungeons around the country," she said.

We had a long chat, and I felt much more comfortable with her than I'd felt with Amy. Christina had a list of questions to ask me – the usual ones – and of course I had a few to ask in return.

"Would we be able to film an actual live session?" she asked.

"Yes," I said, "but only with the slave masked."

"Oh, God, of course! We want to be sure everybody feels comfortable. We're not out to ruin anyone's life!"

I liked the sound of this already; Christina and her colleagues seemed much more knowledgeable about my work and more respectful of it, and of me, than Amy had been. Then she mentioned the dogs.

"We'd love to come with you and film you spending time with them," she said.

"Really?" I was overjoyed.

"Yes. We don't just want to show you in the dungeon, but also the things you get up to outside the dungeon. The things you do when you're not here, just normal stuff."

This was sounding better and better! Before Christina left she confirmed that if I was happy to be involved, they'd be interested in using me and my Chamber.

"The next step," she explained, "will be for the two producers to meet you and have a chat with you in person."

I met Paul and Victor the following week.

*

They arrived from London and as soon as they alighted from the taxi I knew we were going to get along well. Sometimes you can just feel a person's energy and you instinctively sense that all's going to be fine with them. Both men were well dressed and smart. Victor was in his thirties, I would say, and Paul – who owned the production company – seemed a little older. They came into the Chamber, loved what they saw, and even put up with a barking Charlie. We sat for a few hours drinking coffee, eating biscuits and enjoying a satisfyingly intelligent conversation.

Paul explained his vision for the documentary to me and I liked what I heard. As I've said, he'd made the first 'Sex Business' series and in doing so he'd worked closely with escorts and other sex workers, and been allowed entry into otherwise very private lifestyles. He'd also made a documentary about gangs, which had let him into another type of lifestyle altogether. He was thoroughly respectful of the trust that allowed people to open up to him and let him into the most personal areas of their lives and work, and I loved that. He was passionate about what he did. He didn't want to sensationalise anything, but simply to show my life as it was and is.

"We want you just to get on with what you do," he said. "We're going to be like a fly on the wall. We want to show what you do in the room, but also what you do *outside* the room as well."

"That's great." I knew I could work with these men.

"What do *you* hope to get out of the documentary?" he asked.

"I want to show your viewers that the BDSM world isn't full of freaks or life's rejects. But there's one thing in particular I want to get across." (This was something that hadn't been at the forefront of my mind with the earlier production team.) "BDSM can be a very lonely world for some people."

They asked me to explain that in more detail.

"Everyone enters this world for a different reason," I said, "and each person who does so is on their own individual path. Some people get turned on by the sight of a woman in thigh-high boots and they enjoy a little light spanking. For others, being submissive is a deep need, and unless that need is fed, depression can set in. Between those two levels there are a thousand others."

"So we need to emphasise the variety. But what do you mean by 'lonely', Lucina?"

This was one of the main points I wanted viewers of the documentary to grasp. A man doesn't want to be judged or ridiculed by the rest of the world, so he won't admit to his submissive streak. In fact, his best mate could also be doing the same thing, or at least dreaming about it, but neither will ever learn about the other because the subject is taboo. For some subs, this is a very lonely place to be; to feel they're so different, unable to understand where their feelings came from.

"Over the years," I explained, "I've met scores of people who believe they're the only ones in the world with a particular fetish. In fact, they believe there's something wrong with them! Men chat together just as much as women do. They talk about their conquests, and even about escorts and working girls and affairs they're having. Sometimes they boast about those matters. But none of them ever tells his mate, 'Oh, I went to see a Dominatrix the other day'. I mean, who'd understand? This side of their lives is so secret that even the closest of friends will never know about it."

I've had many e-mails from slaves who've been devastated because of a fall-out with their Mistresses. A Mistress/slave relationship can be very intense because of the depth of trust that's needed, and if the relationship goes wrong it can create a massive gap in the slave's life. Most who've been in contact with me in this way just want to talk. They might be happily married but that doesn't lessen the pain; they have to find someone who'll listen to them and understand their feelings. If the documentary worked as I hoped, it would tell every submissive watching it: "You're not alone, and you're certainly not a freak! What you feel is felt by far more people than you realise, so never believe there's anything wrong with you!"

During our long discussion I got this message across to Paul and Victor. Paul understood my wishes and promised to convey the message as best he could.

*

No payment would be involved. The team wanted people to participate in the documentary because of their passion for the industry, not for money. That was good for me. Life provides many motivations, but money has never been high on my list of priorities. I've already spelled out my reasons for doing the documentary, but I was also doing it for the experience – the fun. That's what life's about for me: building up experiences and enjoying them! Even when I was in the papers I tried to see the funny side. I hoped making the documentary would be a giggle, too. In the event, it proved to be just that.

The filming schedule was arranged. Mistress Luci, who works alongside me in the Chamber, was going to play a prominent part in the film. Two other Mistresses from different parts of the U.K. would also feature in the documentary. The first bit of filming would be the 'interview'; basically, the team would interview Mistress Luci and me separately in the Chamber. In the event, this took most of the day by the time the lighting and sound were right, and none of it appeared in the eventual film. Instead, we did a 'studio interview' with all the same questions after the filming had been finished, and they used that.

During our discussions, Paul had said that one of the things he really wanted to see was ball nailing. This had never been shown before on British TV and he was very excited about the prospect. So I asked one of my longest-serving and most loyal clients if he'd take part, and to my surprise he agreed. Cell Man, as I nicknamed him because of his love for being left in the cell for long periods, had first visited me over ten years earlier in the city gate apartment. Back then we'd begun with anal play and with mild breath play using a gas mask. Over the years I think we'd tried almost everything. When you find a Mistress you can trust and a slave who's eager for experience, the path can diverge in very interesting ways. Eventually we'd come to a path of pain.

The first thing most people ask is: "Why would you pay to be hurt?" It's a reasonable question. The answer is that if a slave like Cell Man sees that I'm having fun hurting him, if he knows I'm achieving a 'high', he gets a wonderful buzz out of it. It's the ultimate exchange of power and energy. Cell Man and I finally came to the ball nailing, which I believe I could do now with my eyes closed. He's highly intelligent with his own business and a grown-up family, but he needs to be submissive and let me take total control. When I was deciding which client to ask to participate in filming a ball-nailing scene, he was my first choice. I honestly didn't think he'd be up for it, but he surprised me.

"I'd love to be shown as your slave, Princess Lucina, as long as I can't be recognised."

"We go to great lengths to makes sure all identities are concealed," said Paul.

It demands a lot of trust to let someone into your life like that, and in my case I felt very protective of my clients, especially Cell Man; but I believed and trusted Paul.

Mistress Luci and I planned the day with the utmost precision. Cell Man came in. Mistress Chloe and Mistress Lavinia had also agreed to be involved and were happy to show their faces. There's one shot of Mistress Chloe jumping around with a strap-on and we're all laughing. Paul reiterated that he wanted to capture what we did outside the dungeon, too, and I think this was evident in the final product.

"I hadn't realised how much fun you all have!" Paul said to me later. "I'd underestimated that side of it. I'd always seen BDSM as something quite serious."

"Sometimes it *is* serious," I said, "but in general we have fun, and we've all had a great time making the documentary."

For the filming, a GoPro was used so there was no actual person filming in the room. Mistress Luci and I took it in turns to wear the GoPros on our chests. Victor was always around with his camera, though, and it's surprising how quickly you get used to it. The fact that I trusted the two guys and felt so comfortable with them made all the difference. I doubt if I could have made the documentary with anyone else.

The week after the Cell Man game, we filmed Colin and his tickle torture session. You might not think of tickling as a torture, but it is, and we find it hilarious to do. To have someone tied up while you tickle them is one of the funniest things. While they're laughing and screaming we have tears of laughter rolling down our faces. Colin likes to be dressed up as a sissy and then tied down and tickled. It was good to include this in the documentary because it illustrated the range of our activities and made the point that not all aspects of BDSM are painful. Also, Colin was happy to be interviewed, with his voice disguised. He explained that he'd had the need to be submissive since childhood, and he wanted to emphasise the word 'need'. Submissiveness isn't always a choice. He also explained how alone he'd felt at times, fearing – as many submissives do – that there could be something wrong with him. This was one of the main points I'd explained to Paul. Thanks to Colin, the documentary would enable us to reach people who felt the same as he did.

*

Outside the Chamber, Mistress Luci and I went to Bolton to spend time with the dogs. Paul didn't join us. I think he was concerned about how big some of the dogs were, so he sent Christina, though she too was a little worried about the size of the animals! The team followed us into Pat's with the camera and showed us chilling with the dogs, and then they came on a walk with us and asked us questions about what the dogs meant to us. Afterwards, they wanted to walk around the park with me and Charlie. It was interesting to see people's reactions as I took my daily walk, feeding the pigeons and squirrels as usual, but followed by a cameraman and a sound man. Charlie was oblivious of our companions and was only interested in his sniffs and wees. The team were amazed at the squirrels coming up and taking food out of my hand. This illustrated an important facet of my life: Lucina the animal lover, not Princess Lucina the Dominatrix (though they're the same person, of course: just two sides of the same coin).

I can honestly say I had a great time with the filming. Now and again it was bit stressful, trying to organise everything to fit in, but we had such a laugh along the way. I was more than happy with how it went. But the end result was the main thing, and we didn't get to see the final edit before it went out on TV. I'd trusted Paul not to make us look seedy or silly, but I couldn't really know whether my trust had been well founded until after the broadcast.

*

The day came in December 2018 when the program was to be aired. To put it mildly, I was nervous. Here I was, exposed to everyone who chose to watch. The other Mistresses and I might come across as good or bad, but it was too late now to alter anything.

Seeing yourself on television is a funny experience, but ten minutes into the programme I could tell Paul had kept his word and fulfilled all his promises to show us in our true light. He'd included all the parts I wanted to show, especially where I said I care for the clients and feel protective towards them, and that nobody should feel alone with their fetish. I was more than happy with the outcome. I honestly don't believe the documentary could have been done better.

Messages from viewers started to arrive the following day, both personal and on social media, and they were all one hundred percent positive. A lot of people said it had been 'The first BDSM documentary to show us in a positive light'. Other comments included,

'You have done the BDSM scene justice'. I was bombarded by e-mails from people saying my comments about 'not being alone' and 'not being a freak' meant such a lot to them. This was nothing more than a 'thank you', but it was a 'thank you' that meant a great deal to me.

A few days later, whilst I was walking through the park with Charlie, I encountered Michael, an elderly gentleman whom I'd come to know since he was in the park most days. He'd lost his wife a few years previously, so this was a way for him to get out. We would say "Hello" in passing and exchange a few words. This day he was on the other side of the small woodland from me when we saw each other. I shouted "Hello" as usual.

"Oh, hang on!" he shouted back.

He nearly fell over as he dived through the bushes. His face was full of 'that look' people have when they know what I do.

"I have to tell you," he said, his face beaming, "I saw you on telly. You're a dark horse, you are, ya bugger!"

He laughed, his eyes sparkling and gleaming. I laughed in return.

Since then I've been the talk of the park. All the park keepers now wave at me as I go by. Michael always has a joke with me, saying something like, "Let me know when you have a discount day, Lucina". What's really good about this is that he now has a spring in his step and a gleam all over his face. It's as though having seen the documentary and knowing me personally has brought a bit of life back to him. To affect people's lives in a positive way gives you a lovely feeling. You can't beat it.

For me, the documentary had the same objective as this book: to talk about my experiences and show how much these have changed me, but also to educate people about the ways of the fetish industry. I'm sure I've given people many laughs along the way, but hopefully I've been successful in reaching out to those who've felt lost or confused.

My aim now is to continue what I do and hopefully to reach more lives. My days as a Professional Dominatrix will come to an end in the years to come, but I hope by then to have passed on my skills and attitudes to other Mistresses, who will then carry on the good work.

Chapter 22

Self-pity has never been among my vices, but sometimes it feels as though I've been consigned to a world in which The skies are of ash, the heavens crash upon the earth and all beasts perish in misery. The foundations of the Earth are shaken. All signs have passed before humankind with flood, pestilence and flame...

All right, I'm being a trifle over-dramatic. However, there comes a point when you have to wonder if you're living in a Biblical-style disaster film. Given the dramas that have afflicted every turn of my professional career, I might be forgiven for wanting a taste of good fortune. Perhaps the trail of mishaps and adversity that seems to have defined my adult life has been Fate's way of giving me material for this book. If so, I'd rather my days had been filled with calmness and felicity and these pages had remained blank.

I've taken no pleasure from my farcical courtroom melodramas, and staging my own version of The Towering Inferno didn't rate high on my bucket list. It seems I'm a magnet for incompetence, a candle flame for the moths of bureaucracy, and seduction-personified to mischance. From plague to flood and from fire to the debacle of institutional law, my life has been governed by successive disasters, each branding me a casualty of Fate.

Oh yes, flood. I haven't mentioned that so far.

*

When I first moved into my new Chamber in Stockport the nation was in the grip of one of the coldest winters I can remember. Since the premises are located in the cellar of a large old mill, its walls are relatively impermeable, so it would have made a great indoor swimming pool. Indeed, I'd barely moved in when a pipe burst under the pressure from ice, giving the locals a new place to practise their front crawl. Simply bad luck, or an omen I should have heeded? Regardless, I mopped up the mess and carried on.

There's a space toward the back of the Chamber that's often ornamented with large puddles, especially following long periods of rain. This part of the building isn't used, and as it causes no problems with the day to day running of my business (or anyone else's) it isn't considered important. As to whether I should have seen those puddles as a mere irritation or another omen I failed to heed, who can say?

A few years ago, after a cloud-burst, I arrived at my Chamber to find it had been transformed into a children's paddling pool. A small drain close to the front entrance had failed, allowing water to flow in beneath the door.

"What now?" I cried to the heavens as I stepped through into the reception area. A small family of ducks frolicked in an inch or so of water. At least they were happy.

The damage proved relatively minor. The tsunami had cascaded down the outside steps and through the reception area but it had only reached the lounge. All the working areas remained dry, so a day's mopping was all that was needed before I could reopen for business. Investigations revealed that the flood had been caused by a blocked drain in the street, which had redirected the water towards my Chamber, overwhelming the mill's inadequate drainage system. Council workers were summoned, the drain was unblocked, and my world returned to its customary glory.

A slight aggravation or the last of three omens? Who cared? The Chamber was up and running and it was business as usual. Of course omens, if you believe in such things, are there for a reason. I should have heeded them. All three of them.

*

Days passed into weeks and Britain was finally bathed in summer. The heavy grey Lancashire skies had given way to heavenly blue and all in my garden was rosy. I should have felt alarmed at this point: the roller-coaster was juddering over the brow of a hill and had nowhere to go now except downwards.

A few weeks later, while I was enjoying my Monday at the dog sanctuary, Tony the mill caretaker phoned me. As I said earlier, Tony is efficient and does a good job but he's elderly and verbose.

Summertime in Manchester, he told me, was living up to its reputation: the heavenly blue skies had departed and a monsoon had burst over Stockport.

"I'm concerned about the amount of water that's puddling on the street," he said, "I think it might be heading down the steps to your cellar."

"Thanks for telling me. You've got a key, haven't you?"

"Yes. Can I have your permission to go down and check you've not being flooded?"

"Of course."

Given the history of my dungeon and my usual luck, I expected the worst. He soon rang back.

"It's fine, Lucina, all's well!"

Tony greeted me when I arrived at the Chamber the following morning. He pointed to some new structures beside the entrance.

"See those barriers, Lucina? The Council's put them up. Yesterday's rain caused subsidence and the drains have collapsed."

"So I've been flooded after all, have I?"

"No, you're fine, and the Council are going to excavate new drains next Monday."

This couldn't be another omen, I thought. Everyone knows that omens come in threes, not fours. But on the third day the skies grew heavy with Hell's wrath and a furious tempest burst forth. Noah had been spotted touring local zoos and work had begun on his new Ark. An entire month's rain fell on Manchester in just a few hours and it showed no sign of abating. I made my way to the Chamber in the morning knowing what I'd find. The street had become a beautiful lake; all that was missing were lilies. The family of ducks that had previously frolicked in my reception area now paddled past my car.

I waded through another wondrous waterfall cascading down from the street to my cellar. At the bottom of the steps lay a turgid knee-deep pool. It was obvious that my dungeon was under water. Unable to enter through the front door without releasing the entire contents of this newly-formed reservoir into the bowels of the building, I made my way to the back entrance and through a door into the basement.

It was as though my Chamber were sinking beneath a turbulent ocean. Water poured under the front entrance, adding to the flood that seemed to have filled each room to a depth of several fathoms. A tide raged over the expensive wooden flooring in the lounge and the main dungeon, washing away my hopes. My heart plunged to an abyss of despair. The daemon from my nightmares had returned to haunt reality. After everything I'd been through, was this fair?

The immediate task, with Tony's help, was to divert the water away from my Chamber. This was no easy job. A Dominatrix in wellingtons and a jovial pensioner with a snorkel weren't the right personnel. Indeed, anything less than a team of engineers, a fleet of diggers and the excavation of a new canal would have fallen short of what was needed. But then the rain stopped and new cards were dealt. With no additional water flooding down from the street, we managed to pump the cellar more or less dry.

The next job was to mop the floors clean and turn the furniture upside down so everything could drain. It was hard work but at least I was doing something to remedy the situation, which helped me to feel better. A barricade of sandbags was installed before the entrance like props for a Second World War drama. I wanted to be sure that if the rain returned, the flood would be directed elsewhere.

The clean-up operation took little more than a day and the damage was luckily minimal. The diggers arrived the following Monday to excavate the drain that had collapsed, and business returned once again to normal.

Now, however, I must turn my attention once more to bureaucrats, specifically to the insurance industry. As I remarked earlier, I can't obtain any form of insurance for my Chamber. Therefore, every time I suffer a catastrophe like this, I have to foot the bill myself. Insurance companies that specialise in policies for the adult industry have packages for escort agencies, massage parlours and strip clubs, but under no circumstances will they cover a BDSM Chamber. Why not? BDSM is safe and consensual and no sex is involved!

It's hard not to be angry, but anger is healthier than the heartache that follows yet another setback. There's never dull moment. Fire, flood and pestilence are continual threats and calamity is never far from the door. (For 'pestilence' read 'infestation by bureaucrats'.) We're back to Biblical references, the Seven Plagues of Egypt in particular. But I'm not Moses. And Stockport could never be mistaken for the Promised Land.

*

That wasn't the end of my woes, of course. A few months ago my business was closed by a swarm of bees that had taken refuge in the dungeon. My Chamber is in a city. I'm surrounded by buildings, parkland, trees and even some countryside. So why would a swarm of bees choose to nest in my cellar? I love bees, and they're hugely important to the world, but was my Chamber a fit home for them? Am I perhaps a pawn in a chess game between higher beings? Is Stockport to be the battleground for Judgment Day, my Chamber the host for signs of the Apocalypse? If not, I'm certainly due some better luck!

A highly reputable company promised that the bees would be removed unharmed, which I recognised as code for the exact opposite. They knew I wouldn't engage anyone who didn't promise such care. Of course, the swarm met a bitter and unnecessary end. This felt like a double blow. Not only had my business been closed by the infestation (or, as I'd prefer to call it, the bees' infelicitous choice of home), but I also felt responsible for the murder of the poor insects. There was little I could have done, especially since no one had told me that the highly reputable company had planned in advance to exterminate the swarm. The incident left me feeling low. I hate anything being killed.

*

I'm not going to fill more pages with the melancholy woe of an angry, bitter woman. I'm not indulging my feelings of resentment, just making an impassioned plea for Fate to grant me mercy. I want the mythological relationship between Lucina and the fates to be restored in its proper order! It's hard not to feel exasperated by the constant bombardment of mishap and woe, the malevolent daemon that likes to sit on my shoulder. But if, by Kismet's decree, all that fills my life is to be predetermined by Fate, I shall take what pleasure I can from the hand I'm dealt. As far as possible I'll take responsibility for my own destiny, as I always have, though the naughty daemon makes me wish I could turn some tomorrows into yesterdays. Indeed, every time the roller-coaster of life has plunged me to the fiery pits of Hell, I've clung on in the hope that things will improve. And of course, they do. I've risen from the darkness to be bathed again in the gleaming light of the Promised Land.

In his book 'Me, My World and I', the poet A. V. Barber wrote:

As when riding on a roller coaster, life is often filled with contrasting emotions. We can't escape what life has in store any more than we can get off a ride before it's finished. And all the time, one truth holds true: you only get one chance. There are good times, and there are bad times. Regardless, the rest of the world will just carry on. Life really is just one big track with hills.

To me, it seems that, often, the lows come when you least expect them. You're on the top of your game, everything is going to plan, and then suddenly it all unravels and comes crashing down around you. Time passes, and slowly you lift yourself up from the gloom. Finally, all is well once more.

We become so embroiled in our lives that we barely notice anything else. Who, when riding a roller coaster, takes the time to look at the other passengers? We are all focused on our little corner of the world, and we rarely look beyond the things and people we know.

Time goes by so quickly. One minute you're taking a seat for the ride of your life, and the next thing you know, the ride is all but over. I know that, at my age, I may not be entirely qualified to make such a statement, but the years just seem to fly by, and I am not expecting things to slow down any time soon.

*

After the sad encounter with the bees I wondered: what next? Well, to add to the aforementioned financial stresses on me, electricity supplies to commercial premises have become increasingly expensive to the point of extortion. Also, my landlord has kindly decided to increase my rent by twenty-six percent. Of course I make a reasonable income from my business, but these draconian attacks on my financial reserves have more or less forced me to relax one of my rules: never to rent out the dungeons to non-professionals.

With other Mistresses working in the Chamber, not all of whom I know well, there's always been a risk of theft or damage to equipment. To date, however, that's never happened. It's sensible to take precautions but not to be too suspicious; contrary to tabloid-inspired common belief, most people are honest. I've also allowed photo-shoots in the cellar and those have always passed without trouble or complications. However, couples renting a dungeon so they can indulge their private BDSM fantasies are another matter. I'm always afraid they won't treat my property with the care my fellow-Mistresses have shown. Nevertheless, the need for extra income has now compelled me to put my anxiety on the back burner and countenance such applications. So far so good, I'm happy to say. Two gay men rented time in the Chamber recently and they were a delight; charming people, respectful of person and property. As I observed, most people are honest. It was also gratifying that my dungeon was recognised as a place where couples could explore their kinks and fetishes in a safe, well-equipped environment.

Nevertheless the question keeps recurring: what next? Perhaps a meteor will strike Manchester, missing all other buildings before skidding through Stockport and crashing into my Chamber. Perhaps the planet will be invaded by vampire-like aliens who will use my cellar to hide from the light. I suppose neither of those events is really likely. However, right now I'm off to hire an army of strippers so I can purchase insurance against alien invasions and acts of God!

Chapter 23

My name is Lucina White. I work, I pay my bills and my taxes, I have a family and a pet dog called Charlie, I love to travel and to work in animal sanctuaries, I have a pilot's license and I love to fly. I have hopes and fears, I laugh when I find something funny and I cry when I feel hurt. Also: my name is Princess Lucina and I'm a professional Dominatrix. I don't worship the Devil, nor have I ever eaten children or burned a Bible. Instead, I run a business that I've kept alive by sheer determination (or bloody-mindedness) in the face of serial setbacks, disasters, episodes of bureaucratic harassment and tabloid caricatures. I continue to run that business just as I continue to fly, care for animals and walk my dog. I'm both Lucina White and Princess Lucina. I am one whole, fully-integrated woman, not a split personality. I'm happy inside my skin. I know myself.

Our characters might be moulded at birth or before, but our life's experiences add up to make us who we are and establish our outlook and philosophy. My love of animals, my immersion in foreign cultures and my spiritual beliefs are all facets of me and inform the way I act. I have the great good fortune of knowing wonderful people and I've been privileged to share in their lives. The tragic death of a friend, the fire in my Chamber, the flood, the bees, and even my brushes with bureaucracy, have all affected me. I've travelled to far-off lands, walked with wolves and lived in the canopy of a jungle. I've battled with despair, embraced my dreams and refused to show fear. In BDSM, I've travelled so many roads that to recount every journey would be impossible. It's been exciting, stimulating, sometimes funny and occasionally sad, but I wouldn't change any of it. There have been moments of madness and occasional genius, there have been thrills and there have been spills, and all the time I've been growing as a person.

If you'll forgive the cliché, we must take the rough with the smooth on life's journey. If nothing ever happened to cause us pain, how could we learn to appreciate what can make us happy? And we never stop learning.

*

Thailand taught me that there are people in this world who possess far less than I do, far less than anyone in Britain does, but they find ways to achieve happiness. As Peter said, the Thai people always seem to smile. Perhaps contentment can't be measured by the materialistic trappings of a rapacious world. It involves something more spiritual.

The Thai people work very hard for little reward. The average employee takes perhaps only one weekend off in every month. Yet they seem to find joy in their work. They've learned to appreciate what they have instead of dwelling on what they haven't. A job, no matter the hours, is the difference for them between feeding a family and starving. Thailand has no government infrastructure to offer security, no benefits to cushion the needy. Immersion in such a different culture taught me how many reasons I have to be happy. The experience became part of me.

The time I've spent in Thailand, the people I have met through being a Dominatrix and the life I've chosen to live have enabled me to see a far bigger picture than I'd otherwise have seen. It's like standing back from a portrait in a gallery so I can see everything the canvas portrays. Through BDSM and through visiting Thailand I've learned more about myself as an individual and more about other people than I could have done in any other way.

Few of us want to seem judgmental, but if someone's actions don't conform to social norms they're likely to be labelled, pigeonholed and often derided. Only when we encounter the values of other cultures such as those of Thailand, embrace their beliefs and try to integrate with them can we become truly open-minded. In BDSM, the sharing between Mistress and subservient is honest. During a session, the two individuals aren't controlled by norms, labels or pigeonholes. Only the journey matters, each player drawing gratification from being true to themselves, treading further along the path as meeting follows meeting. My clients come from all walks of life; most are professional, educated and intelligent and all have genuine needs to explore. Why should they be denied the right to acknowledge what they are just because society seeks to marginalise their needs? Let those with no secrets cast the first stone!

We are what we were born to be, but we can wear masks and pretend to conform. I have no interest in judging people on the basis of one-dimensional stereotypes. I've had publicity enough for being who I am, none of it accurate, with the honourable exception of the Channel Five documentary; but my honesty has caused a bit of a stir. What I offer isn't to everyone's taste, but it's to the taste of a surprisingly large number. Does it matter if some people choose to brand me immoral? I provide a much-needed outlet for good people who have nowhere else to turn, and I challenge any preacher or moral philosopher to deem that unethical.

*

Some readers might think it perverse to compare BDSM with conventional sex, but the parallels are real and significant. Sex at its best is the most wonderful experience for a couple in love. It's at least as much mental as physical, it forges and sustains a powerful bond between the participants, it generates and releases powerful emotions, it is (or should be) a voyage in which both bodies and fantasies are explored; and it's great fun. Likewise, BDSM is at least as much psychological as physical, it generates and sustains a strong bond between Dominatrix and submissive, it releases the slave's emotions and gives the Dominatrix a glorious high, it's a continuing voyage of mutual exploration that can lead to lasting friendship; and it's great fun. BDSM, like love-making, is an art, a means of expressing inner desires in whatever ways we choose. It can match the most unlikely partners, often with remarkable results. At its best, love-making leads to the post-orgasmic taste of Paradise. At its best, BDSM leads to 'sub space' for the slave and a wonderful high for the Mistress.

The difficulty with BDSM in an established relationship is that the partners seldom share the same need. You don't begin with a blank canvas; you're surrounded by the clutter and baggage of your personal history. Can that problem be solved? It depends on the two people involved and whether they're willing to accommodate each other's needs fully and non-judgmentally. Starting small, even if thinking big, can be the difference between success and failure. Introducing your partner to something you might both learn to enjoy can be the first step on a wonderful journey. Take time to think about what you might like to experience. Share your thoughts with your partner and make sure you're both on board.

If you decide to take that first step, remember to share the needs of both participants and *always be safe*. At its best, BDSM can help you to create a world of trust and understanding. It's a place where people can be what they feel they need to be rather than what society has made them and expects them to be. Most of all, if you choose to explore BDSM, remember to have fun and enjoy the experience. There's little point in spending time doing something that seems a chore, and you definitely shouldn't embark on anything you find unpleasant. Don't be in a hurry to push your boundaries. Relish your journey and savour every moment.

Just be warned: BDSM can become addictive! Before you know it, your every thought will be consumed and your life will never be the same again. Behind that picture of innocence you like to present in public will be thoughts of a forbidden pleasure that will thrill and titillate even during the most tedious of hours.

*

Has society finally embraced BDSM? It probably hasn't. Public perception of the scene has softened but my profession is still kept in the shadows. Why does it remain taboo? Preconceptions about activities considered 'normal' and 'abnormal' are the root of the problem, but who decides what 'normal' means? Is it normal to jump off a bridge with only a length of elastic between the thrill of a lifetime and certain death? Is it normal to jump from an aeroplane supported only by an oversized silk bed sheet? Is it normal to dive with sharks, or eat scorpions dried on a stick? Is it normal for a consenting adult to be tied down and spanked with a paddle? (That might hurt, but not as much as jumping off a bridge or out of an aeroplane and landing on your head.)

Our boundaries aren't universal or absolute, they're culturally prescribed. On the muddy beaches of northern Germany you'll see people of all ages changing into their bathing costumes with no concern for hiding their bodies. If you do that in a Manchester street you'll be arrested for offending public decency. (You'll also probably contract pneumonia.) Amsterdam and Hamburg are more liberal about the adult industry than London and Manchester are because people are brought up with it. It's much more a part of their culture than it is of ours.

More than one of my clients has compared the sniggering and jokes at the expense of BDSM today, the marginalisation and even ostracism of Dominatrix and submissive, with the attitudes towards homosexuality in Britain half a century ago. Perhaps it's worth remembering that very soon after the law about male homosexuality was relaxed, Gay Pride marches began in London and other cities and their recurrence dramatically altered social attitudes and induced further changes in the law during the decades that followed. Perhaps we need BDSM pride marches, with Dominatrixes dressed in the variety of costumes we wear during sessions leading shackled submissives clothed as minimally as the law allows. Would that be a way of persuading Britain to regard BDSM as 'normal'? It's no longer politically correct to show prejudice against LGBT people, but as things stand, political correctness doesn't extend to participants in the BDSM scene.

*

We all have our part to play in deciding what values will be passed on to the next generation. We're responsible for the way we behave and we have a duty to ensure that we leave a better world for our children. Please don't let us allow current attitudes to undermine our supposed commitment to tolerance. And please, let us do something about the way the law is currently applied and enforced.

We need a world where laws and their enforcement serve to protect society and the individual, not as tools to improve government statistics. Alas, in their efforts to meet crime-solving targets and boost their figures, the authorities prefer to gather low-hanging fruit. 'Ignorance is no defence' makes a mockery of the legal profession. My experience has demonstrated that the honest majority are far more vulnerable to prosecution because of accidental infringement than criminals with deliberate intent. If you wrap a law in enough small print it becomes a trap. I sometimes wonder if 'bureaucracy' is a synonym for 'corruption'.

We live in a country with a democratically elected government. Our MPs are elected to represent us, our opinions and our needs. It's time we all made our needs known, time the ordinary people were considered rather than those who know how to play the game. We're all members of the human race, each unique in our ways. Imagine how life would be in a world driven by understanding, love and cooperation rather than prejudice, greed and corruption.

In my world, anything is possible. The boundaries of BDSM are set only by the imagination. We inhabit the frontier between reality and fantasy in a place of dreams, where the mask of social acceptance can be shed. In this surreal borderland where the human soul is stripped bare and held naked before truth, we find a veritable cornucopia of compulsions and cravings.

I look forward to seeing you there!

AFTERWORD

Two Slaves' Perspectives

I

It's a great honour to be invited to contribute a short testimonial to Princess Lucina's book. I've been one of Her slaves for only a few months, but I've already become devoted to Her, for reasons I'll try to explain.

Many years ago, during a very happy marriage, my wife and I included occasional fem-domme sessions among our bedroom games. We both enjoyed those sessions a great deal and we talked about why. For me, they provided the relief of transferring power and control (however temporarily) to someone I trusted implicitly. This was something I needed to do, because during my working and domestic life I was required to make decisions and provide guidance day after day and shoulder a lot of responsibility, which became wearing. My wife said that for her the sessions provided a feeling of power. They also made her very sexually aroused, so love-making was inevitable so after we'd played those games. It was all great fun and it helped to sustain the intense bond of love between us.

I knew I'd never find another soul-mate after she passed away. There could be no more durable personal relationships for me. Nevertheless, over time, my need for sex reawakened. Fearing that any girlfriend would be at risk of emotional hurt if she became attached to me because I'd be unable to make a commitment, I decided that the only sensible way to deal with my need was to visit carefully-selected escorts. Few of them proved satisfactory for me, though there was (and is) one exception. This lady's professional skills include a measure of domination, which is fun, but it isn't her main focus. I still longed, occasionally, for more intense fem-domme.

To satisfy this longing I visited four Mistresses over a two-year period. One proved to be loud and crude, one was frivolous, one was stupid, untidy and unhygienic, and one was no doubt a good professional but she somehow made it impossible for me to explain what I wanted. After those four failed attempts I more or less gave up. Then, much later, I discovered the Stockport Dungeon website during an internet search. It caught my eye because it was so much more professionally produced and informative than any other domination site I'd seen. My interest duly piqued, I phoned Princess Lucina to request an appointment.

As soon as She answered the phone I knew I was talking to an intelligent and understanding woman, and She honoured me with a booking for a session four days ahead. I found I could tell Her some of my wants without embarrassment, despite never having met Her or spoken to Her before, and with Her consent I explained more of my wishes in an e-mail – which She acknowledged with great courtesy. Our telephone conversation included the following exchange:

"What's your name? I don't think you told me."

"Limp-dick," I replied.

The nickname sprang into my head when Princess Lucina asked the question, possibly because I'd already stated my wish for humiliation. Her laughter in response was equally spontaneous, and it was warm, genuine and appreciative laughter, not forced, and not cold or contemptuous. I knew then that I'd found the right Mistress for me – at last.

This impression was confirmed when I arrived at Her Chamber for the session. Her directions for travelling and parking were exact and clear. As a matter of courtesy I presented myself as a man should when he visits a lady (freshly showered, teeth cleaned, suit and tie and well-polished shoes), and She expressed surprise that I'd made the effort. Surely one should expect the same of any slave! More remarkable, and reassuring, was Her greeting when she opened the door to admit me to the reception area. I was nervous as well as excited, but She immediately put me at ease by smiling warmly and giving me a hug and a kiss before leading me into the lounge and introducing me to Her colleague Mistress Luci and to Her little dog Charlie (a delight!), then guiding me into the dungeon. I was surprised at how easy it was to talk to Her about my wishes and fantasies as I was taking off my clothes.

I was also surprised by how gentle She was – at first. Although She made it clear from the outset that I was now Her property and existed only to serve Her and obey Her orders, She never raised Her voice. She ensured that I had a safe word, but She also made sure I wouldn't need to use it; and while She pursued a number of the activities I'd requested, She did so with restraint, staying well within my boundaries. Afterwards, She gave me a cup of tea and we chatted in the lounge. Her personal warmth enveloped me, so I felt that although W/we were barely acquainted, She liked me and was interested in me.

The effect was to make me hunger for more sessions with Princess Lucina! During the following week I couldn't get Her or Her dungeon out of my head. I had to request another booking, and once again She graciously granted the request. I've now experienced four sessions with Her (three more than with any of the Mistresses I'd visited previously!) and my boundaries are gradually being pushed – not too hard, but definitely pushed. She has an inspired way of enhancing a slave's pain tolerance: She simply tells him (at least, She simply tells me) that he's doing really well and taking stronger punishment than many submissives can. Whether this is true or not, it makes me willing and indeed eager to take more!

Princess Lucina tells me that those four sessions have constituted the beginning of a journey for 'Slave Limp-dick', which is now my name during sessions. I'm starting to grasp what She means: each session brings something new, some more challenging punishments, and I don't yet know where this 'journey' will lead – though I'm becoming more and more keen to find out! During the fourth session, of my own free will, I assigned ownership of my genitals to Her. The signed agreement allows me to use my penis only with one approved escort (my long-term friend) and with no other partner, and it requires me to confess to Her if I ever masturbate. If I ever break the agreement She will have the right to confiscate my penis and testicles. Strange as it may seem, I know that if I *did* ever transgress in that way I'd have to confess it and accept the consequences. Something about this Dominatrix makes it impossible to lie to Her or to conceal information that She might wish to know.

But I've no intention of committing such an error. No doubt my relationship with Her is still young, but already I feel that I'm Her property, no longer a free agent entitled to have sex when opportunities arise. I'm sure I speak for all that have the honour to serve this Mistress: we don't *act the part* of Her slaves, we genuinely *become* Her slaves.

It fully satisfies my longing – and it really is great fun!

II

When I first met Princess Lucina, my now Mistress, I never thought I would become Her slave girl. I had never heard of a slave girl!

Before meeting Her I used to do some adult photography, and through that W/we met via a client of Hers, and I posed as a model in some pictures. I had never been in a dungeon before, and to be honest I had never really thought much about BDSM. I had dabbled in it with a previous partner where we tried various things, but in no way on this scale, and it had been purely sexual.

I walked nervously into the dungeon, really not knowing what to expect. Standing there was a woman wearing a black PVC dress, black high heels and a big smile. I had never met a Dominatrix before but I for one did not think they smiled! She gave me a big hug and I felt a little zing through me. It wasn't sexual, it was more than that, as though the hug had just pressed an unlock button deep inside me. "WTF?" I wondered.

I was surprised how welcoming and comforting She was. She really helped with my nerves and I was looking forward to the next couple of hours. I got changed into some lace outfit and W/we did some poses. Although I was playing a part for the pictures, it felt so natural! This was weird for me. Being bisexual, I was used to finding women attractive, but this was past attraction and brand new to me. I felt *submissive*. This was something I only really 'did' in the bedroom with men, where I liked them to take charge, but outside of that I was not subservient. I am not saying I was a dominant personality but certainly I was not docile or meek.

After the shoot Lucina gave me her number and said to keep in touch and maybe W/we could do another shoot soon! I had to be somewhere, so I thanked Her and rushed off. I had butterflies! Why?

Over the next few days I became a little giddy whenever I thought of Her. It was obvious to me that I fancied Her, but what was the other thing? Why did I feel such a pull towards Her? I texted Her a lot. I tried to act cool, but that failed. Luckily, She didn't seem annoyed by the texts and arranged for me to visit the dungeon again. She said that I could join in a session as a slave girl. I was like, "Hell, yeah!" We booked the session.

I arrived, nervous again, but this time also embarrassed because I fancied Her. I was greeted first by Charlie, Her absolutely amazing little Yorkie. He gave me loads of kisses and I gave him a treat I had brought him. Next was that hug! It was only the second I had had, but just as amazing. She was dressed again in PVC and looked stunning. The session was brilliant. I helped dish out pain to Her slave and She introduced me to bondage, spanking and a little tie and tease. I honestly felt I was in a dream. I pretty much floated out of the dungeon that day.

Over the next few weeks W/we discussed the possibility of me becoming Her slave girl. As previously said, I really hadn't heard of one, but was getting to understand more what it meant. I just wanted to spend time with Her and please Her so I was one hundred percent on board.

I visited Lucina again but this time it was different. It was for a more informal connection and She said to come down just so we could spend some time together. She wasn't sessioning, and a very random thought came through my head: was I in lust with Princess Lucina? This would be the first time seeing Her in 'normal' clothes. What if the feelings weren't the same? But they were! PVC or no PVC, it was the same person, Lucina and Princess Lucina, it didn't matter. I just wanted to please Her and be around her – and Charlie!

Being brand new to the scene I really had a lot to learn and I will say there were many tears on my part. I was a bit of a brat and needed some harsh lessons. The worst is not being punished but knowing I have disappointed my Mistress. That is a psychological gut punch. I am an emotional person, so things go deep with me, but four years on I have learnt so much. She is an amazing Mistress and totally human.

Her love of animals was a massive tick for me and it was a huge draw to Her at the beginning. She has changed my life in ways I can't even describe and I look forward to many more years under Her control.

Other biographies, memoires and history available from Stairwell Books

Tales from the Medicine Cabinet	Ed. Mark P. Henderson
The Tally Man	Rita Jerram
The Great Billy Butlin Race	Robin Richards
The Tao of Revolution	Chris Taylor
Margaret Clitherow	John RD, Wendy Rayne Davis
Serpent Child	Patricia Riley
Looking for Githa	Patricia Riley
The Martyrdoms at Clifford's Tower 1190 and 1537	John Rayne-Davis
Thinking of You Always	Lewis Hill
A Shadow in My Life	Rita Jerram
Tales from a Prairie Journal	Rita Jerram

For further information please contact rose@stairwellbooks.com

www.stairwellbooks.co.uk
@stairwellbooks

www.ingramcontent.com/pod-product-compliance
Lightning Source LLC
Chambersburg PA
CBHW031626160426
43196CB00006B/292